Oskar Schindler

· · · · · · · · · · · · · · · · · ·
AND HIS LIST

Other Nonfiction Books by Thomas Fensch

Television News Anchors (1993)

Nonfiction for the 1990s (1991)

Associated Press Coverage of a Major Disaster:
The Crash of Delta Flight 1141 (1990)

Best Magazine Articles: 1988 (1989)

Writing Solutions: Beginnings, Middles & Endings (1989)

Conversations with James Thurber (1989)

The Sports Writing Handbook (1988)

Conversations with John Steinbeck (1988)

Steinbeck and Covici: The Story of a Friendship (1979)

—plus six others.

Jacket Photo: Oskar Schindler, 1949
Al Taylor/Herbert Steinhouse

Oskar Schindler
AND HIS LIST

The Man, the Book, the Film, the Holocaust and Its Survivors

Edited by Thomas Fensch

With an Introduction by Herbert Steinhouse

Paul S. Eriksson, *Publisher*
Forest Dale, Vermont

Design by Eugenie Seidenberg Delaney

Library of Congress Cataloging-in-Publication Data

Oskar Schindler and his list : the man, the book, the film, the Holocaust and its survivors / edited by Thomas Fensch ; with an introduction by Herbert Steinhouse.

    p.   cm.

Includes bibliographical references and index

ISBN 0-8397-6472-3 (hardcover)

1. Schindler, Oskar, 1908-1974. 2. Righteous gentiles in the Holocaust—Poland—Kraków—Biography. 3. Keneally, Thomas.Schindler's list. 4. Schindler, Oskar, 1908-1974—In literature. 5. Holocaust, Jewish (1939-1945), in literature. 6. Schindler's list (Motion picture) 7. Holocaust, Jewish (1939-1945), in motion pictures. 8. Spielberg, Steven, 1947-   . 9. Holocaust survivors. I. Fensch, Thomas.

D804.3.S32083   1995

940.53'18'092—dc20

[B]

95-13696

CIP

Acknowledgments

The first are the most personal—to my wife, Sharon, to Irvin A. Kraft and Kenneth Kopel, whose contributions have been more than any words can express ....

And to the following, grateful acknowledgment is made for permission to reprint copyrighted material:

American Cinematographer, "*Schindler's List* Finds Heroism Amidst Holocaust" by Karen Erbach, reprinted courtesy of *American Cinematographer;*

The Boston Herald, "Holocaust drama is a Spielberg triumph" by James Verniere, reprinted with permission of *The Boston Herald;*

The Chicago Sun-Times, "'Schindler's List' Follows a Man's Trek to Heroism" by Roger Ebert, copyright © 1994, The Ebert Co., Ltd., reprinted with permission;

The Chicago Tribune, personality profile of actor Ralph Fiennes by Lisa Anderson, Copyrighted *Chicago Tribune* Company. All rights reserved. Used with permission;

(continued page 265)

For all those who perished.

Contents

NEWSPAPER REVIEWS

Preface

······················

"As a concept, as an image, we shrink from it as from damnation itself."

—William Styron

How do we interpret the Holocaust?

How do we look inside the mind of one man, Oskar Schindler?

The 1982 publication of Thomas Keneally's non-fiction novel *Schindler's List* (published under the title *Schindler's Ark* in England) and the 1993 release of Steven Spielberg's film of the same name have brought world-wide attention to the Holocaust and to Oskar Schindler as embodiment of all those who risked their own lives to save Jews and other victims of the "Final Solution."

But the Holocaust and Oskar Schindler remain inexplicable.

In the Preface to his collection of essays, *Unanswered Questions: Nazi Germany and the Genocide of the Jews*, François Furet writes, "by its very excess, nazism remains, forty years after its fall, a sort of enigma for historical rationality. The 'Final Solution,' which is nazism's culmination point, remains the horrifying embodiment of this mystery." (pp. viii.)

In his introduction to *The Cunning of History: The Holocaust and the American Future*, novelist William Styron calls Auschwitz (as embodiment of the Holocaust) "the core of hell" and writes "its unspeakable monstrousness—one is tempted to say its unbelievability—continues to leave us weak with trauma, haunting us as with the knowledge of some lacerating bereavement. Even as it recedes slowly into the past it taxes our belief, making us wonder if it really happened. As a concept, as an image, we shrink from it as from damnation itself." (pp. vii-viii.)

Richard Rubenstein, the author of *The Cunning of History*, suggests that Nazi Germany stepped across a previously "unbreachable moral and political barrier in the history of Western civilization" when genocide became sanctioned by the Nazi government. Rubenstein writes:

> For the first time in history, a ruling elite in the heart of Europe, the center of Western civilization, had an almost inexhaustible supply of men and women with whom they could do anything they pleased, irrespective of any antique religious or moral prejudice. The Nazis had created a society of total domination. Among the preconditions for such a society are: (a) bureaucratic administration capable of governing with utter indifference to the human needs of the inmates; (b) a supply of inmates capable of continuous replenishment; (c) the imposition of the death sentence on every inmate as soon as he or she enters. Unless the supply is more or less inexhaustible, the masters will be tempted to moderate their treatment of the inmates because of their labor value. If the supply is capable of replenishment, the masters can calculate the exact rate at which they wish to work the prisoners before disposing of them. Both use and riddance can be calculated in terms of the masters' requirements, with only minimal concern for the survival requirements of the slaves. Furthermore, there must be no hope that any inmate might eventually return to normal life. Total domination cannot be achieved if camp guards are apprehensive that some of the inmates might be persons to be reckoned with at some future time. Such cautionary calculation could inhibit the extremities of behavior the camp personnel might otherwise indulge in. The Germans were able to create a society of total domination because of the competence of their police and civil service bureaucracies and because they possessed millions of totally superfluous men

whose lives and sufferings were of absolutely no consequence to any power secular or sacred and who were as good as dead the moment they entered the camps. (Pp. 34-35.)

And what of Schindler?

In *The Path of the Righteous: Gentile Rescuers of Jews During the Holocaust,* by Mordecai Paldiel, Schindler explains, "I hated the brutality, the sadism, and the insanity of Nazism. I just couldn't stand by and see people destroyed. I did what I could, what I had to do, what my conscience told me I must do. That's all there is to it. Really, nothing more." (Pp. 168-169.)

That simplistic explanation itself also seems inexplicable.

Even Schindler's widow confessed no one knows exactly why he did what he did during the Holocaust.

There are a number of reasons why others like Schindler risked instant death to save victims of the Holocaust. In *The Path of the Righteous:* (pp. 376-381), Paldiel cites seven types of reasons: religious reasons; performing one's duty (as Schindler explained); a religious duty; a "natural" thing (to do); to preserve the sanctity of life; to avoid the shame of not helping; and to do a conscientious act.

The publication of Thomas Keneally's *Schindler's List,* the release of Steven Spielberg's film and the recent publication of Herbert Steinhouse's early article ask all of us to consider Oskar Schindler's ethics and morality—and to consider all those other Schindlers who risked sudden death at the hands of the Nazis to save others. We are reminded that Schindler's workers gave him a ring at the close of the war, inscribed with a verse in Hebrew: *He who saves a single life saves the world entire.*

We are also reminded that Oskar Schindler undertook the work of saving lives during the blackest days of the Holocaust: a tragedy so deep, a concept so unspeakable, "We shrink from it," as William Styron wrote, "as from damnation itself."

—*Thomas Fensch*

Introduction

Fifty years later. Fifty years after the opening of all the gates of all of the camps. A moment for reflection. For the poet's emotion recalled in tranquility.

And to consider the simplified implications of a much, much longer sweep of history.

So sweeping, so simply summarized, that I might even put it into mock-fable form:

Once upon a long, long time ago, a pious, illiterate villager somewhere in Europe uttered a loud curse. It was directed against all the Jews and others who were unlike him and his immediate kind, and the curse was accidental and thoughtless. Perhaps there was justification for his anger but there was none for the wildness of his indictment. And there was no one, not even a more pious or more literate person, around to tell him so.

Not far away, a rich and educated man, of arrogant monocle and awe-inspiring uniform, recounted to his friends some snide and hoary traditional jests that embraced all Jews and all Poles and all Englishmen and Frenchmen. The friends roared out their laughing appreciation.

Somewhere in the Third World, an administrator strolled unseeingly through a million natives, generously colonizing them for their own good, quietly exploiting them for his Empire's.

The years and centuries passed. The casual strolls became brutality, uprising and mass murder. The militarists' jests became obliterating war. The curses became pogrom became Holocaust.

Add a 'lo and behold' or two and the fable converts to biblical para-
ble. Or prophecy. For there is an Act Three. The colonizer goes home,
leaving ruined lands to tribalism and to genocide; into the Prussian towns
come newer strangers, to be tormented by raised fists; in lonely Eastern
European villages, miraculously, the slandering curses reappear among
people with but a vague folk-memory of having once seen a Jew.

Stripped of its weight of facts and the accoutrements of all the explanations, and so naked, then, in such simplicity, history's sweep becomes
exasperation. Why does it take so long for the learning to stick? Why do
we fall asleep amid the technological marvels of a 20th century, so replete
with the indicators of progress, and awake in the morning in yet another
vicious corner of the terrible 14th, or even in the stench and blackness of the
8th or 9th? Must it always be two steps forward and one back? And By the
Skin of our Teeth? Is the greatest of our human race's crimes, then, the crime
of collective innocence?

Wintry thoughts—as we wander down the final miles of a misbegotten
century. Yet a book like this, in its very existence, demonstrates the need
for toughness, not innocence. The kindly pills of a country doctor go only
so far when it's the radical cut of a surgeon's knife that's wanted. Struggles
for enlightenment, for full respect for minorities of peoples and opinions,
must, of course, continue—within the constraints of judgment and acquired wisdom. They are vital to forward movement. It is the guileless innocence of untoughened tolerance that can prove so dangerous.

For sweet innocence makes us vulnerable when we expose to sunlight
the poisoners, the purveyors of the Great Lie, the disease-carrying rodents
of the sewers. Our unjudging innocents of the media rush to interview
delegates of the publicity-chasing international conspiracy, or to offer
them—naturally with only the noblest of intentions—free time on network
TV programs that play to vast audiences of the untutored gullible.

Leon Wieseltier put it succinctly in his *New Republic* essay, repro-
duced in this book: "The discussion about 'Holocaust revisionism' is not a
'debate' between a 'view' that it happened and a 'view' that it did not happen; it is a war between a truth and a disease."

Or, to shift the critique, what about the re-arrangers of the Titanic's
deck chairs? What do we say to the squabbling intellectuals and the carp-
ing critics—and there naturally are several represented here—who roundly
condemn book or film for *not* being what neither had intended to be: the

all-time definitive Holocaust story? Or simply and fundamentally, *a* legitimate Holocaust story? French film director Claude Lanzmann, whose own magnificent *Shoah* comes the closest to fulfilling that need for definition, has himself voiced that angry criticism of Spielberg's *List*. Must there always be absolutists in our relative world, settling only to possess the moon?

I once met a man in Munich, a ruggedly handsome man, a Good German, who told me just how he had saved 1,100 human beings, and I cannot recall ever having classified it as Holocaust story, definitive or other. I had publicized too many wrenching Holocaust tales, and anyway, by then the survivors were bringing their similar histories by the shipload into the safety of the harbours of the Americas and the veneer of security of the new Israel. What was so intriguing, in 1949, was that this man's saga went far beyond the commonplace. The Holocaust was six million dead. His story was not even a metaphor for that untellable history of assembly-line murder in the villages, the killing-forests, the death camps. It was a marginal story, a warming true-fable of one man's deeds and of a handful who thereby survived—truer and more significant, perhaps, than any once penned by Hans Christian Andersen or the Brothers Grimm of Kassel.

A provocative morality story, then? A universal learning lesson? An eloquent and rare allegory on Good Amidst Evil? It is at least that: the saga of the ambitious opportunist, Nazi party member or more, originally as committed on all but The Jewish Question as any other faithful believer in that dehumanized, violent ideology. Voluntarily or pathologically or after total conditioning, fascists exit from the human race. Here was one who rediscovers our inter-linked world's simplest, most fundamental societal values. At the epicenter of that gigantic lunatic asylum, he assumes the unaccustomed role of Normal Human Being.

Thomas Keneally and Steven Spielberg set out to teach the ignorant, the forgetful and the innocent about some of those basic human values, and about where racism and fascism inevitably lead. The world still needs that knowledge when the same old banners again rise ominously in Germany, ex-Yugoslavia, Italy, the Middle East and elsewhere. We all need it, including apathetic us on this continent of unattained political maturity and creeping dangers on our horizons.

The lesson in realism is to fight early. Oskar Schindler may have learned something as an Alpine skier of the 1930s: that if you kick-start your way from a summit of tolerated racial expletives, or jolly old racial jokes, or so-innocent racial beer-drinking songs, then you may have a following avalanche long before you reach the valley.

Perhaps you will arrive at a similar conclusion as you go deeper into this thoughtful examination of the many-faceted Schindler saga. Thomas Fensch must have agreed long before he set out on this exemplary project. But how the deuce did a professor in Texas ever learn so much about snow and avalanches?

— Herbert Steinhouse

Part One

Oskar Schindler
Circa 1946–1949

The Journalist Who Knew Oskar Schindler

··

An Interview with Herbert Steinhouse

by Thomas Fensch

Montreal, December 19, 1994.

Poldek Pfefferberg kept the story of Oskar Schindler alive in his heart waiting for someone to really listen.

Thomas Keneally listened and brought Schindler's story to life in his book, Schindler's List.

Steven Spielberg made the story bigger than life in his film, "Schindler's List" so all the world could see and hear.

And everyone who read and saw and heard wondered "Why?" Why did this unlikely hero do what he did? To save 1,100 lives.

Perhaps part of the answer could be found in the dusty cellar trunk of a Canadian journalist who knew Oskar Schindler.

Herbert Steinhouse met Oskar Schindler after World War Two and got to know him quite well. As a journalist, Steinhouse documented and verified the Schindler story, only to find in the late 1940s, no one wanted to hear any more about the Nazis and their atrocities to the Jews. So he locked the story away.

When Steinhouse read Keneally's book and saw Spielberg's

film, he knew it was time to unlock the trunk and add his missing piece to the puzzle of Oskar Schindler ....

Steinhouse, a native of Montreal, graduated from McGill University early in World War II. He delivered factory-new bombers to the world's war zones for the Royal Canadian Air Force for three years, then went to Europe right after V.E. Day to work as an information officer for the United Nations Relief and Rehabilitation Administration (UNRRA) in 1945 and 1946.

He left Europe for a graduate degree at the New School for Social Research in New York City, married, and then returned to Europe as a journalist early in 1948, with his wife Tobie, eventually to work out of Paris for the American Joint Distribution Committee, the AJDC (which employees invariably called "The Joint"). There, Steinhouse wrote publicity feature stories about the plight of World War II's surviving displaced persons. In 1949, he became the Canadian Broadcasting Corporation's news correspondent for western Europe. In the late fifties he wrote the critically praised political novel on contemporary France and Algeria's long war of liberation, The Time of the Juggernaut *(William Morrow, New York).*

Now in his early 70s, retired in Montreal, Steinhouse speaks forcefully and dramatically about the Schindler story. He hesitates only to recall if minor incident "A" happened weeks before or after minor incident "B" all those decades ago ....

"...by 1948, Itzhak Stern was surviving in Paris with his brother and their wives, and along with many others. They finally had got out of Germany and were all in a holding pattern, waiting for the American Joint Distribution Committee to help get them immigration papers to ... anywhere. Canada ... South America ... Israel ...."

And you met Stern when you were working in Paris for the AJDC, when he was waiting for those papers ....

"Yes. I worked there for about a year. My artist bride and I had gone completely broke. I had first freelanced—covered the '48 Italian elections, done a lot of feature writing. I was trying to avoid political writing then, and was doing positive stories on Europe's reconstruction and so forth. I remember Salzburg, and a piece on Mozart. The Bavarian Alps and a feature on Richard Strauss. One of the last interviews done with Strauss, who died two weeks later. On France's first ambitious plans to harness the Rhône and provide an economic infrastructure ....

"Finally I saw an advertisement. Two of us were short-listed, Art Buchwald and me. I got it and Buchwald was turned down, for insufficient press experience. I had never even worked on a newspaper—although I had done a lot of work similar to the AJDC's for UNRRA and so on, and I had been the editor of my college daily. Whereas Buchwald, as I recall, had been the editor of the Pacific edition of *Stars and Stripes*, with ten times my newspaper experience. He went across the Seine to the old Paris *Herald Tribune* with a couple of sample pieces—humorous articles—and he became famous, the most popular feature on the paper. They finally had to start paying him. He was very, very funny from the start. Later, I told him that he owed his entire career to me ....

"So working for the European headquarters of 'the Joint' on the Left Bank, one day I heard about this unusual man, always hanging around the waiting room all day over at our Emigration Department on the Champs Elysees. His name, it seemed, was Itzhak Stern.

"I was running the AJDC's public relations and information department. We were putting out nice little feature stories and photos aimed especially at the American, British and Canadian media. I guess I was curious about this Mr. Stern.

"But first—it just came to me—I was told this year by an old friend from Chicago, when he read my article, that he had briefly introduced me to the Schindlers in Austria in 1946, and I have absolutely no memory of that. Absolutely none.

"But back then, when I was working with UNRRA, James Rice headed the Joint Distribution Committee in Austria. The Schindler party came down from the hills, where they had been hiding, into Linz, and tried to get help through him. October, 1945. Rice was, as I was eventually to be, very skeptical. We all met so very many of, in quotes, 'The Good German.' Each told what could well have been a true story with proof of having saved a man, a family, a Communist or Socialist, a Russian, Pole, Jew, foreigner, an escapee from a transport—whatever. Jim Rice met Oskar and his wife Emilie then, who presented documents through the *Schindlerjuden*, their so-called bodyguards, three of whom were musicians. I met them in '48 and was convinced that they had never held a gun in their lives. Jim said he introduced me to the Schindler party in 1946 when I came through Linz. He later got them all to Munich and pleaded their case. All of them were underweight still—this was barely six months after they got out of the camps and the factory. The musicians had lived in the Plaszow camp, and worked in Schindler's factory and played music for Amon Goeth ...."

Which kept them alive ....

"Which kept them alive. Violins and accordion for those SS parties. And also informed Schindler, when he had not attended.

"So when James Rice met up with the Schindler group, Oskar did not say: 'I saved a Jew.'...He simply said: 'I saved twelve hundred Jews.' How could you possibly believe it? The Schindler figure was anything between eleven hundred, which is what I think Spielberg settled on—Keneally, if I am not mistaken, says twelve hundred—and what some *Schindlerjuden* later claimed could have been fifteen hundred, sixteen hundred, as there was a lot of going and coming ....

"But the famous Schindler list was eleven hundred. I have a copy. I think I once counted off the names, eleven hundred."

How did you get a copy of the list?

"How did I first get a copy of the list? I don't remember. I suppose through Schindler."

Really?

"Well, he carried things around with him. He carried photocopies. He carried documentation. He was working hard to get out of Germany and find a country to accept him ...."

To go anywhere.

"He'd go anywhere. He had applied to Canada. For him and his wife. The Canadians already had started to secretly 'park'—as favors to the CIA, or I guess even for the old OSS, top-ranking Gestapo officers and SS 'sources of information'—all sorts of murderous people .... But the 'bright lads' who ran immigration policy including the RCMP (Royal Canadian Mounted Police) who controlled the first stamp, the security clearance—

they went mainly by the book. Which said that anybody who had been a Nazi ... and they had the records. Schindler might even have been with Germany Military Intelligence, the Abwehr, in 1939. Maybe the SS, too, though that I still doubt. So that was the end of that. Forget it. For Canadian immigration back then, no case was analyzed on its merits. Blanket condemnation, blanket decision."

So you met Schindler through Stern.

"Yes, but this is where I'm a little hazy about which came first—because I was living in Paris where my office was, but was making so many trips into Germany, where the new material was, where I was taking pictures, where I was writing the stories, and then back to Paris, do the office assignments, run the lives of the others ... then back to Germany to do something else.

And to get back to Stern: who was this unusual man who hung about our Emigration Department?

"The JDC was providing fundamental help only to Jews, which was its mandate, and because the funds it raised in England or Canada and, above all, in the United States, were strictly for this welfare organization to feed and to help Jewish survivors. That was the basis of their Schindler dilemma, of the problem of a well-intentioned James Rice and of the JDC's executive.

"So here was this man, waiting for his own papers but unlike anybody else, turning up every day. He would arrive early, pants freshly pressed if a little shiny. Shoes polished. Hair neatly trimmed, a good looking shirt—the same one, but good enough. And almost elegant, proud.

"And he would sit there, without any apparent reason. Everybody else awaiting a visa—for Brazil or Central America or the USA—would be at home. It could take six months—a year, longer if they were told they had a spot on the lungs, or perhaps if someone in the family was still medically unacceptable ....

"But Itzhak Stern would come around and sit. He would be alone. He would read his newspapers and just sit. Was he the contact man of a group? The news-gatherer? The coordinator?

"I got intrigued and introduced myself. 'Have you had breakfast?' He said, 'Yes, don't worry about me.' At which point I started to worry about him.

"So I began taking him around the corner to a café off the Champs

Elysees, where we would sit with croissants and coffees—lots of good croissants—I kept stuffing him.

And I kept my notebook out and he'd tell me his story, bit by bit. We'd use about three different languages ...."

English?

"He had no English, as I recall. He was learning French and he had been in France for a year by then. My French was fluent, my German was passable—good enough for conversation but sometimes mixed up with my bit of Yiddish. Like my problems with skiing. Never knew whether I was doing French parallel skiing in Austria or deep-snow Austrian skiing in France.

"Hell, to this day my Spanish can get mixed up with my Italian. Order *vino rosso* when I mean *vino tinto!*"

So you and Stern had coffee every day ...

"While I took notes. I don't know if we talked at first about Schindler but he began telling me his own story ... his older brother's story. And introduced me to his brother, Nahum Stern. Joined us for breakfast. Nahum's story confirmed Itzhak's and the factory. Maybe the name Schindler came up then—I can't remember now. That was late summer or early fall, '48.

"My wife and I decided to do a bit of Christmas skiing in Bavaria. At either Garmisch-Parkenkirchen or in Hitler country, Berchtesgaden. The American Army ran both places as R & R centers. Gave you skis and equipment free and set you up for a dollar a night, room and board. We'd first spend a week in Munich, then go down to one of these R & R centers.

"So there we were, at the U.S. Army press villa out in the suburbs of Munich. Not a hotel left standing in downtown Munich. The center was totally destroyed, including Hitler's famed Beer Hall, Europe's finest museums and most theaters, the entire area around the railroad station. I had seen worse—Kassel, Hamburg—but the destruction in Munich was still terrible.

"I was typing a story up in my room, I remember, and my wife was out somewhere, when this puffing, ancient taxicab pulled up in front and three men, in their 20s, got to the building door, where the Army Police refused to let them in.

"No Germans or DPs (displaced persons)—only people accredited by the American civilian or military occupation. My own accreditation read

Full Colonel, which enabled me primarily to get a better berth on the train and a second cup of coffee.

"They asked for me, which was surprising. I saw all this from my window. I came down. They said, 'Herr Schindler wants to see you. We are his bodyguards.'

"And my natural reaction was, "Who the hell is Herr Schindler?'

"They introduced themselves. Polish Jews. And I with a busy day lined up, trying to cover a few more stories before we could go off skiing. I was a bit resentful; they were determined. As if I'd had a royal summons. The Queen wants to see you, the King wants to see you.

"Bemused, I said, 'Right, I'm not busy. I have nothing else to do' (laugh), and went off with them in their taxi, to a café down near the railway station. The Schindlers had a single-room place there, in one of the few apartment houses in the area that was still more or less standing. Their official address was up in the city of Regensburg, where they and the *Schindlerjuden* shared AJDC and UNRRA rations, on which they were presumed to survive. Later I found that, of course, they were all using the rations to take to Munich, the headquarters of Germany's black market, around that same railway station. Oskar was playing the black market as best he could. Very minor stuff. I am talking about a man who a few years before had been a millionaire. In gold and diamonds and American currency.

"I remember asking, 'How did you know I was in Munich? How do you know who I am?' I never got a proper answer. Much later I surmised that the *Schindlerjuden* could have settled on me through Itzhak Stern. He might have been in touch by some sort of networking arrangement and sent a signal to Munich. They knew exactly where to find me out in the suburbs with their 'Herr Schindler wishes to see you.'

"But why me? For it was obvious by then—in fact they told me— that they had given up on all other methods. They now thought, after much discussion, that their best tactic would be to try to get the Schindler story out. Some country would pick it up. Maybe Canada, and I was a handy Canadian. Maybe they'd make it into the United States, the whole lot of them. I was working for an American organization. I was a journalist and I suspect somebody also put in a report that I was young—25, 26 at the time—and so, easy to manipulate, easy to handle, easy to bribe. What they did not know was that I had spent some tough times in post-war Germany, had helped in the process of getting ten million victims of Fascism out of the concentration camps, the slave labor setups and so on—into our hospitals, off the roads.

"And, by God, I was hardly naive. There wasn't a new story anyone could tell me then. And I was always very political. Tough and unforgiving of Germany. And of the Germans, for what they had swallowed and permitted. But I also had to keep fighting tendencies to over-generalize, to indulge in reverse racism, to condemn a whole people. The point was, I was politically sophisticated, not exactly the patsy they may have been looking for.

"Anyway, it wasn't that sophistication that made me skeptical. I just couldn't believe his story as it started to pour into my notebooks.

"Stern's story, I believed. That there'd been 'A Good German' somewhere, in Hanover, or in Frankfurt, or on an eastern farm, who had saved a family, a man, two brothers, or somebody off a train headed for the death camps—those were credible stories and my world was full of them. There was no reason *not* to believe them.

"Then somebody comes along and says, 'Help us. I saved eleven hundred people.' And the *Schindlerjuden* around the table, his so-called bodyguards, all nod (Steinhouse nods as if a crowd of bystanders were nodding in unison): 'Yes, Yes, Yes, Yes, Yes,' as we talked in a variety of languages. Perhaps I believed, maybe, ten percent.

"We kept meeting. When I realized that the Schindlers weren't eating, I bought them lunches, dinners. He charmed us. The wives liked one another. When I asked Schindler which black market restaurant he enjoyed, naturally it just happened to be the one where the Rosner brothers had been hired to play. As we talked, they played, just behind us. And the more we talked the more notes I took. The ten percent rose to twenty percent. His credibility level went up. And other people continued to confirm, including AJDC-Munich.

"There were a couple of anecdotes I still remember:

"One was that just before we left to ski, and with Oskar and Emilie, who, as usual, looking daggers at each other in the restaurant—they truly disliked each other—more than that, hated each other—nonetheless, they asked insistently: 'is there anything we can do?' When I said, 'I am very busy on stories I still must write,' and my wife said, 'While he works I shall take a taxi out to Nymphenberg Castle'—Mad King Ludwig's of Bavaria.

Within it was the factory noted for the delicate white Nymphenberg porcelain—long world-famous. She planned to see both castle and factory.

"'Good,' the Schindlers said quickly, 'Good, we'll take you.' I was irritated. I knew enough by then about Oskar Schindler, and from his own lips, to know that for ten years or so he had done little in life except through bribery. An SS officer here or a Commandant there. Part of his inherent personality. Probably always had been.

"'No gifts,' I warned my wife, who hardly needed the warning. 'They haven't the money, but they'll try to compromise us anyway.'

"They went off together, toured the castle, toured the factory. There was a gift shop and the Schindlers kept offering and my wife kept on politely refusing.

"But in the taxi back, sure enough Emilie Schindler pulled out a small package and pressed it on my wife 'with our compliments.' And once again my wife said, 'No; no; no.' Whereupon Emilie Schindler got very annoyed, or pretended to be, and demanded, 'What do you expect us to do with it? We're not going to leave it in the taxi. We're not going back. You *must* take it. It's nothing—a souvenir, a keepsake.' I may have been mistaken. They were proud and perhaps only wished to reciprocate.

"My wife had to accept it, a little tea-pot or something. Sent it home to her mother-in-law. A cleaning lady apparently broke it soon afterwards.

"The other anecdote that comes to mind was curious, in a way. By then Munich was full of what we called 'The Too-Late Heroes.' It was an R & R center. The GIs who had done the real fighting had long ago gone home. The Army of Occupation now consisted of nice young farm boys from Wisconsin or Idaho, who knew about corn and potatoes but not a lot about life, and who were loose on the town. Three Bavarian beers and they would try to gang up on the German girls.

"One evening we came out of our Munich restaurant, the Schindlers and us. We had eaten well and were walking it off. The two ladies were in deep discussion out in front and Oskar and I were some ten feet behind, strolling slowly.

"Suddenly, six GIs, drunk as hell, descended on the women and started to paw them. Put their hands on my wife and on Emilie. Mistook them for young Germans (laughs). Which in Emilie's case was almost true. She was born in 1908, I think, so we're talking of her at 40. Born in the same year, if I remember correctly, the exact same year, as Oskar. They married at 20.

"My bad temper flared and I became the hero and rushed forward to shout at them in English. Told them to take their bloody hands off the women and got into a bit of a fistfight with a couple of them. It was silly. They were only 17 or 18. I swung at them a few times and soon the U.S. military police—they were everywhere in Munich in those days—arrived from nowhere. I said something or other—to just get them out of there and to leave them alone. It all ended amicably.

"And I turned around, and where was Oskar? Oskar had evaporated. Oskar, who was taller and stronger than me and still in his prime, built like a football player, who had been a motorcycle racer and a downhill skier, had vanished.

"Eventually I found him. My first reaction, of course, was, 'How could this guy who claims to have saved eleven hundred people at such risk to his own life turn out to be such a coward? Why did he leave it to me to protect his wife?' Whether or not he hated her was beside the point (laughs).

"It was only later when I got a bit more logical that I realized that, in fact, it had been not only the shrewdest thing to do but the *right* thing to do. He was hoping for immigration papers. The last thing he needed was to end up on a police docket. He had to protect the main thing—their main chance. Instinctively he had been craftier and smarter, and probably more courageous, than me with my my foolhardy heroics."

You were talking earlier about Oskar and his millions in diamonds and gold and dollars. Did you ask him how it disappeared? Or did you understand how it disappeared?

"I definitely understood *that* it all disappeared. That they were living, since '45, almost entirely off the proceeds of the small-potatoes black market. Selling the clothes and cans of food the *Schindlerjuden* sent him from abroad. And he lived with several of them in Regensburg. And they had rations from UNRRA and its successor organization, and from the JDC. None of which he was entitled to, as a German. The *Schindlerjuden* yes, but the Schindlers themselves did not have refugee status and the United Nations officially owed them nothing.

"The few *Schindlerjuden* already in the U.S. kept in touch with each other, and divided up the responsibility and kept sending him parcels. Either he and Emilie stayed alive on them or he used them in the black market. I couldn't tell which.

"Everybody, especially the American soldiers and officers, played the black market in those days. Some even made small fortunes. I guess I was one of the very few who tried to remain virginal.

"After the Christmas skiing I got fully involved. I must say I worked harder as a young journalist on that Schindler story than I ever did, before or since, to research a story. I got material from Prague and Krakow. Notarized corroboration. Letters of attestation from Jews in Brussels and Paris. All taken down by a notary under oath and analyzed.

"Eventually my acceptance of the story got up to sixty or seventy percent. Because there was virtually nothing that did not fit, from wherever I got it—from French-Jewish organizations and other organizations, and, as I said, from sources in Prague and from Krakow, from Zionists and Communists, even from some then still-secret American-Jewish wartime dossiers.

"One man had worked in the Schindler factory in Krakow, but, prior to that, had known him in the mid '30s. He was the son of a rabbi in Svitavy, Schindler's hometown, and he had grown up as a next door neighbor of the Schindlers. He wrote telling me about Schindler as a neighbor.

"This fellow said that as a man who was a Sudetenland Fascist, was a member of the Henlein party which was later absorbed into the Greater Germany's Nazi party, Schindler apparently had been a true believer in everything but one. That was the racial policy. He had been friendly with several of the Sudetenland Jews. He'd speak with his neighbor and the neighbor's father, the rabbi. They'd talk about the sophisticated Yiddish literature in Poland and Czechoslovakia, about the folk tales and the mythology and the anecdotes and the ancient Jewish traditions of the villages of eastern Poland, or Moldova.

"And what all that showed, of course, was unlike the portrait painted later by the Spielberg film.

"The film seems to accept a character study where a man, in September, '39, crosses the border and settles down in Krakow as your average carpetbagger. Like any Northerner of the American Civil War who went south to grab a lumber or textile factory, or an old plantation in Savannah or Charleston. Spielberg seems to suggest this as the only original motivation. That, in fact, Schindler had no idea just how bad things were in the ghetto until he went out horseback riding on a hill overlooking the ghetto ...."

A key scene in the film ....

"It's a key scene. And I think this is in Keneally's book as well ...."

He was riding with one of his mistresses at the time ....

"He was with one of his mistresses at the time. And he saw this little girl in the red dress. The film had been black and white. Suddenly it's color. The sweet little girl in the red dress who gets shot in the street. And that seems to be presented by Spielberg as a—as *the* basic reason why Schindler the Nazi suddenly changed heart. Paul's revelation on the road to Damascus.

"Suddenly he is the simple humanist. Suddenly he starts operating to get people out of the ghetto and into his factory, to outsmart the vicious system.

"That's all well and good and dramatic and could be partly truthful, but I am stuck with, from some of my documentation, the anomaly of the man who was long fascinated by Jewishness, by all the fabulous material of the nineteenth century, of the eighteenth, who had nothing but basic respect for Jews, it seemed, even when he agreed with his party on all but its racism. He thought that complete nonsense, apparently.

"Yet he believed in the Greater Germany.

"He was a Czech, but he didn't consider himself a Czech. He was a *German* national, German in every respect. Deep in the Nazi party and maybe the Abwehr, maybe even the SS, say some British researchers, and agreeing with everything except the racial policies.

"It's never been explained. Like many other aspects of the mystery of Oskar Schindler. Important things that don't seem ever to get fully explained.

"In my original article I tried to guess at answers—in the plural—to the fundamental question: What *was* Oskar Schindler's motivation? Because he may have been saving eleven hundred people, but by God, only by the skin of his teeth. He was arrested at least twice, maybe three times. He was in jail, in German jails, in Krakow. The others weren't all fools. Everybody seemed to know what he was up to. One of the Commandants, the one he said he pushed down a stairway, said, 'Oskar, you tried to kill me. And don't think you can get away. We all know who you are. You're a Jew-lover, and you'll get to Auschwitz just as fast as your Jews.'"

You saw Schindler in Munich, got well acquainted and really began to believe his story. And then ...?

"After I was through with all those testimonials and notarized documents, and the documentation that Schindler himself had given me, it was all so extensive and iron-clad that *you couldn't disbelieve it any more.*

"A little later—I can't remember exactly when—late January, 1949, probably, I was in touch with all the Paris *Schindlerjuden* and we decided we would throw a party. Schindler, of course—I don't remember if Emilie came or not—had no papers to allow him out of Germany. The *Schindlerjuden* reserved an Alsatian restaurant in north central Paris and I said, 'I'll provide Oskar.'

"So I drove down to Munich, piled Oskar in the Jeep and sneaked him across the frontier over a black marketeers' route and got him to Paris without being caught.

"It was a joyous occasion. Everybody lifted a glass and we came out with the traditional Polish toast, 'May he live a thousand years. Thanks. Thanks. Thanks. A thousand thanks. May he live a thousand years.'"

And the Al Taylor photos were from that party?

"Yes. The party was on a Friday night. They toasted with tears in their eyes. It was the first time since '45 any of them had seen Oskar Schindler.

"The joy on their faces made the story irrefutable. Oskar was crying. Someone was playing an accordion. The tears were streaming down his face. A party became an annual event, subsequently, after Oskar was able to get out of Germany.

"Friday night, the partying. For Saturday and Sunday I arranged with Itzhak Stern and Schindler to come to my office and confront each other. I'd heard their individual stories but had never been with the two together privately. They hadn't seen one another in almost four years. Since May, 1945. Al Taylor shot many rolls of film. To make sure I wouldn't miss anything—there were no reliable tape recorders yet—I got my own secretary to take dictation. Plus a Polish-speaking girl who was a very good interpreter. Somebody else for German and Yiddish.

"There was this truly emotional reaction. They had seen each other at the party the night before, but here they were freely together.

"In the simplified film version, and to a lesser extent in the book, Stern is portrayed as Schindler's main confidant. You'd think Schindler never made a move without Itzhak Stern being involved. You'd think it was Itzhak Stern who was writing down the famous list and putting people on and taking people off ....

"Here were the two of them again, together for the first time in four years. The emotion shows on their faces, in Al Taylor's photos.

"I pretended to forget everything I had ever heard. We went back to square one and, jointly, they told the entire story, repeating most of what I already had on paper. When one of them forgot an incident or detail or a name, the other would supply it. Itzhak Stern had a fabulous memory, better than Schindler's, certainly better than mine. He kept providing prompts and Schindler would say, 'Yes, yes, that's exactly how it happened.'

"We continued on Sunday morning. Then, either Sunday or Monday, I put Schindler in my Jeep and we returned to Munich. I came back to Paris, got to work on the story and wrote 10,000 words ...."

> *Steinhouse never saw Schindler again, although they kept in touch by mail for a while. He sent off the completed story and documentary evidence and the best photos to his New York literary agent, but the USA preferred to forget the Second World War. The chill of the Cold War began its sweep across Europe and no major editor wished to read about "A Good German." Or else no one believed the Schindler story. No publication bought it, none published it.*
>
> *Steinhouse went on to other stories. He worked for Reuters, the British news agency, in London, then returned to Paris, spent a year in Asia and eventually joined the Canadian Broadcasting Corporation, becoming a radio and television correspondent. He and his wife Tobie later moved back to Montreal, where he spent another 30 years as a producer, then executive, with the CBC before retiring.*
>
> *The literary agent eventually returned Steinhouse's story to him, who let it lie dormant in a cellar trunk in Montreal for 40-odd years, until the release, in December, 1993, of the Steven Spielberg film version of* Schindler's List. *He dug out the article and photos, discovering the pictures still in pristine condition, and sold all to an enthusiastic* Saturday Night, *one of Canada's major magazines, and then quickly also sold the story to*

The *(London England)* Sunday Telegraph; *to* Die Weltwoche, *a weekly newsmagazine in Zurich; to leading reviews in France, Germany, Italy and elsewhere, even Iceland. Only the U.S. media declined, as they had before, with not a single major publication courteous enough to reply to the enquiry or return the copies of photos and documents.*

He has also given permission to reprint the Al Taylor photos to various charitable and non-profit organizations and has deposited everything with the U.S. Holocaust Memorial Museum in Washington, D.C., and the Yad Vashem archives in Jerusalem.

In the 1980s, Al Taylor, his old friend, was the victim of a vicious New York mugging and died in a hospital, a welfare case. All of Taylor's vast holdings of cameras, prints and negatives from a long career as a photographer-writer were lost, including many other Schindler photos.

Steinhouse later wrapped up the Schindler story, quickly resuming the factual record without notes.

"Schindler, his wife and a mistress and a couple of the *Schindlerjuden* were able to leave Germany for the Argentine in the summer of '49. JDC money had come through, via the New York *Schindlerjuden* who had formed an association. The JDC's hands were free of unwanted legal precedent.

"They were generous; boat tickets for him and Emilie and enough to start on something new in the Argentine. Schindler decided that he would raise nutria for the luxury fur market. They settled about a hundred miles from the capital. Emilie planted a garden—fortunately, because that kept them alive.

"Oskar built his cages and fences for his nutria. Nutria were indeed then out-selling mink. But no one had told him that those nutria were wild nutria captured from the jungle. No one had experimented with nutria raised in captivity.

"A year or so later, he discovered them all quite dead. Then he tried his hand at modest farming at another location. That also failed.

"He was optimistic and hopeful—as he always was.

"Eventually he returned to Germany alone, leaving Emilie in the Argentine. Deserting her. That was in 1958.

"He then opened a small cement factory in Germany and again lost his shirt and his benefactors' money. It turned out in the end, and especially according to his wife, that Oskar Schindler was a salesman, a dreamer—and a very bad honest businessman. (Steinhouse laughs).

"He knew how to play the black market and he had known how to become a millionaire. Under wartime conditions of bribery and gifts he made money. But as a straightforward entrepreneur he apparently made a mess of things, in Argentina and again back in Germany.

"He was never to be happy in Germany. His story came out briefly on television in the early '60s. By this time he was living in Frankfurt, where a German recognized him on the street (Steinhouse dramatically pauses between words) and ... spit ... into ... his ... face, and called him a 'Jew kisser.' Which was, of course, one of the things the SS had had against him back in Krakow and for which he had been put in jail. That he had kissed a Jewish girl."

That kiss was in the movie ....

"Yes. So in Frankfurt it caught up with him. Then through various intercessions the German government under Konrad Adenauer gave him a medal, which was very nice, and later a small pension.

"In the meantime he was hungry and depressed and living in a one-room place near the railroad station and still depending, in the 1960s, on handouts from the *Schindlerjuden.* Sometimes he thought of suicide. Then the *Schindlerjuden* group in Israel, which included some of his best friends, like Itzhak Stern, invited him to come to visit.

"That became an annual event. He'd get to Israel and everybody would throw parties. He'd be a big hero, extroverted and happy, and they would all sit at café tables together and he'd drink and drink and drink. He became an alcoholic. And then he wouldn't know what to do in Israel, so he'd go back to Frankfurt. And the next year he'd receive another invitation. His story was publicized in Israel. He was welcomed into the Yad Vashem as a Righteous Gentile. He planted the traditional carob tree at Yad Vashem and went back to Frankfurt.

"And in 1974 he died.

"He had made it clear he wished to be buried as a Catholic in Israel. Friends came from Israel and made arrangements with the archbishop in Frankfurt; his body was exhumed and reburied in the Catholic cemetery on a slope of Mount Zion. Almost all the mourners were Jews.

"And that seemed as if it would be the end of the Oskar Schindler legend, which up to then had been little publicized. A medal pinned on him by Konrad Adenauer, and a tree in Jerusalem. Poverty and alcoholism, from which he died. His wife was still in Argentina. Thomas Keneally hit upon his story quite by chance, in 1980, in Los Angeles."

....

What is the significance of Steinhouse's work, given that his article was never published until 1994, well after the 1982 U.S. publication of Thomas Keneally's Schindler's List?

Quite simply, Steinhouse's early research validates all the rest of the previously publicized *Schindler material.*

Since Thomas Keneally did not have the opportunity to meet Schindler, he, of necessity, had to create out of his novelist's imagination conversations between Schindler and Amon Goeth, and with others now long deceased.

For that reason, Keneally's book, authentic as it is, nevertheless is officially labeled fiction.

Holocaust deniers could, if they wish, dismiss the book as figments of a novelist's imagination.

And those same Holocaust deniers could dismiss the Spielberg film as the product of a Hollywood producer most noted for science fiction.

But Steinhouse's story denies them their denial. Locked in that dusty cellar trunk in Montreal was further proof of the story that began with Pfefferberg and Keneally and Spielberg, proof researched and documented, complete with photographs of the principle players, Schindler, Stern and the Schlinderjuden. *Maybe after all these forty-five years and more, the timing is just right.*

The Man Who Saved a Thousand Lives

by Herbert Steinhouse

Paris, February, 1949.

At a table outside a Paris café recently, three men sat deep in conversation.

"All Germans are bad," the oldest one said. "But *der Oskar*, now there is a fine German." And his two companions nodded grave agreement with this contradiction each had heard so often in the past.

The men varied widely in appearance, and every now and then their talk revealed the equally-wide discrepancies in their interests and their preoccupying thoughts. The old one was a factory owner, once prosperous in his native country, then suddenly ruined by the common disaster of European Jewry and now, with a swiftness that had astonished everyone, plumped-out, active, again the owner of a factory which this time stood in a land whose language he hardly knew, a man worth almost a hundred million francs three years after he had arrived in Paris penniless and beaten.

On his right sat a stern, gaunt man with thick eyebrows and a high forehead flanked by grey temples. Younger and taller than the other two, he called himself a journalist since he had always listed that profession in his passport. Back in prewar Kracow he had indeed basked under a certain reputation and had even been prominent in the literary cafés. Today he earned a thousand francs here and there as an insecure "stringer" correspondent for Yiddish dailies in New York and London. He needed a new

20

suit badly and clung with desperation to his reputation of intellectual.

The third man, sipping a glass of sparkling soda-water, wore his grey pin-stripe neatly, and his carefully-knotted tie was immaculate. He had an honest round face with keen and steady eyes and his manner alternated between poised attentiveness and passionate speech. He had been an accountant in the past, a Chief Accountant he would say, and now he did nothing but maintain a daily vigil in the waiting room of the Emigration offices of the large American Jewish welfare agency, the Joint Distribution Committee, near the Champs Elysées. Some day, he hoped, his visa for some South American country would come across a desk in those offices and he would part company with the tense visa-hunters with whom he shared the waiting-room benches. He pressed creases into his trousers and shined his shoes each morning and lived in the future. He would, he knew, be a respected Chief Accountant once more. He and his wife would have clothes and smart luggage, perhaps even a small car.

Each man thought constantly of his own problems—of production and markets and competition, of insults from editors and how to buy a typewriter, of ships and official rubber stamps and life in a strange country where the climate would be hot and the people hostile. But when one mentioned his own preoccupation, even casually, the others shrugged coldly and rudely turned away. Interest appeared only when there was talk of the common experience that had first thrown together the three widely-different Kracow Jews. For these men, each in a way typical of some thousand or more others who meet and carry on almost identical conversations in the cafés and bars of Durban, New York, Toronto, Wroclau, Haifa and Rio de Janeiro, are "Schindler Juden," linked by a chain of once-shared anguish and hopelessness, and by a similar affection and gratitude for the man who saved their lives, the good German, Oscar Schindler.

Can there be such a person as "the Good German?" Jews the world over, in bitterness and in anger, today might well howl down the suggestion. The scattered remnants of Poland's Jewry, survivors of the Warsaw, Lodz and Vilna ghettos, survivors of Auschwitz, Belsen and Maidenek, would be incredulous at the question itself. They had learned their generalization painfully. The prayed-for salvation of an uprising of bystanding "decent" Germans that would overthrow the criminal madmen never did come. Instead, the Frankfurt worker had helped make I.G.Farben gas for the extermination chambers and the slovenly-uniformed Bavarian peasant boy had dutifully driven the transports to the railway station. An entire people without human values, the Jewish survivor would say. An entire people without decency, without remorse and beyond redemption!

As Jews, the thousand and more men and women who owe their existence to Oscar Schindler today have the dilemma of sharing such a general attitude while simultaneously never forgetting the deeds and character of the one exception who seems to prove the rule. A few purists might point out that Schindler is a *Volksdeutsche* hailing from the Sudetenland. But upon almost the entire group of *Schindlerjuden* the distinction has been wasted. Culturally and politically, Oscar Schindler had always thought as a German. Czechoslovakia's traditions and history meant little to him. His prewar vacations were spent skiing at Garmisch and Bad Reichenhall, never in the High Tatras. He spoke and wrote German almost exclusively. He could have been, but for geographic accident, any average citizen of Stuttgart, Leipzig or Hanover. When the *Schindlerjuden* repeat that "all Germans are bad but *der Oskar* is a good German," they reveal the carefully-compartmentalized mind on the subject that has kept the dilemma from becoming too disconcerting.

There exists only trifling disagreement over the actual facts of the Schindler story. To any display of disbelief, to the "but no German could ever have done all that!" retort which an account of the legend often provokes, the *Schindlerjuden* present a stubborn united front and surprisingly unconfused and uncontradictory versions of the tale.

One of the handful who know even the most intimate details of the story is Isaac Stern, the first of the group to have met Oscar Schindler and ever a confidant. Stern is our Chief Accountant, the refugee in Paris whom we met above. It was from him that I first heard of the man Schindler.

They had met in Kracow in 1939. "I must admit now that I was intensely suspicious of Schindler for a long time," Stern confided, beginning his story. "I suffered greatly under the Fascists. I lost my mother in Auschwitz quite early and I was very embittered."

At the end of 1939, Stern directed the accountancy section of a large Jewish-owned export-import firm, a position he had held since 1924. With the occupation of Poland in November, the head of each important Jewish business was replaced by a German trustee, or *Treuhandler,* and Stern's new boss was a man named Aue. The former owner became an employee, the firm became German and Aryan workers were brought in to replace many of the Jews.

Aue's immediate behaviour had aroused Stern's curiosity. Although he had begun Aryanizing the firm and firing the Jewish workers in accordance with his instructions, Aue at the same time left the discharged employees' names on the social insurance registry, thus enabling them to maintain their all-important workers' identity cards. He secretly gave these hungry men money as well. Such exemplary behaviour could only impress the Jews and astonish the wary and cautious Stern. Only with the end of the war was Stern to learn that Aue had been Jewish himself, that his own father was murdered in Auschwitz in 1942, and that the Polish he pretended to speak so poorly actually was his native tongue.

Not knowing all this, Stern had no reason to trust Aue. Certainly he could not understand the man's presumption when, only a few days after having taken charge of the export-import firm, Aue brought an old friend who had just arrived in Kracow in to see Stern and had said, quite casually, "You know, Stern, you can have confidence in my friend Schindler." Stern had said nothing, had exchanged courtesies with the visitor and had answered his questions with care.

"He wanted to know what kind of Jew I was. He asked me many questions like was I a Zionist or assimilated or what have you. I told him what everyone knew, that I was Vice-President of the Jewish Agency for Western Poland and a member of the Zionist Central Committee. Then he thanked me politely and went away.

"I did not know what he wanted and I was frightened," Stern continued. "Until December 1 we Polish Jews had been left more or less alone. They had Aryanized the factories, of course. And if a German asked you a question in the street it was compulsory for you to precede your answer with "I am a Jew ..." But it was only on December 1 that we had to begin wearing the Star of David. Then it was, just as the situation had begun to grow worse for the Jews, that the sword of Damocles was already over our heads, that I had this meeting with Oscar Schindler."

On December 3 Schindler paid another visit to Stern, this time at night and to his home. They had talked chiefly of literature, Stern remembers, and Schindler had revealed an unusual interest in the great Yiddish writers. And then suddenly, over some tea, Schindler had remarked "I hear that there will be a raid on all remaining Jewish property tomorrow." Recognizing the intended warning, Stern had passed the word around and effectively saved many friends from the most ruthless "control" the Germans had thus far carried out. Schindler, he realized, had been attempting to encourage his confidence, although he could still not fathom why.

Oscar Schindler, a Sudeten industrialist, had come to Kracow from his native town of Zwittau, just across what a few months earlier had been a border. Unlike most of the carpet-baggers who joyously rushed into prostrate Poland to gobble up the nation's production, he received a factory not from an expropriated Jew but from the Court of Commercial Claims. A small concern devoted to the manufacture of chinaware, it had lain idle and in bankruptcy for many years. In the winter of 1939-1940 he began operations with 4,000 square metres of floor space and a hundred workers, of whom seven were Jewish. Soon he managed to bring in Stern as his accountant.

Production started with a rush, for Schindler was a shrewd and a tireless worker, and labor, by now semi-slave, was as plentiful and as cheap as in any industrialist's fondest dream. During the first year the labor force expanded to 300, including 150 Jews. By the end of 1942 the factory had grown to 45,000 square metres and employed almost 800 men and women. The Jewish workers, of whom there were now 370, by this time lived in the Kracow ghetto. "It had become a tremendous advantage," says Stern, "to be able to leave the ghetto in the daytime and work in a German factory."

Outward relations between Schindler and the Jewish workers began and continued on a carefully circumspect plane. In these early days he had little contact with all save the few who, like Stern, worked in the offices. But comparing their lot with that of the Jews trapped in the ghetto from where deportations had by now begun, or even with those who slaved for other Germans in neighbouring factories, Schindler's Jewish workers grew to appreciate their position. Although they could not understand the reasons, they recognized that *der Herr Direktor* was somehow protecting them. An air of quasi-security grew in the factory and the men soon sought permission to bring in families and friends to share in their comparative haven.

Word spread among Kracow's Jews that Schindler's factory was the place to work. And, although the workers did not know it, Schindler helped his Jewish employees by falsifying the factory records. Old people were recorded as being twenty years younger; children were listed as adults. Lawyers, doctors and engineers were registered as metal workers, mechanics and draughtsmen, all trades considered essential to war production. Countless lives were saved in this simple manner as the workers were protected from the extermination commissions who periodically scrutinized Schindler's records.

At the same time, most of the workers did not know that Schindler spent his evenings entertaining many of the local SS and Wehrmacht officers, cultivating influential friends and strengthening his position wherever possible. His easy charm passed as candour, and his personality and seeming political reliability made him popular around Nazi social circles in Kracow.

Stern remained unimpressed by the air of security, however. They were all perched on a volcano's edge, he knew. From behind his high bookkeeper's table he could see through the glass door of Schindler's private office. "Almost every day, from morning until evening, 'controls,' visitors and commissions came to the factory and made me nervous. Schindler used to keep pouring them vodka and joking with them. When they left he would ask me in, close the door and then quietly tell me whatever they had come for. He used to tell them that he knew how to get work out of these Jews and that he wanted more brought in. That was how we managed to get in the families and relatives all the time and save them from deportation." Schindler never offered explanations for his confidences and never revealed himself as a die-hard anti-fascist, but gradually Stern's trust in the man began.

Schindler maintained three other links to "his Jews." Each worked in the factory's office. One was Isaac Stern's brother, Dr. Nathan Stern, a man who lives today as a respected member of Poland's small Jewish community. Magister Label Salpeter and Samuel Wulcan, both old ranking members of the Polish Zionist movement, were the other two. The four also were part of a group that served as a connecting link to the outside underground movement. And in this work they were soon joined by Hildegeist, a former leader of the Socialist Workers' Union in his native Austria who, after three years in Buchenwald, had been taken on in the factory as an accountant. A factory worker, the engineer Pawlik, subsequently to reveal himself to the others as an officer in the Polish underground, led these activities.

Schindler himself played no active role in all this, but his protection served to shelter the group. It is doubtful that so few men did effective resistance work. The mechanism built up in this manner, however, did provide the *Schindlerjuden* with their first cohesiveness and a semblance of discipline that later was to prove useful.

While friends and parents in the ghetto were being murdered in the streets, were dying of disease or were being sent to nearby Auschwitz, daily life in the factory continued in this minor key until 1943. Then, on March 13, came orders to close the Kracow ghetto. All Jews were moved to the forced labor camp of Plaszow, outside the city. Here, in this sprawling series of installations that included subordinate camps throughout the region, conditions even for the Jewish graduates of the terrible Kracow ghetto were shocking. The prisoners suffered and by the hundreds either died in camp or were moved to Auschwitz. The order to complete the extermination of Jewry had already been given and willing hands on all sides cooperated to carry out the command as efficiently and quickly as possible.

Stern and Schindler's other workers had also been moved to Plaszow from the ghetto but, like some 25,000 other inmates who inhabited the camp and worked outside, they continued spending their days in the factory. Falling deathly ill one day, Stern sent word to Schindler urgently pleading for help. Schindler came at once, bringing essential medicines, and continued his visits until Stern recovered. But what he saw in Plaszow had chilled him.

Nor did Schindler like the turn things had taken in his factory. Increasingly helpless before the frenetic Jew-haters and Jew-destroyers, he found that he could no longer joke too easily with the German officials who came on inspections. The double game was becoming more difficult. Incidents happened more and more often. On one occasion, three SS men walked onto the factory floor without warning, arguing among themselves. "I tell you, the Jew is even *lower* than an animal," one was saying. Then, taking out his pistol, he ordered the nearest Jewish worker to leave his machine and pick up some sweepings from the floor. "Eat it," he barked, menacing the man with his gun. The shivering man choked down the mess. "You see what I mean," the SS man explained to his friends as they walked away. "They eat anything at all. Even an animal would never do that."

Another time, during an inspection by an official SS commission, the attention of the visitors was caught by the sight of the old Jew Lamus who was dragging himself across the factory courtyard in an utterly depressed state. The head of the commission asked why the man was so sad, and it was explained to him that Lamus had lost his wife and only child a few weeks earlier during the evacuation of the ghetto. Deeply touched, the commander ordered his adjutant to shoot the Jew "so that he might be reunited with his family in heaven"; then he guffawed and the commission moved on. Schindler was left standing with Lamus and the adjutant.

"Slip your pants down to your ankles and start walking," the adjutant ordered Lamus. Dazed, Lamus did as he was told.

"You are interfering with all my discipline here," Schindler said desperately. The SS officer sneered.

"The morale of my workers will suffer. Production for *der Vaterland* will be affected." Schindler blurted out the words. The officer drew his gun.

"A bottle of *schnapps* if you don't shoot him," Schindler almost screamed, no longer thinking rationally.

"*Shtimt!*" To Schindler's astonishment, the man complied. Grinning, the officer put the gun away and strolled arm-in-arm with the shaken Schindler to collect his bottle at the office. And Lamus, trailing his pants along the ground, continued shuffling across the yard, waiting sickeningly for the bullet in his back that never came.

The increasing frequency of such incidents in the factory and the evil his eyes had seen at the Plaszow camp probably were responsible for moving Schindler into a more active anti-fascist role. In the Spring of 1943, he stopped worrying about the production of chinaware appliances for Wehrmacht barracks and began the conspiring, the string-pulling, the bribery and the shrewd outguessing of Nazi officialdom which finally were to save so many human lives. It is at this point that the real Schindler legend begins. For the next two years, Oscar Schindler's ever-present obsession was how to save the greatest number of Jews from the yawning mouth of the Auschwitz gas chamber that beckoned only sixty miles distant from Kracow.

His first ambitious move was to attempt to help the starving and fearful prisoners at Plaszow. Other labor camps in Poland, such as Lemberg and Maidenek, had already been liquidated and their inhabitants destroyed. Plaszow seemed doomed. At the prompting of Stern and the others of the "inner-office" circle, Schindler one evening managed to convince one of his drinking companions, General Schindler—no relative but well placed as Chief of the War Equipment Command in Poland—that Plaszow's camp workshops would be ideally suited for serious war production. At that time they were being used only for the repair of uniforms. His namesake the General fell in with the idea readily and important orders for wood and metal work were given to the camp. As a result, Plaszow was officially transformed into a war essential concentration camp. And though conditions hardly improved, it came off the list of labor camps which then were being done away with. Temporarily at least, Auschwitz's fires were cheated of more fuel.

The move also put Schindler in well with Plaszow's Commander, the Hauptsturmfuehrer Goeth, who with the change now found his status elevated to a new dignity. When Schindler requested that those Jews who continued to work in his factory be moved into their own sub-camp near the plant "to save time in getting to the job," Goeth complied. From then on, Schindler found that with little danger he could have food and medicines smuggled into the barracks. The guards, of course, were bribed and Goeth never was to discover the true motives of Schindler's request.

He began to take bigger risks. Interceding for Jews who were denounced for one "crime" or another was a dangerous habit in Fascist eyes but Schindler now started to do this almost regularly. "Stop killing my good workers," was his usual technique. "We've got a war to win. These things can always be settled later." The ruse succeeded often enough to save dozens of doomed lives.

One August morning in 1943, Schindler played host to two surprise visitors who had been sent to him by the underground organization that the American Jewish welfare agency, the Joint Distribution Committee, then operated in Occupied Europe. Satisfied that the men indeed had been sent by Dr. Rudolph Kastner, fabulous head of the secret JDC apparatus who was at the time leading a shadowy existence in Budapest with a sizable price on his head, Schindler called for Stern. "Speak frankly to these men, Stern," he said. "Let them know what has been going on in Plaszow." "We want a full report on the anti-Semitic persecutions," the visitors told Stern. "Write us a comprehensive report." "Go ahead," urged Schindler. "They are Swiss. It is safe. You can rely on them. Sit down and write."

To Stern the risk was purposeless and foolhardy, and he flared up. Turning angrily to Schindler, he asked, "Schindler, tell me frankly, isn't this a provocation? It is most suspicious." Schindler in turn became angry at Stern's sudden mistrust. "Write!" he ordered. Stern had little choice. He wrote everything he could think of, mentioned names of those living and those dead, and turned out the long letter which, years later, he discovered was circulated widely and helped to bring courage or settle uncertainties in the hearts of the prisoners' relatives scattered around the free world outside Europe. And when the underground subsequently brought him answering letters from America and Palestine, any doubts he still might have had of the integrity or judgment of Oscar Schindler vanished.

Life in the Schindler factory went on. Some of the less hardy men and women died but the majority continued doggedly at their machines, turning out chinaware fixtures for the German army. Schindler and his "inner-office" circle by now had become taut and apprehensive, wondering just how long they could continue their game of deception. Schindler himself still entertained the local officers, but with the change of tide that followed Stalingrad and the invasion of Italy, Fascist tempers were often out of control. A penstroke could send the Jewish workers to Auschwitz and Schindler along with them. The group moved cautiously, increased the bribes to the guards at the camp and the factory and, with Schindler's smuggled food and medicines, fought for survival. The year 1943 became 1944. Daily, life ended for thousands of Polish Jews. But the *Schindlerjuden*, to their own surprise, still found themselves alive.

By the Spring of 1944 the German retreat on the Eastern Front was on in earnest. Plaszow and all its sub-camps were ordered emptied. Schindler and his workers had no illusions about what a move to another concentration camp implied. The time had come for Oscar Schindler to play his trump card, a daring gamble that he had devised beforehand with the help of his small group.

He went to work on all his drinking companions, on his connections in military and industrial circles in Kracow and in Warsaw. He bribed, cajoled, pleaded, working desperately against time and fighting what everyone assured him was a *Verlorene Sache*—a lost cause. He got on a train and saw people in Berlin. And he persisted until someone, somewhere in the hierarchy, perhaps impatient to end the seemingly trifling business, finally gave him the authorization to move a force of 1000 Jews—700 men and 300 women—from the Plaszow camp into a factory at Brnenec in his native Sudetenland. Most of the other 25,000 men, women and children at Plaszow were sent to Auschwitz, there to find the same end that several million other Jews had already discovered. But out of the vast calamity, and through the stubborn efforts of one man, 1000 Jews were saved temporarily. One thousand half-starved, sick and almost broken human beings had had a death sentence commuted by a miraculous reprieve.

One evening in January, 1949 some thirty-five *Schindlerjuden* gathered privately at Aux Armes de Colmar, an Alsatian restaurant in the north of Paris, to fête their friend Oscar Schindler who was then passing through the city. Members of the group had come in from Switzerland, Brussels and Marseille for the event. All were gay and exuberant, and the warm night echoed with their laughter as they surrounded the beaming and perspiring Schindler. *"Sto Lat!"* they toasted him with passion as they roared out the traditional Polish song, "A hundred years may he live!" Glasses of white wine flashed in the air, and on raised arms all around, sleeves slipped back to reveal the tattoos of the concentration camp.

The speeches were full of florid tributes. "It was known throughout Poland that whoever went to Schindler's factory was safe," said the industrialist movingly. "He did not do it out of crass stupidity, nor out of scheming for the future," the journalist told the animated group. "At the Sudetenland factory they sneered at us as *Schindlerjuden*, said a textile worker. "Today we are proud of that name."

Schindler spoke with joyful tears in his eyes, fervently stammering his thanks for the warm demonstration. "Germans today seem to share a collective innocence," he told them bitterly, "not the collective guilt they should." When his speech was over, he rushed from table to table, embracing each of "his children," as he called them, still fighting back his happy tears. Again he was toasted.

As we ate our Alsatian meal, everyone eagerly plied me with new details of the common experience and confirmed the stories originally recounted by Stern as well as those I had heard from Schindler himself when I had visited him a few months earlier in his modest room in a Munich suburb. The saga was brought up to date.

The move of the group from the Polish factory to the new quarters in Czechoslovakia, had not been uneventful. One lot of 100 did go out directly in July, 1944, and arrived at Brnenec safely. The remainder, however, found their train diverted without warning to the concentration camp of Gross Rosen where many were beaten and tortured and where all were forced to stand in even files in the great courtyard, doing absolutely nothing but putting on and taking off their caps in unison all day long. At length Schindler once more proved successful at pulling strings. By early November all of the *Schindlerjuden* were again united in their new camp.

And until liberation in the Spring of 1945 they continued to outwit the Nazis at the dangerous game of remaining alive. Ostensibly the new factory was producing parts for V2 bombs but actually, as everyone assured me, the output during those ten months between July and May was absolutely nil.

Jews escaping from the transports then evacuating Auschwitz and the other easternmost camps ahead of the oncoming Russians found haven with no questions asked. Schindler even brazenly requested the Gestapo to send him all intercepted Jewish fugitives, in the interest, he said, of continued war production. A hundred additional people were saved in this way, including Jews from Belgium, Holland and Hungary. "His Children" reached the number of 1098: 801 men and 297 women.

The *Schindlerjuden* by now depended on him completely and were fearful in his absence. His compassion and sacrifice were unstinting. He spent every bit of money still left in his possession, and his wife's jewelry as well, on food, clothing, medicines and for *Schnapps* with which to bribe the many SS investigators. He furnished a secret hospital with stolen and black-market medical equipment, fought epidemics and once made a 300-mile trip himself carrying two enormous flasks filled with Polish vodka and bringing them back full of desperately-needed serum. His wife cooked and cared for the sick. Emilie Schindler earned her own reputation and praise.

In the factory some of the men began turning out false rubber stamps, military travel documents and the special official papers needed to protect the delivery of food bought illicitly. Nazi uniforms and guns were collected and hidden, along with ammunition and hand grenades, as all eventualities were prepared for. The risks mounted and the tension grew.

Schindler, however, seems to have maintained virtually unshakable equilibrium throughout this period. "Perhaps I had become fatalistic," he said later. "Or perhaps I was just afraid of the danger that would come once the men began to lose hope and acted rashly. I had to keep them full of optimism."

But two real frights did disturb his normal calm during the constant perils of these months. The first was when a group of workers, lost for some means of expressing their pent-up gratitude, foolishly told him that they had heard the illegal radio broadcast a promise to name a street in post-war Palestine "Oscar Schindler Strasse." For days he waited for the Gestapo to come around and drag him away. When the hoax was finally admitted he could no longer laugh.

The other occurred during a visit from the local SS Commandant. As was customary, the SS officer sat in Schindler's office drinking glass after glass of vodka and getting drunk rapidly. When he lurched perilously near an iron staircase leading to the basement, Schindler, suddenly yielding to temptation, made one of his rare unpremeditated acts. A slight push, and then a howl and a dull thud from the bottom. But the man was not dead. Climbing back into the room with blood pouring from his scalp, he bellowed that Schindler had shot him. And running out, cursing with rage, he had flung over his shoulder, "You will not live until any liberation, Schindler. Don't think you fool us. You belong in a concentration camp yourself, along with all your Jews!"

Schindler understood "his children" and catered to their fears. Near the factory he had been given a beautifully-furnished villa that overlooked the length of the valley where the small Czech village lay. But since the workers always dreaded the SS visits which might come late at night and spell their end, Oscar and Emilie Schindler never spent a single night at the villa, sleeping instead in a small room in the factory itself.

When Jewish workers died they were secretly buried with full rites despite Nazi rulings that their corpses be burned. Religious holidays were observed clandestinely and celebrated with extra rations of black market food.

Perhaps the most absorbing of all the legends that *Schindlerjuden* on four continents repeat is one that graphically illustrates Schindler's self-adopted role of protector and saviour in the midst of general and amoral indifference.

Just about the time the Nazi empire was crashing down heavily, a phone call from the railway station late one evening asked Schindler whether he cared to accept delivery of three railway cars full of near-frozen Jews. The cars were hermetically sealed at a temperature of 5 degrees above zero, Fahrenheit, and contained almost a hundred sick men who had been locked inside for ten days, ever since the train had been sent off from Auschwitz with orders to deliver the human cargo to some willing factory. But when informed of the condition of the prisoners, no factory manager would hear of receiving them. "We are not running a sanitarium!" was the usual word. Schindler, sickened by the news, ordered the train sent to his factory siding at once.

The train was awesome to behold. Ice had formed on the locks and the cars had to be opened with axes and acetylene torches. Inside, the miserable relics of human beings were stretched out, frozen stiff. Each had to be carried out like carcasses of frozen, shriveled beef. Four were unmistakably dead but the others still breathed.

Throughout that night and for many days and nights following, Oscar and Emilie Schindler and a number of the men worked without halt on the frozen and starved skeletons. One large room in the factory was emptied for the purpose. Three more men died, but with the care, the warmth, the milk and the medicines, the others gradually rallied. All this had been achieved surreptitiously, with the factory guards, as usual, receiving their bribes so as not to inform the SS Commandant. The men's convalescence also had to be effected secretly lest they be shot as useless invalids. Later they became part of the factory labor force and joined the others in the motions of feigning war production.

Such was life at Brnenec until the arrival of the victorious Russians on May 9 put an end to the constant nightmare. The day before, Schindler had decided that they would have to get rid of the local SS commander just in case he suddenly remembered his drunken threat and got any desperate last-minute ideas. The task was not difficult for the guards had already begun pouring out of town in panic. Unearthing their hidden weapons, a group slipped out of the factory late at night, found the SS officer drinking himself into oblivion in his room and shot him from outside his window. In the morning, once certain that his workers finally were out of danger and that all was in order to explain to the Russians, Schindler, his wife Emilie and several of his closest Jewish friends discreetly disappeared and were not heard from until they turned up, months later, deep in Austria's U.S. Zone.

For the Nazis he had known all the answers. But at the end he had decided that, as an owner of a German slave-labor factory, he would take no chances on Russian troops casually shooting him before asking for character references or his particular views on the Fascist system.

In the four years that followed, the *Schindlerjuden* regained their health and scattered to many countries. Some joined relatives in America, others found their way, legally or illegally, to Israel, France and South America. A majority returned to Poland but many of these drifted out again and began the life of DPs in Germany's many UNRRA, later IRO, camps. Most inevitably lost touch with their good friend Oscar Schindler.

For him, everyday life became difficult and unsettled. A Sudeten German, he had no future in Czechoslovakia and at the same time could no longer stand the Germany he had once loved. For a time he tried living in Regensburg. Later he moved to Munich, depending heavily on Care parcels sent him from America by some of the *Schindlerjuden* but ever remaining too proud to plead for help. Polish Jewish welfare organizations traced him, discovered him in want and tried to bring some assistance even in the midst of all their own bitter postwar troubles. Ultimately the problem of effecting some sort of restitution was passed on to the Joint Distribution Committee.

He began to receive a full JDC ration of food and cigarettes, living like any Jewish DP in the country and being kept alive while a permanent solution and recompense were sought. He became as anti-German in his sentiments as any of the Jewish DPs who now became his only friends. He proved useful to American authorities, and brought a heap of dangerous hostility upon his own head, by presenting the CIC with detailed documentation on all his old drinking companions, on the vicious owners of the other slave factories that had stood near his, on all the rotten group he had wined and flattered, while inwardly loathing, in order to save the lives of helpless people.

Such is the Schindler story that a thousand people in many different countries today tell. The baffling problem that remains is what actually made Oscar Schindler tick? It is doubtful whether any of the *Schindlerjuden* have yet discovered the real answer. One of them guesses that he was motivated largely by an obsession of guilt, since it seems a safe assumption that he must have been a member—perhaps an important one—of the Henlein Party, Czechoslovakia's prewar Fascist movement, in order to have earned himself a factory in Poland and the trust of the Nazis. Another agrees with this hypothesis but refines it on the strength of a rumour. Schindler first parted company with the Nazis, says this theorist, when a young, hot-headed German stormtrooper entered his house and savagely struck his wife in front of him during the 1938 march into the Sudetenland.

Inquiries in Czechoslovakia have produced many who knew him but more confusion than elucidation. One witness, Ifo Zwicker, not only was among the Jews whom Schindler saved but by a happy coincidence had lived for years in Zwittau, Schindler's birthplace and home town. Yet after enthusiastically confirming the now-familiar Schindler saga, Zwicker could only add, uncertainly, "As a Zwittau citizen I never would have considered him capable of all these wonderful deeds. Before the war, you know, everyone here called him *Gauner* (swindler or sharper)." But was the *Gauner* so slick and so disingenuous that he had become an anti-fascist because he knew his old friends were doomed? Hardly the answer to explain a conversion in 1939 or 1940, or to account for a hundred serious risks of quick death!

The only possible conclusion seems to be that Oscar Schindler's exceptional deeds stemmed from just that elementary sense of decency and humanity that our sophisticated age seldom sincerely believes in. A repentant opportunist saw the light and rebelled against the sadism and vile criminality all around him. The inference may be disappointingly simple, especially for all amateur psychoanalysts who would prefer the deeper and more mysterious motive which may, it is true, still lie unprobed and unappreciated. But an hour with Oscar Schindler encourages belief in the simple answer.

Today [1949], at forty-one, Schindler is indeed a man of convincing honesty and outstanding charm. Tall and erect, with broad-shoulders and a powerful trunk, he usually has a cheerful smile on his strong face. His frank, gray-blue eyes smile too, except when they tighten in distressed memory as he talks of the past. Then his whole jaw juts out belligerently and his great fists are clenched and pounded in slow anger. When he laughs, it is a boyish and hearty laugh, one which he and all his listeners enjoy to the full. "It's the personality more than anything else that saved us," one of the group once remarked.

In 1948, the continuous efforts being made by many people on his behalf finally bore fruit. After years of trying, the JDC received authorization for his permanent exit from Germany. The organization then presented him with a cash grant, a visa for Argentina and a boat ticket, and helped him bring to an end the drifting confusion and poverty of the post-war years. Oscar and Emilie Schindler boarded a boat in Genoa and sailed towards their unknown future. Many of "his children" waited in South America to greet them.

Part Two

The Author and the Book — How Thomas Keneally wrote "Schindler's List"

Making Novels of Life's Ethical Dilemmas

by Pedro E. Ponce
The Chronicle of Higher Education, Feb. 2, 1994

Thomas Keneally stumbled onto one of his biggest inspirations while buying a briefcase.

Mr. Keneally was shopping in a luggage store in Beverly Hills, Cal., in 1980 when he first heard the story of Oskar Schindler. Poldek Pfefferberg,[1] the store's owner, told of how he and his wife were among the 1,200 Jews whose lives were saved by Schindler, who ran a factory in wartime Poland for the Nazis.

Schindler managed to persuade his superiors that his workers were essential to the German war effort. Mr. Pfefferberg had helped him provide workers with food and other supplies from the black market.

A 'Documentary Novel'

Mr. Keneally, an Australian writer who now teaches in the graduate writing program at the University of California at Irvine, turned the story into a book, *Schindler's Ark*, published in 1982 in Britain, where it won the Booker Prize. It was released in the United States the same year as *Schindler's List*.

While he based the book on interviews with many people who knew Schindler, Mr. Keneally wrote what he calls a "documentary novel," not a

---

[1] Pfefferberg Americanized his name to Leopold Page.

standard biography. "I thought of him as very much partaking of the paradoxes that are favored by the novel," he says of Schindler's contradictory character. "Paradox is what turns novelists on. Linear valor is not as important to them as light and shade."

Steven Spielberg's film of the story was released in December [1994], and critical acclaim for it ... thrust the book onto the best-seller lists.

Mr. Keneally admits that he wasn't sure how Mr. Spielberg would handle the story. "It wasn't clear that that gulf could be spanned" between blockbusters like *Jaws* and *E. T.* and a serious story of the Holocaust, he says.

But he praises the finished product. "You get very much the sense that these people are a fragment of a great cataclysm," he says about how the film avoids sentimentality. He also likes how Mr. Spielberg faithfully portrayed Schindler's moral ambiguity.

Ethical dilemmas have been at the center of Mr. Keneally's thinking and fiction for some time. Born in Australia in 1935, he was raised in Sydney and studied for the Catholic priesthood at St. Patrick's College in New South Wales. There, he says, he spent considerable time thinking about the boundaries of his faith. "Posing moral questions has had its impact on me," he says. "All those questions are, in a way, novels."

'Dropped off a truck'

He abandoned his studies in 1959, disillusioned with a church hierarchy that he says refused to change with the times. "A lot of people started to leave because they didn't find the church a sympathetic-enough environment," he remembers. "You were either in the elect, or you dropped off the back of the truck."

As a youth, he had always written, inspired by the epics of Sir Walter Scott. No longer committed to the priesthood, he decided to take up writing in earnest.

It wasn't until he had published his third novel, *Bring Larks and Heroes* (1967), that he began to receive attention. More raves followed with the publication of *The Chant of Jimmie Blacksmith* (1972), a novel about the plight of Australia's aborigines. In the last decade, he published six more novels, including *To Asmara* (1989), a best-selling story about the Eritrean revolt against Ethiopia in the 1980's.

Mr. Keneally writes frequently about seminal events in the history of nations. Despite his painstaking research, he says that "you can't do it right for everyone," when writing about events that affect so many people.

Mr. Keneally is now working on a novel about Irish settlers in New South Wales at the turn of the century. And this year [1994], Merchant Ivory, the British company responsible for producing such films as *A Room With a View* and *The Remains of the Day*, is set to film *The Playmaker*, Mr. Keneally's 1987 novel about prison inmates in Australia when the country was a British penal colony.

Mr. Keneally also applies his moral sensibility to politics in his native land. In 1991 he helped found the Australian Republican Movement, and he served as its chairman until [1993].

The organization leads a growing movement in Australia to sever ties to the British monarchy. "Ethnically, we're no longer British," he says, referring to the influx of Chinese, Vietnamese, and other people into Australia since the end of the British Empire. "That's [a movement] not represented by a symbol of privilege like the British monarchy."

Time to teach

In between his writing and political careers, Mr. Keneally also finds time to teach. He taught at Australia's University of New England in the late 1960's and at New York University from 1988 to 1990. He was a visiting professor at Irvine in 1985 and has been a distinguished professor there since 1991.

Mr. Keneally says he wants students to "shake the tree," constantly challenging themselves in their work. When choosing students for Irvine's renowned graduate writing program, he looks for "the person who can write about ordinary events but in a way that gives them the reek of the unexpected, the utterly individual."

In addition to his writing courses, he teaches comparative literature. One of his recent offerings was "Imagining War and Peace." Using examples ranging from Ireland to East Africa, Mr. Keneally and his students explored the ways in which literature represents major historical conflicts.

Despite the political and moral commitments of his fiction, Mr. Keneally has no rigorous working methods. To start a project, he says, he dictates ideas onto a tape while strolling the beach in California or Sydney. Once his ideas begin to take shape, he transcribes the tape onto a laptop computer.

As for how he gets his ideas, Mr. Keneally says, "It's pretty much like falling in love. You can't choose it. That's what happened with Schindler. I was just trying to buy a briefcase."

Keneally's Luck

································

*'Schindler' Author Wins Attention
for Rest of His Respected Oeuvre*

by Fritz Lanham
Houston Chronicle, April 24, 1994

Thomas Keneally fairly beams with good humor. He's fathered 25 literary offspring over the past three decades, and one of them, a precocious 12-year-old named *Schindler's List*, is a paperback best seller, more than a million copies having tumbled off the presses since December.

And, he happily reports, his most recent novel published in the United States, *Woman of the Inner Sea* (1993), "is being much helped by the fact that its big sister was kissed by Mr. Spielberg."

Keneally, 58, has long been a successful and respected as well as prolific writer. The hard-cover version of *Schindler's List* (originally published in London in 1982 under the title *Schindler's Ark*) won the coveted Booker Prize, the most prestigious literary award in Great Britain, and sold about a million copies worldwide.

With the extraordinary success of Steven Spielberg's film *Schindler's List*, which dominated the [1994] Academy Awards and is being hailed as a classic, Keneally has become something approaching a household name.

Reporters seek him out, and he's tapped for speaking engagements. He was invited to be on hand at the Oscars. "I'm amply rewarded for my trouble," he says, meditating on the recent sales figures for his books.

The Australian-born Keneally was in Houston recently to speak at a Houston Forum dinner honoring cultural patron Dominique de Menil. In an interview before the event, he praised the film, which he's seen six or seven times, for conveying the ambiguity of Oskar Schindler's character.

"The more you look into the Schindler story, the more remarkable, not the less remarkable, the story becomes," Keneally said.

In a Beverly Hills luggage shop in 1980 he first heard of the German industrialist who saved 1,200 Jewish workers from almost certain death in Nazi concentration camps ... He'd stopped in to buy a briefcase. When the proprietor, Leopold Pfefferberg, a *Schindlerjude* himself, learned that Keneally was a writer, he insisted on telling the story.

In the course of researching the book, Keneally interviewed 50 Schindler survivors. Oskar himself was beyond reach, having died six years earlier.

Keneally doubts that Schindler could have cast much light on his own motives. One Holocaust survivor, years after the war, spent a night drinking with Schindler and asked him several times why he risked his life to save the Jews. Schindler gave a different answer every time, Keneally said.

"He wasn't the sort of man who stood back and analyzed what he was doing."

Keneally would have asked Schindler about "the list." Late in the war, Schindler was ordered to shut down his factory in Poland. He talked German authorities into allowing him to move his Jewish laborers to his native Czechoslovakia and open another plant. The list contained the names of the workers assigned to the new factory. As the workers well knew, not being on the list might mean a trip to the gas chambers of Auschwitz.

The Spielberg movie implied that Schindler and his Jewish accountant, Stern, had control over the list. The reality was less tidy, Keneally said. After Schindler and his associates, the list went into the hands of a Jewish functionary named Goldberg, who apparently took bribes to add or bump names. There are people alive today who were bumped from the list—and still blame Schindler.

Keneally doesn't think Schindler himself took bribes—the amounts would have been trivial compared to what he made on the black market—but that area remains fuzzy.

While Schindler had a good thing going, exploiting slave labor to produce goods he sold both to the German military and on the black market, his actions can't be reduced to mercenary motives, Keneally said.

Late in the war he turned to the black market to buy weapons for his workers so they could defend themselves. He also took into his factory Jews who were so weak that they obviously couldn't be considered "essential workers." He was taken into custody and interrogated several times. No one knows how close he came to getting shot for his activities.

"I think if the war had lasted another four or five months, he could have been in serious trouble," Keneally said.

"He was the sort of man who would have been very surprised to have been shot. Even if he'd been arrested again, it may be that his contacts (in the German government) would have sworn by him—the people he'd supplied with fancy food, fancy drink, even sex. But ultimately, if the war had gone on and on, he would have gotten too outrageous for even them to handle."

The cover of *Schindler's List* calls it a novel—a label that has occasioned considerable confusion. Actually, it's a carefully researched, true account that incorporates some of the storytelling devices of fiction.

Keneally calls it "a documentary novel," "a nonfiction novel," a "faction," and professes to be "astounded that people are so mystified about where it fits, given that you have had a number of famous American books that are in this genre, like *In Cold Blood* and *The Right Stuff* and *The Executioner's Song* and *The Armies of the Night.*"

What dialogue there is in the book is based on survivors' recollections of what was said, or what they were told was said. Keneally did not fuse events for dramatic purposes. Indeed he sent parts or all of his manuscript to some 20 Schindler survivors to make sure he was telling the story the way it happened.

Schindler's List may soon be joined on the screen by another Keneally novel, *The Playmaker*, scheduled to be filmed by the team of James Ivory and Ismail Merchant, known for their adaptations of such literary works as *Howards End* and *A Room With a View.* Set in Australia in the 18th century, when the country was a British penal colony, *The Playmaker* centers on a group of inmates and their keepers trying to stage a version of George Farquhar's comedy *The Recruiting Officer.*

Keneally, who has taught creative writing at the University of California at Irvine since 1991, has just started a novel about the catastrophes that befell Ireland in the mid-19th century—the potato famine, political oppression, massive emigration. Keneally is of Irish Catholic ancestry and once studied to be a priest.

He also intends to continue agitating for an end to Australia's membership in the British Commonwealth. He has been chairman of the Australian Republican Movement since 1991, and he takes the matter seriously.

Australia's future is as a Pacific Rim country, not as an adjunct European one, he said. Having the British queen as Australia's head of state doesn't help forge ties with Asian countries. He expects Australia to become a republic by the year 2000.

"To get on with our neighbors," he said, "I think we have to show that we're not deluded about our place in the world, that we've gotten the news that the British Empire no longer exists, and that we are trying to produce a more appropriate system for the sort of country we now are."

"Schindler's" Author Gives Film a Standing Ovation

························

by Valerie Takahama
The Orange County Register, January 2, 1994

Author Thomas Keneally has attended screenings of *Schindler's List* with luminaries such as President Clinton, Hillary Rodham Clinton, director Steven Spielberg and actors Liam Neeson and Ben Kingsley.

But the person whose reaction resonated most strongly with the Australian novelist and professor at the University of California, Irvine, was a Jewish woman from New York whose siblings perished in a forced-labor camp during a so-called health *aktion*, a weeding-out of the weak.

"She found it wonderful. It made her weep, but I've got a strong sense that it's the right kind of tears," Keneally said from his home in Sydney, Australia.

That as evocative and deeply honest a film—one that can elicit healing tears—has come from the director of *E. T.—The Extra-Terrestrial* and *Raiders of the Lost Ark* has stunned many critics. But it was no surprise to Keneally, who is effusive in his praise of the film.

"I hate to put the kibosh—the mockers, as we say in Australia—on it, but I think this could be like *Lawrence of Arabia*," he said. "I think it's a really big film in its import and in its technical achievements and in its bravery."

Keneally, who saw the movie for the first time only a month ago, found the story of Oskar Schindler during a chance meeting in 1980 with Leopold

Page, one of the more than 1,000 Jews saved by Schindler. On tour promoting a book, Keneally had broken his briefcase and went looking for a new one in Page's Beverly Hills luggage shop. As they waited for Keneally's credit-card clearance, Page found out his customer was a novelist and announced that he had "the story of the century."

The novel was published to critical acclaim in 1982; as *Schindler's Ark*, it won Britain's prestigious Booker Prize for fiction. The film rights were sold to Spielberg the next year, and Keneally, for one, is grateful that it has taken a decade to make it to the screen.

"Mind you, I think if he'd made it in early '80s as was originally planned, it might not have been as good a film. He's changed," Keneally said. "We're all like that. Given a particular story in one decade and again in another, we'd all tell it differently. As we age, we get wiser or sillier or whatever."

Keneally, who has said that as a writer he stuck to the facts of Oskar Schindler story "down to the smallest detail of calorie allowances," noted a few factual lapses in the film. But he saw them as true to the story.

"There was a big roundup of people in Krakow in June 1942, and then there was the liquidation of the ghetto in 1943. These two incidents were put together in the film because anything else would be dramatically defusing—and yet the way it's told is true to the events according to survivors."

Keneally said he was initially drawn to Schindler's story in part because the German's motivations and character were ambiguous. Schindler risked his life to save Jews, but he was a hard-drinking adulterer and war profiteer who used bribes and gambling to enjoy the good life.

"The big fear the author of the original work would have with a film is whether or not it retains the ambiguities, and it's there in spades. I'd say it's triumphantly ambiguous," he said.

Still, the "little director" in his head might have made a change: "I would have had Oskar playing in the black market right up to the end. His factory never produced any viable goods, but he was still making a killing on the black market. The film doesn't tell you this.

"But then you think, what would you have dropped to put that in? There were a few matters of emphasis, but I'm not going to argue with a master filmmaker like Steven."

He was particularly impressed by Spielberg's depiction of the clearing of Krakow's Jewish ghetto and searches of buildings using dogs and stethoscopes.

"You see the lights suddenly coming on in flashes. It tells a world of horror without driving audiences from cinema. The movie takes you through the mill, but you emerge triumphantly at the other end a different and exalted person."

He also praised the director's deft use of lists, one of the film's visual motifs.

"The last time I saw Steven—it's not as if I'm in his pocket, but we had a long lunch—and I said, when it was published in England, it was called *Schindler's Ark* because of the Ark of the Covenant, so I asked him, 'Why don't you call it *Schindler's Ark*?' He said because he wanted to make a lot about lists.

"When you think about it, he's right. This is all about lists and the most horrible kind of bureaucracy. The whole film is full of recurrent lists; there are right lists and wrong lists. And every time you see a folding table and chair and an inkwell on the table in an open-air place, you get the shivers. You know people are going to be divided, and it's going to be done with that extra bureaucratic correctness that those lists represent."

Keneally said he hoped Spielberg's cinematic triumph would lead the public back to the novel. And that appears to be happening: Simon & Schuster's Touchtone edition has been published as a movie tie-in with a new cover, and it's already gone back to press seven times for 275,000 copies.

"What's remarkable is that if a book becomes a film, that doesn't mean the book's any better than it was when it was originally published, but it has impact in the public's mind. It's irrational but welcome," said Keneally, whose 1972 novel, *The Chant of Jimmie Blacksmith*, was filmed by Fred Schepisi, and whose 1987 novel, *The Playmaker*, will be Peter Weir's next film.

"I'm hoping, too, that the movie will draw attention to other beloved children who aren't as favored, who don't go dancing with Spielberg. That's really what novelists are about. Above all, they want their works read and appreciated."

Part Three

The Producer and the Film— Steven Spielberg, His version of "Schindler's List" and the critics

Spielberg's "List"

Director Rediscovers His Jewishness while Filming Nazi Story

by Edward Guthmann
San Francisco Chronicle, Dec. 12, 1993

Heartbreak and tragedy aren't the qualities you expect from Steven Spielberg. Fantasy and whimsy—yes. A warm inner glow—yes. A celebration of "the inner child"—yes. Dinosaurs and cuddly aliens and bicycles sailing in front of the moon—you bet.

But not genocide.

And yet, in his newest and bravest film, "Schindler's List" ..., Spielberg abandons the cinematic qualities that made him the world's most successful movie-maker, and turns his attention to a three-hour epic about the Holocaust. Filmed in black and white, "Schindler's List" has virtually no special effects, was shot largely with hand-held cameras, includes full-frontal nudity and explores the nightmare of the Nazi concentration camps with unsparing fidelity.

It doesn't sound like a Spielberg film, and Spielberg knows it. Last spring, while shooting "Schindler's List" in Krakow, Poland, close to the notorious Auschwitz death camp, Spielberg enthused, "This has been the best experience I've had making a movie.... I feel more connected with the material than I've ever felt before."

Today, speaking in his spacious adobe-style office complex at Universal Studios, home to his hugely successful Amblin Entertainment, Spielberg says that "Schindler's List" has changed his life—that the making of the film has reconnected him with his Jewishness, brought him closer to his family and enriched his life in ways that he's still trying to figure out.

"I'm recovering from this movie," Spielberg says. "And my wife [actress Kate Capshaw] thinks the recovery is going to go on for a long time. She says that I'm not myself. And I'm glad I'm not myself."

Looking back on the months he spent in Poland, where he was joined by his wife, their five children, his parents, his rabbi and numerous other relatives ("I would've gone crazy without them"), Spielberg says that the making of "Schindler's List" was unlike anything he's done before. "It wasn't like making a movie. I know what that process is—I've done it enough times in the past. This was like going to have an experience."

Dressed in loafers, a green pullover and khaki chinos, Spielberg is informal, thoughtful and gentle in manner during a one-hour interview. It's unusual for him to devote so much time to publicizing one of his movies—they're usually sold through massive marketing campaigns—but "Schindler's List," an obvious labor of love, demands that special attention. As Kathleen Kennedy, the former president of Amblin Entertainment, said last spring, "I've never seen him so passionately involved in something."

Nearly every film maker goes through a postpartum depression at the end of a project—a time when he or she feels abandoned and lonely, as if a beloved child had walked out the front door and said good-by forever. In Spielberg's case, that condition was exacerbated by the subject matter of "Schindler's List." One gets the impression that Spielberg, at 46, has gone through a heartbreaking, life-changing experience.

Hearing it put this way, Spielberg brightens and says, "*Exactly*! I have trouble saying those words but that's exactly what it is. Because when *you* say those words, they sound noble. When *I* say those words, I feel like I'm sounding pretentious. So I've not made that statement to anybody in the press, even though it's true."

Based on a best-selling 1982 novel by Australian writer Thomas Keneally, "Schindler's List" tells the true story of Oskar Schindler, a notorious Nazi war profiteer who succeeded in bribing and finagling high-ranking Nazi officials—often by drinking them under the table—and who, for reasons that remain mysterious, risked his life by saving more than 1,100 Jews from Nazi death camps.

He was the least likely of saviors. A roué and a scoundrel, partial to

Panama hats and double-breasted silk suits, Schindler first hired Jews as un-paid workers in his enamelware factory on the outskirts of Krakow. In 1944, when the Nazis shut down the factory and gave orders to send his workers to Auschwitz, Schindler established a munitions factory on the Polish/Czechoslovakian border, and persuaded officials to release his "list" of workers to him—claiming they were necessary to the war effort. In a stroke of unconventional casting, Irish actor Liam Neeson plays Schindler. Ben Kingsley co-stars as Itzhak Stern, the Jewish accountant who assisted him.

Filmed in a documentary style that's often grim and unforgivingly re-alistic, "Schindler's List" paints a vivid portrait of Schindler, and re-creates the horrors of Hitler's Final Solution: the purging of the Jewish ghetto in Krakow, when Jews were forced from homes and businesses; the trans-porting of camp prisoners in railway cattle cars; the horrors of the Plaszow death camp, where brutal Nazi commandant Amon Goeth (played by Ralph Fiennes) carried a pistol and executed Jews with the airy disregard of a man swatting flies.

Unlike many Jewish children of the '50s, whose parents struggled to block out the past, Spielberg always knew about Hitler and the 6 million Jews he exterminated. He couldn't help it: His grandmother was living in Cincinnati and teaching English to Holocaust survivors. It was in her home that Spielberg, just 5 at the time, saw concentration camp numbers tattooed on their forearms.

"I can't remember a time I wasn't conscious of it," he says. "My par-ents talked about the atrocities, without using that word. They didn't say 'the Holocaust,' either. But they talked about it all the time…. They would say, 'We're telling you so that it should never happen again.'"

Spielberg first read "Schindler's List" in 1982, when MCA-Universal President Sidney Sheinberg saw a New York Times review and brought it to his attention. "I was drawn to it because of the paradoxical nature of the character," Spielberg says. "It wasn't about a Jew saving Jews, or a neu-tral person from Sweden or Switzerland saving Jews. It was about a Nazi sav-ing Jews.

"I was fascinated by him: He was a gadabout, a fastidious womanizer who bought favors left and right. He provided women, cognac, perish-ables—things you couldn't get except through the black market. He threw good parties, pimped and did some wenching himself. He had a great awareness of his charisma and he used it as if Eastern Europe during World War II were one great confidence game."

During the making of "Schindler's List," Spielberg was driven by one question: "What would drive a man like this to suddenly take everything he had earned and put it all in the service of saving these lives? I've asked a lot of survivors, both here and in Poland, 'Why do you think Oskar Schindler saved your life?' And most of them say, 'It's not important why he saved my life. It's only important that he did it.'"

Originally, Spielberg had planned to make "Schindler's List" in the mid-'80s, but he had trouble finding a suitable script. Screenwriter Kurt Luedtke ("Out of Africa") labored for four years, and finally gave up without finishing. Spielberg searched two years for another writer, and finally hired Steven Zaillian ("Awakenings"), who built his script not only from Keneally's book, but from interviews that Spielberg conducted with surviving members of the *Schindler-juden.*

In the end, the long delays worked to the film's advantage. It wasn't until this year [1993], after all, that the U.S. Holocaust Memorial Museum opened in Washington, D.C.—a coincidence that Universal Pictures observed with a "Schindler's List" benefit screening last month [November 1993]. The timeliness is underscored by the rise in neo-Nazi political sentiments in Europe, by the bloody "ethnic cleansing" in the former Yugoslavian republics, and by the fact that Holocaust survivors, many of whom stayed silent for decades, are starting to speak out more—lest the world repeat its mistakes.

For Spielberg, the delay was beneficial for another, more personal reason. Until recently, he admits, "I knew I wasn't mature enough to make this movie.... I think it's lucky I didn't make the movie earlier, because I think I would have made more of a 'Color Purple' type of movie—more of a celebration of sentiment." By the time he shot the picture, he says, "I wasn't interested in making a poem out of 'Schindler's List' at all. I don't think anything about the Holocaust rhymes."

"Schindler's List" also coincided with a time of powerful spiritual reconnection for the film maker. Last spring, when Spielberg flew to Poland to start production, he says, "I was feeling proud to be a Jew and I was feeling fulfilled by being able to state this without fear of not belonging."

It wasn't always so. Raised in Scottsdale, Ariz., where the Spielbergs were "the only Jews on a block of 200 homes," Spielberg came to shun his religious identity. "It was a *shondeh* [shame] for me when I was growing up, because I was brought up in a gentile neighborhood where there were no Jews in my school. I just felt like I was on the outside, that I wasn't part of anything. And I blamed a lot of it on my Jewishness and my Semitic looks and attitudes."

Spielberg's sense of exile only worsened in his last year of high school, when his family moved to Saratoga, Calif. "It was the only time I've experienced active and hostile anti-Semitism," he says. "I was beaten up and had pennies tossed at me in study hall. My mom had this old Willys Army jeep, and she would pick me up from school and take me home, which was well within walking distance. I became this target. Nobody held back and nobody apologized, and it was something that really opened my eyes."

Desperate to fit in, Spielberg drew back from his religion and became what he calls "a storefront Jew. I wanted to belong to the majority and Jews weren't it then. And I think that as I grew up, I stopped caring about that sort of thing. My Judaism became less of a *shondeh*."

Today, Spielberg says, "I've never identified more as a Jew as I have in the process of researching and producing and directing this film. I mean, the best thing that probably could happen to me because of this film is that I've reconnected as a Jew."

Looking back, he adds, "I can see how I took baby steps [toward spiritual reconnection] even before 'Schindler's List,' in the sense that I had children which made me responsible for how they were going to be brought up." Spielberg chose to raise his children in the Jewish faith, but says he was eager to make their religious education "fun," and not the "punitive" ordeal he remembered from his youth.

"So I went shopping for Hanukkah books to read to my kids, and ... And I found myself really becoming a bit of an amateur teacher to my kids. I started out talking about the holidays when they got presents and the holidays that were nonpresent days, and why the nonpresent holidays could be just as much fun. And I got very interested again in Judaism."

So did his wife. When Capshaw converted to Judaism two years ago, Spielberg went through the conversion with her, and "learned more in one year than I had learned all through formal Jewish training," he says. "I don't think I was really trained properly. I think it would have stuck with me a lot longer had the training been less like going to the dentist and having my teeth pulled."

A rebirth in more ways than one, "Schindler's List" also gave Spielberg a new, pared-down way of working, one that borrows from documentary film and photo-journalism, and avoids the elaborate, often showy camera style he'd developed over the years—a style that's earned him a lightweight reputation and caused some critics to dismiss him as a glib practitioner of quick-sell, easily marketed formulas.

"A lot of my films have technique and I'm conscious of it," he says. "I know what I do when I set up a shot ... but on this film I didn't want to do anything that would be disrespectful to the true nature of those events and those times. I had to let the facts tell the story.

"It was a liberating experience to work that way. It freed me from so many 'good habits' that would have been 'bad habits' if I had used them on this movie. And I'd love to work like that again, or at least start looking at reality the way I did on this movie. It frightened me, but it didn't put me off ever doing anything like this again."

Spielberg says he's not abandoning the fantasy-adventure genre that made him the world's pre-eminent movie director. "I'm not a born-again film maker or anything like that. I simply got into a territory of film making that I've always aspired to evolve myself into. It doesn't mean I'm going to just do this over and over again. I'm still considering a fourth 'Indiana Jones' film, and it's no secret that I'm playing with 'The Bridges of Madison County' [Robert James Waller's romantic best-seller]—which is as far away from 'Schindler's List' as you can imagine.

Before he chooses his next project, Spielberg says, he's determined to take time off and recover from the emotional drain of "Schindler's List." "When I think about this movie," he says, "I think of it as having had an experience that took a lot out of me, that I'll always have with me. Nobody can ever take that away from me."

Spielberg's Obsession

by David Ansen
Newsweek, Dec. 20, 1993

There was a man named Oskar Schindler. A German Catholic businessman and confidant of the Nazis, who during the Holocaust protected and rescued some 1,200 Jews from almost certain death. In Poland today, where Schindler once ran his profitable enamelware factory during World War II, there are fewer than 4,000 Jews left. Around the world there are more than 6,000 descendants of the "Schindler Jews" he saved. But to this day nobody can say with certainty what made this unlikely hero risk his life when so many others failed to lift a finger. A hedonist in love with cognac, night life and motorcycles, a womanizer incorrigibly unfaithful to his wife, a war profiteer, gambler, black-market dealer and heavy drinker, this gregarious, urbane and spoiled young man may have been motivated by nothing more complicated than simple decency, but then decency was neither simple nor easy to find in a German businessman in Eastern Europe between 1939 and 1945. To any sane observer, there has always been an unfathomable mystery about the systematic evil the Nazi regime perpetrated—like a moral black hole, it seems to defy the laws of nature while being a part of that nature. But sometimes the good is equally mysterious. The conscience of Oskar Schindler is a wonderful conundrum.

Another unlikely man, Steven Spielberg, has chosen Schindler to be the vehicle through which he tells the story of the Holocaust. "Schindler's List," adapted by Steven Zaillian from Thomas Keneally's prize-winning 1982 nonfiction novel, is not a movie anyone could have predicted from the most commercially successful filmmaker in the world (his 15 movies have grossed more than $4 billion). Following close on the trampling heels of "Jurassic Park"—the world's all-time box-office champ—the contrast couldn't be more startling. It's not just that the subject matter is a departure for a man renowned for his lyrical and rollicking boys' adventures; after all, he did make "The Color Purple" and "Empire of the Sun." But Spielberg's very nature as a filmmaker has been transformed; he's reached within himself for a new language, and without losing any of his innate fluency or his natural-born storytelling gift, he's found a style and a depth of feeling that will astonish both his fans and those detractors who believed he was doomed to permanent adolescence. More than three hours long, shot almost entirely in black and white, with a cast filled with little-known Polish and Israeli actors, "Schindler's List" plunges us into the nightmare of the Holocaust with newsreel-like urgency—and amazing restraint.

The master of escapism comes to terms with the Holocaust in the year's most shattering movie, 'Schindler's List'

So often when Hollywood directors pump themselves up to make a major statement, their filmmaking becomes as inflated and ponderous as a politician's rhetoric. Spielberg *deflates* his style: gone are the majestic boom shots, the pearly-slick sheen, the push-button sense of wonder. Maybe the biggest surprise is that Spielberg resists the easy, bludgeoning sentimentality that is the peril of films about the destruction of the Jews. This movie will shatter you, but it earns its tears honestly. His impeccable craft (aided by Michael Kahn's superb editing and Janusz Kaminski's starkly beautiful cinematography) holds you riveted for 196 minutes. But this time the abundant virtuosity is in the service of a harrowing authenticity.

Spielberg knew instinctively that his old methods were inadequate to tell this story. "I have a pretty good imagination. I've made a fortune off my imagination. My imagination is dwarfed by the events of 1940 to 1945. Just dwarfed," Spielberg told NEWSWEEK's Cathleen McGuigan at his East Hampton, N.Y., summer home. "And so I couldn't imagine the Holocaust until I went to Cracow, and to Auschwitz-Birkenau for the first time." His primary goal was to "bear witness" to the *Shoah* (the annihilation). "And I didn't want a style that was similar to anything I had done before. First of all, I threw half my toolbox away. I canceled the crane. I tore out the dolly track. I didn't really plan a style. I didn't say I'm going to use a lot of handheld camera. I simply tried to pull the events closer to the audience by reducing the artifice."

Zaillian's ambitious, sinewy screenplay artfully balances Schindler's story with the larger chronicle of the fate of the Jews of Cracow, all the while rarely straying from the facts documented in Keneally's extraordinary book. In several ways, the movie makes Schindler—played with gruff, complex grace by Irish actor Liam Neeson—a less heroic, more ambiguous figure than he is in the novel, in which the reader knows immediately of Oskar's good deeds. The Oskar we first encounter—a cagey, manipulative bon vivant buttering up Nazi officers in a nightclub for the good of his business ventures—is a man on the make, using the war to make his fortune. But unlike some Germans, he is not averse to using Jews as well to pad his pockets. He welcomes their investment in his factory and is happy to employ their slave labor. He's a great front man; it's the Jew Itzhak Stern (Ben Kingsley), his accountant, who has the real savvy to run the business. (Though Stern is real, his movie character is a composite of several *Schindlerjuden*, or "Schindler's Jews.")

There is nothing clear-cut about Oskar's transformation into a man of virtue. In Neeson's subtle, lived-in performance, he's a man who backs into heroism almost against his will, his cupidity inconvenienced by his conscience. But from a hillside, where he is riding horses with his mistress, he is a witness to the Nazis' vicious destruction of the ghetto, and he begins to sense that the men and women working in his factory will have no future unless he does something about it. Spielberg's depiction of the murderous day and night when the Germans liquidate Cracow's ghetto has a sickening reality. The accumulation of details—the women rolling their jewels into bread to swallow; a hospital nurse mercifully poisoning her terminally ill Jewish patients to save them from a crueler death by machine-gun fire—will lodge in your mind forever.

When the drama moves to the Plaszow Forced Labor Camp, the film introduces Commandant Amon Goeth. The sadistic Nazi is a familiar movie trope, but Ralph Fiennes, the brilliant young English actor who plays him, finds fresh horrors that owe nothing to Hollywood clichés. Goeth is a man of cool monstrosity—to start his day, he picks off Jewish workers with a rifle from his balcony. The flicker of insecurity that Fiennes finds in the character makes him all the more frightening. Spielberg, who gave us cartoon Nazis in his Indiana Jones movies, has found a new set of eyes. The dazzling fantasist has become an unblinking reporter.

Confronted with the horrors of Auschwitz-Birkenau, the ghastly sight of children hiding from capture in outhouse cesspools, Spielberg never loses his nerve or his tact. "Schindler's List" doesn't succumb to melodrama, or to hagiography. The first word we hear spoken is "Name," as Jews railroaded into Cracow disembark from a train and give their identities to government functionaries. It is a film filled throughout with names and faces—a testimony to the 6 million Jews who died, and the 1,200 who survived because of Oskar Schindler. No one film can begin to convey the totality of that annihilating chapter in history. But no dramatic film, from Hollywood or anywhere, has told so much so eloquently.

Spielberg grew up, in Cincinnati, Ohio, Haddonfield, N.J., and Phoenix, Ariz., hearing stories from his relatives about the mass extermination of his people. His grandmother gave English lessons to an Auschwitz survivor who taught the young boy numbers using the numerical brand the Nazis had tattooed into his arm. But he never heard the word "Holocaust" until he was in college. "My parents referred to it as 'those murdering sons of bitches.' Those murdering sons of bitches broke that Jewish pianist's fingers so he could never play the piano again."

When he was 7, the family moved to Arizona from New Jersey, abandoning their observant Orthodox ways. "I didn't have any Jewish friends growing up in Phoenix. I felt like I was the only Jewish kid in my high school." Eager to assimilate ("I would always try and negotiate for conformity"), Spielberg remembers feeling "ashamed because I was living on a street where at Christmas, we were the only house with nothing but a porch light on." He'd try, in vain, to get his father to put up a red light. But he never experienced anti-Semitism until the family moved to Saratoga, Calif., when his father got a job with a Palo Alto computer company. It was Spielberg's senior year in high school, and he encountered kids who would cough the word Jew in their hands when they passed him, beat him up and throw pennies at him in study hall. "It was my six months of personal horror. And to this day I haven't gotten over it nor have I forgiven any of them."

Until now, his Judaism was never touched upon in his work. The young hero of "E.T.," growing up in a broken home and feeling like an alien himself, may have been a metaphorical stand-in for Spielberg, but ethnicity was left far out of the picture. The fantasies he concocted in his spectacular career were the ultimate triumph of assimilation: he colonized the world with his imagination.

'I really believe had I done "Schindler's List" first, I would not have had the appetite or interest in a dinosaur movie'

●

"Schindler's List" lurked in the back of Spielberg's mind for a decade, ever since Sidney Sheinberg, MCA/Universal's president, bought it for him in 1982. "I wasn't ready to make it in '82 because I wasn't mature enough. I wasn't emotionally resolved with my life. I hadn't had children. I really hadn't seen God until my first child was born. A lot of things happened that were big deals in my personal life that I didn't give interviews about. But they changed me as a person and as a filmmaker. And they led me to say I want to do it now, I need to make it right now."

His longtime producer Kathleen Kennedy thinks his second marriage, to Kate Capshaw (who converted to Judaism), has brought a new balance to his life. "He has a personal confidence now and isn't trying to prove anything to himself anymore." "I wanted to tell people who had told me to be ashamed of my Jewishness," Spielberg says, "that I was so proud to be a Jew."

His urgency to make the movie was spurred by the "ethnic cleansing" in Bosnia and other atrocities. "It was a combination of things: my interest in the Holocaust and my horror at the symptoms of the Shoah again happening in Bosnia. And again happening with Saddam Hussein's attempt to eradicate the Kurdish race. We were racing over these moments in world history that were exactly like what happened in 1943."

Keneally had been the first writer to attempt a screenplay from his own book. But his effort was the length of a mini-series. Kurt Luedtke ("Out of Africa") worked on it for three years before throwing in the towel. At various times both Sydney Pollack and Martin Scorsese considered directing "Schindler," and it was Scorsese who brought in Zaillian (writer-director of "Searching for Bobby Fischer") to attempt to crack the book. When Spielberg finally decided he must make it, he paid his first visit to

Auschwitz-Birkenau. His reaction—anger—surprised him. "I was deeply pissed off. I was all ready to cry in front of strangers, and I didn't shed a tear. I was just boiling inside. Freezing day, and I was so hot. I felt so helpless, that there was nothing I could do about it. And yet I thought, well, there is something I can do about it. I can make 'Schindler's List.' I mean, it's not going to bring anybody back alive, but it maybe will remind people that another Holocaust is a sad possibility."

"I couldn't find any Jews in Poland to be the Jews in the movie because Hitler had murdered them all"

....

Shooting in Poland, in the haunted places where these events occurred (Schindler's factory still stands), was the most intense professional experience of his life, and it was made more bizarre by the fact that he had to complete post-production work on 'Jurassic Park' from Poland. How can I reconcile dinosaurs and the Holocaust? he kept asking himself. "It didn't work in my mind." Two or three times a week he would receive transmissions beamed by satellite from the United States to the huge parabolic dish in the front yard of his Cracow house. After 12-hour workdays on the set, he'd come home to his wife and five kids—and after dinner and bedtime stories he'd trudge to his monitor to focus on smoothing out the jerky dinosaur movements. "I was not in a mind-set to be involved with 'Jurassic Park' but I had a duty to myself and to the special effects."

Spielberg was not prepared for the kind of personal reaction "Schindler" evoked. "I was frightened every day.... I sound pretentious, like some kind of European artist or something. Because I've not had personal experiences in the making of my films. A lot of my films have been made for you, just like somebody makes a hamburger just the way you want it. That's been my modus operandi. Now I go to Poland and I get hit in the face with my personal life. My upbringing. My Jewishness. The stories my grandparents told me about the Shoah. And Jewish life came pouring back into my heart. I cried all the time. I never cry on sets making films. I've often protected myself with the movie camera. The camera has always been my golden shield against things really reaching me. I put that thing in front of my face, it stops the bullet. I can't tell you the shots I did on

'Schindler's List' or why I put the camera in a certain place. I re-created these events, and then I experienced them as any witness or victim would have. It wasn't like a movie.

"So every single day was like waking up and going to hell, really. There were no jokes on the set. No funny outtakes to show at the wrap party. Twice in the production I called Robin Williams just to say, Robin, I haven't laughed in seven weeks. Help me here. And Robin would do 20 minutes on the telephone."

In one of the most painful scenes in the film, the inmates of the labor camp are rounded up, forced to strip and to run past doctors. We see women pricking their fingers for blood to rub some pink into their cheeks, for those who look healthy will be allowed to stay and work. The rejects will be sent to Auschwitz and the ovens. The sequence took three days to shoot, and after the first day Spielberg was "trying to find a way not to come back to work." The scene was hard on everyone involved. "None of us looked. I said to the guy pulling the focus on a very difficult shot, 'Do you think you got that?' And he said, 'I don't know, I wasn't looking.' And when the man on focus doesn't look, you know, it's interesting."

Spielberg's actors recall his energy, his spontaneity, his calm professionalism and, in Ben Kingsley's words, his "lovely childish enthusiasm." To prepare Neeson to play Schindler, Spielberg gave the actor home movies of Steve Ross, the charismatic late head of Time Warner, and a kind of father figure to the director. Ross, to whom the film is dedicated, became Spielberg's private prototype of the movie's hero. "I think Schindler loved people. I've often said that he and my late great friend Steve Ross had a lot of similarities." Neeson ultimately used some of Ross's expansive body language in his portrayal.

The Poles generously welcomed the movie people to Cracow, but there were a few ugly incidents. In a hotel bar, an old German-speaking businessman approached Israeli actor Michael Schneider and asked him whether he was a Jew. Yes, the actor replied, and the man drew a finger across his neck and pulled an imaginary noose above his throat, saying, "Hitler should have finished the job." An enraged Kingsley had to be restrained before a brawl ensued.

Spielberg found when his German actors put on Nazi uniforms, he became unintentionally hostile toward them. But that changed the day the company had a Passover Seder. "All the German actors showed up. They

Spielberg's Hits

· · · · · · · · · · · · · · · · · ·

He has directed four of the ten top-grossing films of all times.

Year	Film*	Gross In Millions
1993	Jurassic Park	$860.0
1982	E.T.	701.1
1990	Ghost	517.6
1977	Star Wars	513.0
1989	Indiana Jones Last Crusade	494.8
1991	Terminator 2	488.7
1990	Home Alone	474.7
1975	Jaws	458.0
1990	Pretty Woman	454.4
1989	Batman	411.2

*Spielberg films are shaded   Source: VARIETY

put on yarmulkes and opened up Haggadas [the Seder text], and the Israeli actors moved right next to them and began explaining it to them. And this family of actors sat around and race and culture were just left behind."

These scenes from his four months in Poland keep haunting Spielberg; he's finding it hard to come down from the experience. "Schindler's List" has forced him to re-examine his life as a filmmaker. "My problem is I have too much of a command of the visual language. I know how to put a Cecil B. DeMille image on the screen. I can do a Michael Curtiz. If my mojo's working I can put one tenth of a David Lean image on the screen. But I've never really been able to put my image on the screen, with the exception of 'E.T.' perhaps. And certainly not until 'Schindler' was I really able to not reference other filmmakers. I'm always referencing everybody. I didn't do any of that on this movie."

Spielberg talked for more than four hours, but he wasn't satisfied that he'd said everything he wanted to say. A few days later he called back with a final thought. "I came to realize, the reason I came to make the movie, is that I have never in my life told the truth in a movie. My effort as a moviemaker has been to create something that couldn't possibly happen. So people could leave their lives and have an adventure and then come back to earth and drive home. That was one of the things I thought: if I'm going to tell the truth for the first time, it should be about this subject. Not about divorce or parents and children, but about this."

And he did. When you drive home from "Schindler's List," you have seen all the truth you can handle, and are grateful for it.

With Abigail Kuflik in New York and Charles Fleming in Los Angeles

Making History:

How Steven Spielberg Brought "Schindler's List" to Life

·······················

by Anne Thompson
Entertainment Weekly, Jan. 21, 1994

The cold could snap bones. And for the actors filming the Auschwitz-Birkenau concentration camp scenes during their first weeks on location in Poland, the work itself was a chilling business that tore them out of their own place and time and engulfed them in nightmarish history. In one horrific scene, 300 naked actresses in shorn wigs crowded into an Auschwitz shower and were told to stare up at the menacing nozzles. As Jewish prisoners just transferred into the death camp, they were supposed to appear unsure if the fixtures would produce water or gas—if they were meant for cleansing or for killing.

Their tears were real. Israeli actress Miri Fabian held a young girl close. She herself had been born in a concentration camp and had not yet told her mother that she had taken the role. The tension was unbearable. She had trouble breathing, then began hyperventilating, and was barely able to finish filming the sequence.

Other Auschwitz scenes played out against similarly haunting visions of hell. One member of the company recalls "guard dogs going mad everywhere, huge burly guards with whips, chaos, blinding snow, a red haze coming from the chimney stacks." And this was just the beginning. For the next 2½ months, Steven Spielberg, directing with precise, singular vision, led the cast and crew of *Schindler's List* to the heart of the Holocaust's horror. "I said to myself, 'How can I bring truth to these impossible images?'" Spielberg admits. "There wasn't even an attempt to alleviate the sadness. Constantly, every week, somebody would lose it."

Miraculously, the finished work brings audiences to the same awful place, securing Spielberg's position as perhaps the nation's preeminent filmmaker. He is a front-runner ... , alongside *The Piano's* Jane Campion, for the Best Director Oscar, an honor that the Academy has begrudged him so far, placating him only with 1986's Irving G. Thalberg Award for his work as, ironically, a producer. *Schindler's* very existence is a victory against astounding odds. It took a decade to adapt journalist Thomas Keneally's sprawling 1982 novel for the screen—and the film's tight schedule required Spielberg to edit his other 1993 triumph, *Jurassic Park*, from Poland early last year. This month ... , *Schindler's*, which has made an impressive $10 million in limited release, opens in more than 250 theaters, with more to come—a heartfelt monument to an event so ghastly that it stands oceans away from the reaches of art. This is the story of how Spielberg, an entertainer until now associated with soaring flights of fancy, hunkered down and bridged that gulf.

Steven Spielberg, 46 and known to brood on occasion, has lately been cheery in a way that befits a director who has new critical esteem to go with four of the 10 biggest movies in history—*Jaws* (1975), *Raiders of the Lost Ark* (1981), *E.T.* (1982), and *Jurassic Park* (1993). Standing outside his Amblin Entertainment office at Universal Studios in jeans and sneakers, his salt-and-pepper beard matching long hair unfettered by his usual baseball cap, he greets Marvin Levy, Amblin's marketing consultant, who offers glad tidings. The National Society of Film Critics has just given *Schindler's* Best Picture and Spielberg his first Best Director honor this year; other groups had chosen Campion. "Great! Wonderful! This means we've swept all five critics' groups!" Spielberg says with a grin.

When *Schindler's List* was published, Spielberg had recently finished *E.T.*, mining his boyish nightmares and fantasies to great effect but earning a reputation as the Peter Pan of filmmaking. MCA president Sidney Sheinberg brought the novel to Spielberg's attention. The story, a moving record of what happened to 1,100 Polish Jews—the *Schindlerjuden*—whose lives were saved when German war profiteer Oskar Schindler "bought" them as factory workers to spare them from the death camps, intrigued Spielberg. After scanning one review, he recalls saying to Sheinberg: "It'll make a helluva story. Is it true?"

Keneally himself had been talked into writing the book while standing in a Beverly Hills leather-goods store, waiting for a credit-card authorization from the proprietor, Schindler survivor Leopold Page (born Poldek Pfefferberg). Page had first helped sell Schindler's story to MGM in the 1960s. The studio hired *Casablanca* coscreenwriter Howard Koch to work on the film, but the dubious character of Oskar Schindler—a womanizing, boozing bear of a man who profited from the war by employing Jews— may have made his story a difficult sell. The project was dropped and lay dormant for years before Spielberg decided to take it on.

Page, 80, insists that from their first meeting, Spielberg knew he would do the movie. "When I met him," he recalls in thickly accented English, "I asked him, 'Please, when are you starting?' He said, 'Ten years from now.'" But as those years passed, Page worried that he wouldn't live to see the film.

"*Schindler's* was on my guilty conscience," says Spielberg. "Page was heaping on the fact that he was going to die."

Spielberg gave the film away twice before deciding to tackle it himself

Like Schindler's motivation for saving his employees, Spielberg's reluctance to take on the project was both spiritual and pragmatic. He gave the project to two other directors, Sydney Pollack and Martin Scorsese, before tackling it himself. "He didn't think he was ready," explains the film's screen-writer, Steven Zaillian *(Awakenings, Searching for Bobby Fischer)*. "He didn't have kids yet. He had to come to terms with his Jewishness. He kept putting it off."

Spielberg wasn't the only one who doubted his abilities. Australian director Fred Schepisi *(Six Degrees of Separation)* implored him not to do it, warning him that his big-studio gloss would be the film's downfall. "Give it to me," he told Spielberg. "I don't think you have the courage to not use the crane and dolly."

"Survivors would come up to me in Poland and say, 'What a strange choice,'" recalls Spielberg, "and I'd have a sinking feeling in my heart, [worrying that] the world wouldn't accept *Schindler's List* from me." Now, as he sits cross-legged in a soft armchair in his office, the fear has fallen away. Spielberg leans forward and boasts: "There is not one crane shot!"

While Spielberg was making other films, the *Schindler's* script was proving no easier to crack than it had been two decades earlier. Keneally himself took the first pass, writing a 220-page tome that was more miniseries than movie. "In my draft, Schindler had relationships with a whole range of people," he says. "I didn't coalesce the stories enough."

Unhappy with Keneally's lack of focus, Spielberg next hired ex-journalist Kurt Luedtke, who had won an Oscar for *Out of Africa*. Luedtke labored for 3½ years before giving up, unable to conquer his own doubt about the heroism of Schindler, who had begun his Moses-like mission merely as a way to make a buck. "As a reporter," says Spielberg, "he had some journalistic conflicts about not believing the story."

Spielberg then handed the project to Scorsese. "I thought Marty would do a great job with it," explains Spielberg. "He wouldn't back down from truth or violence. But the minute I gave it to Marty, I missed it. I'd given away a chance to do something for my children and family about the Holocaust." So the two directors worked out a trade in which Spielberg handed Scorsese a project he'd been developing—*Cape Fear*—and reclaimed *Schindler's* for himself.

Back on the film, Spielberg read the script Scorsese had commissioned from Zaillian. At 115 pages, it was strong but "too contained" and without enough Jewish faces, says Spielberg. "I didn't tell the story from the survivors' point of view," says Zaillian, "but from Schindler's. I wanted it clear that he didn't do what he did out of friendship. He didn't feel sorry for them. He did it because it was the right thing to do."

Spielberg kept asking Zaillian to add more material and treated him to a field trip to Poland for inspiration. "By the time we were done, we had 195 pages," says Zaillian, who originally penned the savage liquidation of the Jews in the Krakow ghetto—some of the film's most brutal scenes—at only two pages. Spielberg insisted on stretching the evacuation into a grueling episode that ultimately took three weeks to film.

"He thought I had lost my mind," recalls Spielberg. "But really, I felt very strongly that the sequence had to be almost unwatchable."

While some critics have faulted *Schindler's List* for telling its tale from the Germans' point of view, Spielberg knew how he wanted to present the story. "I said, 'Look, I don't want to go all the way into *The Diary of Anne*

Frank, where we're telling a detailed portraiture of a family in hiding. It wasn't the story of eight Jews from Krakow who survived—it was a conscious decision to represent the 6 million who died and the several hundred thousand who did survive with just sort of a scent of characters and faces we follow all through the story."

Fighting Universal, Spielberg refused to shoot in color for video release

As he developed the script, Spielberg waged a quiet battle with Universal. The studio was concerned that he was making an apparently uncommercial project even more difficult. He knew he wanted to shoot the movie in documentary-style black and white with Polish émigré Janusz Kaminski *(The Adventures of Huck Finn)* as his director of photography. Universal chairman Tom Pollock begged Spielberg at least to shoot in color and then transfer to black and white, so the studio could eventually release color videocassettes. The director refused. "It would have looked like pink and white," he says.

Disputes over how to tell Schindler's story were just as intense. "The studio, of course, wanted me to spell everything out," says Spielberg. "I got into a lot of arguments with people saying we need that big Hollywood catharsis where Schindler falls to his knees and says, 'Yes, I know what I'm doing—now I must do it!' and goes full steam ahead. That was the last thing I wanted. I did not want to bring in a *Camille* moment, some kind of explosive catharsis that would turn this into *The Great Escape*."

Finally, MCA's Sheinberg gave *Schindler's List* the green light on one condition: Spielberg had to film *Jurassic Park* first. "He knew that once I had directed *Schindler's* I wouldn't be able to do *Jurassic Park*," says Spielberg. (He does plan to produce, but not direct, a *Jurassic* sequel.)

As casting began, Spielberg first focused on the character of Itzhak Stern, a composite of several of the men who ran Schindler's enamelware company while the boss pursued women and good relations with the Nazis. "Stern whispered in Schindler's ear," says Spielberg. "He's the unsung hero." The role went to Ben Kingsley, the Oscar winner for 1982's *Gandhi* and the biggest name in a non-American, nonstar lineup. As Nazi commandant Amon Goeth, the film's emblem of evil, Spielberg cast Ralph Fiennes (pronounced Rafe Fines), whom he had seen as Heathcliff in a little-seen remake of *Wuthering Heights*. South African actress Embeth Davidtz was handed the role of Helen Hirsch, the reluctant recipient of both Goeth's and Schindler's odd affections. Spielberg cast Israelis, many of them children of survivors, for the key Jewish speaking roles and used local Catholic Poles for the remaining Jewish faces.

While Spielberg had tested Irish actor Liam Neeson ... at the start of the casting process and had spurned interest from Kevin Costner and Mel Gibson, it wasn't until December 1992 that he firmed up his choice. After seeing Neeson on Broadway in *Anna Christie*, Spielberg went backstage with his wife, Kate Capshaw, and her mother. Overcome by the performance, Spielberg's mother-in-law met Neeson, who put a comforting arm around her. As they were leaving, Capshaw turned to Spielberg and said, "That's what Schindler would have done."

When the *Schindler's* company arrived in Krakow in February, the punishing Polish winter welcomed them with temperatures of 15 below. "Nobody complained about how we were suffering from the cold," says cinematographer Kaminski, 34, who hadn't returned to Poland since he had left 12 years earlier ... "because our suffering was so little compared with what the actual prisoners were subjected to." But their reception was cold in other ways. A clash with the World Jewish Congress over Spielberg's request to film inside Auschwitz-Birkenau wasn't resolved until Spielberg proposed an ingenious compromise: A train would be backed into the camp and then be shot emerging into a mirror replica of Auschwitz's interior that had been built just outside the actual camp. And during their stay in Krakow, the filmmakers were welcomed with anti-Semitic symbols scrawled on local billboards. One night, Kingsley and a friend were unwinding at the bar in the Hotel Forum, a hangout for the cast and crew. "Good night, Jew," a middle-aged German businessman said to Kingsley's friend. Kingsley lost his temper, screaming at the man until crew members hustled the offender off the premises.

Meanwhile, Spielberg was fighting his own shooting schedule. Some days, he and Kaminski filmed as many as 55 setups, often with a hand-held camera. Screenwriter Zaillian, a novice director who had just completed his first film, *Searching for Bobby Fischer*, recalls the process with amazement. "They were shooting fast, with a cool, unsentimental, matter-of-fact approach. On one shot, the camera pans over to catch something.

The first three times it didn't quite catch the action completely." Spielberg simply decided to continue, imperfections and all. "Okay," he said, "let's move on to the next one."

"Actually," says Neeson, "Steven's direction on *Schindler* was a bit like Woody Allen. We didn't know how he was going to shoot a scene. You just had to be prepared in *not* being prepared." In fact, many of the film's most important shots were mapped out at the last minute. Just before filming the pivotal scene in which Schindler persuades Goeth to let him remove 1,100 of his prisoners to safety, Spielberg shouted to Neeson, "I know how to do it! You're going to be outside, and I'm going to be inside with the camera on you, and I'm gonna just keep the camera steady and you walk into the shot and walk out again. The scene is so important I'm going to throw it away."

"He wanted it to *not* be perfect," says Zaillian. "It was a catch-what-you-can style of filming, which is just as hard to do as to plan out every shot."

The Schindler Jews who visited the set provided their own memories

If the crowning achievement of *Schindler's List* is its authenticity, credit may belong to the Schindler Jews who offered their own experiences to the filmmakers. Page, who accompanied the cast and crew, recalled masquerading as a recruit when he realized that the Germans were shooting every Jew they caught hiding during the Krakow ghetto annihilation: "I told them I had been ordered to clear the road. They started to laugh. An order is an order. They had time to kill me later. I was among the last 40 to get out of the ghetto alive."

Among the other survivors who lent their memories was Nuisa Horowitz, who as an 11-year-old factory worker was kissed by Schindler—an offense that briefly landed him in jail. Horowitz's story became the basis of a scene in which a family presses its diamonds into bread and then eats them during the liquidation of the ghetto. And Page pointed out the actual bluff from which Schindler, on horseback, watched the SS officers attack the ghetto. "There's only one place that Schindler could have parked his horse to watch," Spielberg says with visible enthusiasm. "A lot of it I just got from witnesses who came back: 'Oh, this didn't happen over here, this happened over there!'"

Another survivor told of the Plaszow prisoners pricking their own fingers and coloring their cheeks with blood during a horrifying endurance test in which prisoners were forced to run naked to prove their health—and sent to death camps if they were judged too sickly to work. Spielberg pushed verisimilitude to an obsessive level when he asked for volunteers to prick their fingers; two agreed to do it. For the health sequence, he paid all the extras who were required to run naked double the California-extra day rate of $65—more than the average monthly salary in Krakow.

To give the audience one last dose of realism, Spielberg decided to fly 128 surviving *Schindlerjuden* to Jerusalem to appear in the film's final sequence, in which, following Jewish tradition, they place stones on Schindler's grave. Since the idea for the sequence came to Spielberg midway through filming, his production team scrambled to import the survivors.

The night before Spielberg filmed the coda, the actors met their real-life counterparts at a party at the King David Hotel. "We had such a time that night," says Neeson. "It was wonderful to hear all these anecdotes from all these people, little gems of stories about what somebody did for somebody one day, nothing horrific." Former prisoner Henry Rosner, who had once played his violin at Goeth's villa, played once again, and Spielberg sat surrounded by Holocaust survivors. "He was so exhausted he wasn't sure he'd get through the evening," says Caroline Goodall, who plays Schindler's wife. "But I've never seen him look so happy."

With 126 roles and 30,000 extras, it came in at a third of Jurassic's cost

On cue, Spielberg can rattle off the number of shooting days for all of his films. (*E.T.*: 60; *Hook*: 125). *Schindler's List,* with its 126 speaking parts and 30,000 extras, came in at 71 days—about the same as *Jurassic Park*—and $23 million, about a third of *Jurassic's* cost.

This was the good news. The bad news—at least to Universal—was that the film originally ran close to four hours. Cutting the film to a just-releasable 3 hours, 14 minutes became an ordeal. Kaminski and producer Gerald Molen miss the gruesome delivery of a boxcar full of frozen corpses to Brinnlitz, Czechoslovakia. "It was a striking visual," says Molen. And Neeson lost his favorite scene: a game of 21 between him and Goeth for Goeth's maid, Helen Hirsch, that is only implied in the final cut. "We did this amazing game," says Neeson, "and he shot it wonderfully, turning over the cards. As Ralph studies the cards, I'm looking at him with loathing. It shows the lie that Oskar has been living."

Spielberg, however, dismisses the scene as "too Hollywood. It was *The Cincinnati Kid.* Everything that reminded me of another movie I cut out of *Schindler's List* because I made a career of reverberating my past in my films, if not flagrantly, then subtly. I knew by the fourth setup that the scene was too entertaining and it would be cut. I did not," he adds, "want this to be a Hollywood story in any way."

At one theater, the audience signs a scroll of thanks to Spielberg

At Wometco's Shadowood 12 theater in Boca Raton, Fla., manager Morrie Zryl, a child of Holocaust survivors, tells each audience not to be surprised if some among them cry and sing during the movie, and that anyone whose relatives were victims or survivors of the Holocaust should sign the scroll in the lobby. There are now 18,000 names. They are being sent to Spielberg.

"I was relieved to find that survivors seemed to like it," says Keneally. "they find it cathartic." Although the movie has won almost unanimously admiring reviews, there are notable voices of dissent; a review in the *Forward*, an influential Jewish newspaper, lambasted Spielberg for hailing a Nazi hero while depicting Jews as ineffectual victims.

Still others, including Keneally, have been put off by the apocryphal climactic scene in which Schindler breaks down before making his getaway at the end of the war, crying for the Jews he could have saved if he had tried harder. In fact, Schindler disappeared quietly into the night, his car packed with jewels. "It was absolutely necessary," insists Spielberg. "He's not speaking for himself, he's speaking for all of us, what we might do someday."

These days, Spielberg is spending time with his wife and their five kids (one each from their first marriages, two together, and one adopted), overseeing the production of three Amblin films as unlike *Schindler's List* as possible—*The Flintstones, The Little Rascals,* and *Casper, the Friendly Ghost*—and weighing what to direct next. Going back to making conventionally commercial pictures may prove difficult—while *Schindler's* may have been liberating for Spielberg, it did require him to change. "The whole idea was that if I made a real good chair the same way all my life and everyone feels comfortable sitting in it, it's kind of tough to suddenly build a car," Spielberg explains. "My intuition led me to conventional choices, so I used a lot of mind over instinct."

At least one instinct paid off: The first scene in *Schindler's List* came to Spielberg toward the end of filming, when he was shooting a Sabbath prayer sequence at Brinnlitz. It is a tight shot, in color, of two candle flames. "That gave me the idea to start the film with the candles being lit," he recalls. "I thought it would be a rich book-end, to start the film with a normal *Shabbes* service before the juggernaut against the Jews begins." When the color fades out in the film's opening moments, it gives way to a movie in which black-and-white tendrils of smoke convey unspeakable horror as they curl from the ovens into the stark sky. Only at the end do the images of candle fire regain their warm luster. They represent "just a glint of color," says Spielberg, "and a glimmer of hope."

(Additional reporting by Tim Appelo and Jess Cagle)

Witness

·······················

Is Spielberg's "Schindler's List" More than a Ride in a Holocaust Theme Park?
And How Has the Film Imagined the Unimaginable?

by Simon Louvish
Sight and Sound magazine, March 1994

Steven Spielberg's latest venture, *Schindler's List*, raises an old question about the limits of imagining the unimaginable. The Holocaust is not a new subject in film, and has defeated many well-meaning efforts to overcome the over-familiarity of those iconic images of Nazi concentration camps and their abused inmates. These images have lost their power to shock. We face a classic syndrome of 'compassion fatigue'.

In the late 70s, when documentarist Claude Lanzmann embarked on his massive nine-hour epic on the Holocaust, *Shoah*, he abandoned the familiar imagery completely. Rejecting archive footage, Lanzmann constructed his entire enterprise from a rigorous series of talking-head interviews framed in the director's own quest for answers in the current locations of the actual events. This was done partly because Lanzmann claimed it was not possible to determine which archive footage came from which camp, or which date. Film of Treblinka has come to be used as Auschwitz and vice versa. Lanzmann's obsession was to provide a precise and indeed pitiless verification of the events through their survivors' memories. The word was all; the picture, a means to an end, although in the final analysis the faces of the speakers, as they struggle sometimes reluctantly to fulfill Lanzmann's brief, convey a world of painful emotion.

Steven Spielberg, at the opposite end of the scale, goes back to the old dramatic principle of narrative film-making: show, don't tell. The Holocaust will be painstakingly reconstructed, in all its horror and misery. The transport trains will roll, the ghetto will be populated and depopulated, even the chimneys of Auschwitz-Birkenau will belch forth anew in the full depiction of that particular hell on earth, albeit recreated in 'documentary-style' black and white, often with handheld cameras and with wide-angle lenses darting about, even allowing at times the soft focus of an ersatz snatched shot.

A great deal of trepidation has accompanied this project. American Jewish committees have expressed concern. An outcry prevented Spielberg from using the actual location of Birkenau camp. His riggers and painters made up the fading houses and frames of Krakow's surviving Jewish ghetto. Was this to be a *Jurassic Park* with Nazis replacing T-Rex and Raptosaurus? Could the Hollywood brat survive a close encounter with the ghosts of a very European cataclysm?

Schindler's List, based on Thomas Keneally's *Schindler's Ark* (the book was published as *Schindler's List* in America, presumably because the mass American audience was not expected to know the word Ark), contains in its concept another pitfall. As Keneally remarks at the start of his book, it is the tale of the archetypal "good German": the righteous man who might redeem Sodom. Oskar Schindler was a playboy businessman who, by setting up a metal factory employing Jewish slave labour to manufacture first ordinary metalware and then, supposedly, shell casings for the German war effort, saved over a thousand Jews, randomly picked from the ghettos and mostly unqualified for manual labour, from certain death in the last years of the war. Gradually progressing from an almost detached opportunism to a paroxysm of subterfuge and cunning, his exploits extended (allegedly—some accounts tell it otherwise) to rescuing 'his' labourers in person from the very jaws of Auschwitz and snatching children away from the SS by convincing the guards that their little hands were needed to polish the narrow shell casings from the inside. Six thousand descendants of the original *Schindlerjuden* live today, mostly in Israel, and have kept alive the memory of this extraordinary man.

Spielberg has used this tale as an anchor for his reconstruction. He is clearly aware of the magnitude of his task. All the Hollywood brat's prodigious cinematic experience, as film-maker and film-watcher, is brought into play. A Sabbath candle's wispy smoke cuts into the sinister steam of a thrusting transport train. The SS liquidators of the Krakow ghetto clatter up courtyard stairs in an after-image of the Cossacks in Einstein's *Strike*. People remaining illegally in their houses hide in coal cellars, under floorboards, even inside a piano as the footsteps of the murderers echo. The children hiding in the stoves of the emptied labour camp, later, evoke echoes of *Jurassic Park*'s brats hiding from the brute Raptors, but also of any action drama's tricks of the trade.

In his previous Second World War epic *Empire of the Sun* (1987), Spielberg misjudged J. G. Ballard's stone-faced narrative and sentimentalized the young boy's journey through the Japanese war machine. Given his practically unlimited resources, 'show, don't tell' became a literal commandment. When Ballard recounts the whole of Shanghai on the move in panic as the Japanese approach, Spielberg shows us the whole show in frame with an old-style cast of thousands. Very little is left to our imagination, therefore our imagination is atrophied for the duration: we are, as is the principle in the contemporary American film, passive consumers of the emotions pasted so powerfully on the screen. The result is what psychologists call, I believe, "flattening of affect"—everything is the same if represented in the same manner: *Terminator 2, Total Recall*, science fiction fantasy, crime, romance, *Home Alone*, Holocaust, war. Finally the penny has dropped and Spielberg, for one, has understood that this method can no longer hold water if he wishes, as he does, to undertake that great taboo of the American film—to educate, not only entertain.

If you want to send a message, use Western Union—that old shibboleth of Hollywood's moguls. In truth, of course, 'entertainment', even at its blandest, always purveyed values. Good or bad, well intentioned or reckless—we did not require Golden Turkey Medved to tell us that movies make morals. At least Spielberg has now dropped the pretence—he could hardly stand up and say that *Schindler's List* was made purely to amuse us. This is, in fact, a return to one of Hollywood's more honourable traditions, that of the 'social conscience' film. From *I Am a Fugitive in a Chain Gang* (Mervyn LeRoy), through *Intruder in the Dust* (Clarence Brown), or *Crossfire* (Edward Dmytryk) and indeed back to Griffith and Vidor, this is part of Spielberg's heritage and he has plainly yearned to connect his obvious penchant for the gargantuan with that nagging need.

What other agenda is he following? The Holocaust has, of course, featured in Hollywood films before. Its main purpose, throughout the 50s and 60s, was clearly politically partisan—to justify the State of Israel. Thus the Holocaust served as backdrop to Otto Preminger's *Exodus* (1960) and other Zionist lieders such as Daniel Mann's *Judith* (1965) and Melville Shavelson's *Cast a Giant Shadow* (1966). Only in the 70s did Hollywood, in the shape of the television series *Holocaust*, begin to tackle the thing in itself, and then in a highly sanitised mode. It occurred to me then, watching parts of that series, that the Germans might have tried to make the Jews into soap, but the Americans succeeded. Such dubious thoughts are part and parcel of my Israeli heritage. We became so familiar with the institutional commemorations of the Holocaust, such as the *Yad Vashem* memorial, to which every visiting head of state has to pay homage, preferably on bended knee, that we coined the unkind of phrase: there's no business like Shoah business. This crack was reinforced as memorialisation became an industry, spawning countless books including coffee-table volumes of lost letters, portraits of the dead, lists, endless lists. And cynicism grew as right-wing politicians such as Menachem Begin used the Holocaust to justify the bombing of Beirut in the 1982 Lebanon War.

The Zionist view of the Holocaust, to which Spielberg is heir, is the outcome of an inherent ambivalence: the natural requirement to respond as Jews somehow, some way, to the enormity of our national, or ethnic, or religious trauma, and the Israeli ethos of being a phoenix risen from the ashes, a rejection of the victim complex, subjects rather than objects. In this syndrome we too, like Ballard's boy Jim, identified in part with the oppressor German, the soldier with the gun, rather than with the bedraggled, cowed and sheeplike diaspora Jew. None of this is in Spielberg, who like most American Jews, having lived a fantasy Zionism, is locked into the cult of the victim, victims like fellow artist Art Spiegelman's cartoon Jews, the mice of *Maus*, harmless creatures menaced by the fat Nazi cats. Of course, the Nazis themselves represented us as rats, in *Der Ewige Jude*— the Eternal Jew (Fritz Hippler, 1940).

This cult of victimhood, which Spielberg can't escape from, is now a growing force in a particular American discourse, the cult of 'survival' and 'endurance'. The new Holocaust Museum in Washington can hardly contain its visiting crowds, and has plugged into a certain 'politically correct' idea of everyone as a survivor of some real or imagined trauma. Young

1. *Roundup of Jews, Krakow, Poland, 1939*

2. *Barbed-wire fence separating the Jewish neighborhood of Podgorze from the rest of Krakow, about 1940.*

3. *Segregated streetcar (For Jews/Not for Jews), Krakow, Poland, 1940-1941*

4. *Jews forced to dig ditches as German soldiers look on. Krakow, Poland, 1939-1940.*

5. *Jewish children in the Krakow ghetto, November 15, 1939*

6. *Amon Goeth on his horse in the Plaszow concentration camp, March, 1943 - September, 1944.*

7. *Deportation from Krakow to death camps, Krakow, Poland, 1940-1943*

8. *Herbert Steinhouse in Paris, 1949, as he wrote his original Oskar Schindler article.*

9. *Herbert Steinhouse in retirement, in Montreal, December, 1994*

Dir.Oskar Schindler
Regensburg,Nürnbergerstr.25.   München,12.Aug.49.

        Mr.
        Steinhouse
        Amerikan Joint Distributions Committee
        II9 Rue Saint-Dominique
        Paris.

        Sehr geehrter Herr Steinhouse!

        Ihnen durch Herrn Horowitz diese Zeilen und recht herzliche
Grüße zu übermitteln,ist mir eine große Freude.Immer neue Hindernisse
in unseren Auswanderungsprojekt,verhinderten Ihnen positive Mitteilungen
zuzusenden,jetzt haben wir es Gott sei Dank geschaft und verlassen in
spätesten einer Woche Deutschland.
        Trotz der großen Hilfsbereitschaft aller Joint-Stellen,verzö-
gerten immerwieder neue Hindernisse und Komplikationen unsere Ausreise,
jetzt endlich haben wir unsere Pässe inder Hand und fahren in das neue
Leben,hoffendlich geht alles gut.
        Wir könnten unsere Reise in die neue Heimat nicht antreten,ohne
Ihnen,lieber Herr Steihouse für Ihre liebenswürdige Unterstützung und
große Hilfe,die Sie meinen Plan entgegengebracht haben,aufrichtig zu
dahken,ich hoffe sehr Ihnen noch im Leben zu begegnen,um diesen Dank
persönlich auszudrücken,vor allem danken auch meine jüd.Freunde für die
Unterstützung,die es Ihnen ermöglichte,mit auszuwandern.
        An Herrn Dir.Beckelmann habe ich ein directes Dankschreiben ab-
geschickt.Wenn auch die mir für Europa ausgezahlte Hilfe,durch den un-
glücklichen Kurs nur 40%der erhofften Marksumme brachte,konnte ich doch
alle Verpflichtungen erfüllen und die erfprderlichen Dinge für die Aus-
wanderung besorgen.Die Maschinen-Pläne müssen eben in einer anderen Art
ihre Verwirklichung finden.Auch der Umstand,daß die Schiffskarten in
Buenos Aires zu einem späteren Zeitpunkt bezahlt werden können,verhindert
glücklicherweise eine sofortige Verringerung der dortigen,bescheidenen
Substanz,für meine Existenz-Gründung.
        Mit der Bitte,mir nach Fertigstellung einen Entwurf unserer
Geschichte,durch den Joint in Argentinien zuzuleiten,schließe ich mein
Schreiben mit den herzlichsten Grüßen und Handkuß für Ihre Frau Gemahlin,
mit den besten Grüßen und Wünschen für Sie und Ihre werten Mitarbeiter,
        Ihr dankbarer und sehr ergebener:

10. *August, 1949 letter, in German, from Oskar Schindler to Herbert Steinhouse.*

Dir. Oskar Schindler
Regensburg, Nurnbergerstrasse 25   Munich, 12 August, 1949

Mr. Herbert Steinhouse,
c/o The American Joint Distribution Committee,
    119 Rue St. Dominique,
    Paris, FRANCE

Very Esteemed Mr. Steinhouse,

        It is a great pleasure for me to send you, through Mr.
Horowitz, these words and my most hearty greetings.

        Constant new difficulties for our project to emigrate
have hindered our departure, but now I can send you positive news,
thank God, because we have succeeded and are able to leave Germany
in one week, at the latest.

        Despite all the AJDC departments' great desire to prove
helpful, handicaps and complications always delayed our leaving.
But now, finally, we have our passports in hand and we can travel
into the new life with the hope that all will go well.

        We could not have undertaken our journey to our new
homeland, dear Mr. Steinhouse, without your gracious and kind-
hearted assistance which you brought to my plans. We send you our
most deeply felt thanks.

        I very much hope to meet you again in this life, and be
able to express this gratitude personally. Above all else, I thank
you on behalf of my Jewish friends for the great help which made
it possible for them to join us in emigrating.

        I have sent off a letter of thanks directly to Director
Beckelman. Despite the help received for our European expenses, it
unfortunately came to only 40% of the marks I had hoped for, owing
to the bad exchange rate. Still, I did fulfil all our obligations,
and we also acquired the necessities for our journey. Plans for
the machinery blueprints will have to await some other means of
execution. Luckily, the fact that our ship tickets to Buenos Aires
may be paid for later prevents any immediate diminution to the
modest amount needed for the start of my existence there.

        I ask you please to send me, through AJDC in Argentina,
a copy of the article upon its completion. I end my writing with
heartfelt greetings, and kiss the hand of your esteemed wife, and
with best regards and thanks to your valued colleagues,

        Yours gratefully and most faithfully,

                        (signed) O. SCHINDLER

11. *English translation by Herbert Steinhouse*

12. *Marketplace in the Krakow ghetto, 1940-1941*

13. *Entrance of Oskar Schindler's "Emalia" factory at #4 Lipowa Street in the Zablocia section of Krakow. The factory still exists and was used in the Steven Spielberg film version of "Schindler's List."*

women in college who have been harassed, even verbally, by male fellow students are classed as 'abuse survivors'. Hollywood is never far behind these trends. One can see in Oliver Stone's current release *Heaven & Earth* a typical example of the cult of endurance, this time of the Vietnamese woman surviving the horrors of her country's own holocaust. But Stone's despicable farrago of syrupy sentiment and misjudged bathos (did you know the Vietnam war was just bad karma?) serves only to point up Spielberg's awareness of the pitfalls lurking for his own eulogy to the victims of war.

Spielberg has taken on an impossible task and has almost succeeded. His central drama, displacing our unredeemable anguish at the fate of the victims to the dilemma of the good German Schindler, is intelligently handled. Steven Zaillian's screenplay has improved on Keneally's worthy but dull non-fiction book. (I know it won the Booker Prize for fiction, but some mysteries are beyond my ken.) In the book Schindler is portrayed as fairly sympathetic to the Jews from the outset, but in the film he starts out as an opportunist who thinks he has come across a great scam to make big bucks. The brilliantly cast Liam Neeson is credibly directed as he is drawn further and further into a moral morass where his basic worth as a human being is to be tested. That most men and women in his position failed that test in those dreadful circumstances points to the glory of Schindler's reluctant sainthood. This central hub of the story works.

But Spielberg is not content. His craft as a storyteller vindicated, he wishes to utilise his grand resources to show us the Shoah, no holds barred. The muddy camp, the brutal executions, the hordes of exhausted Jewish prisoners, the transports, the mass exhumation and burning of corpses. He wants to show us hell.

He cannot. Let us quote another, more authoritative source on the Holocaust, the Italian Primo Levi who chronicled his Auschwitz experience in his searing book *If This Is a Man*. Here is his description of the camp at the brink of liberation, in 1945: "Ragged, decrepit, skeleton-like patients at all able to move dragged themselves everywhere on the frozen soil, like an invasion of worms...." This cannot be recreated. Finding a handful of thin actors to demonstrate the 'selections' of fit or unfit prisoners to be sent to work or to destruction does not convey it 'as it was'. The actors cannot act this state of being which another Holocaust writer, the forgotten 'Katzetnik' (aka Yehiel Dinur), described as being on another planet, a wholly separate and different mode of being.

We cannot be consumers of this image. We can only unleash our inadequate imaginations in response to the stories that we hear. In this, Claude Lanzmann, I believe, was right, though he too had another agenda: more Zionist than Spielberg, he conceived of his *Shoah* as the ultimate justification for the State of Israel. But his own obsessive rigour defeated this abstract ambition. What we remember from *Shoah* is not the shrill call of polemic but the hypnotic gaze of all those talking heads. The light behind the eyes, illuminating dark memories.

Documentary and fiction, we are told, appear as different genres and cannot, some might say, be compared. But in fact neither genre has a claim to automatic veracity, to 'true life' as against the 'story'. Documentaries, too, tell tales, sometimes with greater mendacity since we assume that we're seeing it 'as it is'. Not so; we have to exercise our judgment either way. So *Shoah* challenges us to hear and see the witnesses and like a judge to make up our own minds about the stories they relate.

Shoah, too, has a 'righteous gentile'—the Polish courier Jan Karski, who, called upon by two Jewish activists, is persuaded to go into the infamous Warsaw ghetto to see for himself so he can tell the world, the British and the Americans, what is happening in Europe to the Jews. This interview takes up roughly 40 minutes of Lanzmann's nine-hour film. The old man, tall and aristocratic, walks forward and settles in a chair. He says; "I will now go back 35 years." Then his eyes fill with tears, he shakes his head, blurts out, "No, I do not go back," and walks out of the frame, clambering over his interviewer. Lanzmann's camera pans back to an empty chair. Then the old man, having composed himself, returns.

Again and again, Lanzmann's strategy is to leave in what other filmmakers cut out. Where other directors use meaningless cutaways to cover dialogue where picture is missing, Lanzmann uses them even to cover the pauses in the courier's account. He wants us to feel the difficulties of memory, the gap between reality and recollection. And then the witness speaks, and we are forced to listen, forced to seek the images in our own minds. The director impels us to pay attention. We cannot walk away untouched. Lanzmann is cruel both to his interviewees and to his audience. You will sit here. You will tell. You will listen. This is important. You are not allowed to leave.

Spielberg's melodrama is compelling in more traditional ways. Narrative drive, sinuous camera movements, impeccable cutting, glistening nocturnal lighting. It is 'back to basics', to old-fashioned craft values: the *noir* lighting in the commandant's office in Auschwitz as Schindler seeks to bribe with diamonds the ox-like figure seated before him, a bar of shadow hiding his eyes; the shimmering infernal fire of the crematorium chimney. It all has a terrible beauty, the cinematographer's seductive lure. The nicely crafted performances: Liam Neeson as Schindler. Ben Kingsley as the Jewish accountant Stern, Ralph Fiennes as the tormented brute Amon Goeth. Spielberg even gets away with everyone talking in *zese strange Cherman accents, hein?*—which jar at the beginning, and then become steadily more acceptable. It is, all in all, probably his second best film to date, *Close Encounters of the Third Kind* being, for sentimental reasons, my favourite.

But at the end of the day, the most Spielberg can do is to draw his spectators, for the three hours the film runs, into his Holocaust theme park. See, the amazing Schindler factory. Quake at the imminent departure of the train transports. Shiver as you pass beneath the Dantesque archway with snow falling over "Arbeit macht frei". Like Schindler, perhaps, you stand on a hill overlooking the ghetto, gaping at sights and sounds that you cannot comprehend.

In the first post-war generation, when the events were fresh in European minds, some film-makers tried the impossible. Among many films based on Holocaust stories, two in particular—Gillo Pontecorvo's *Kapo* (1960) and Andrzej Munk's *The Passenger* (1963)—concentrated on recreating the camps, albeit with limited resources. Munk's is by far the more interesting film, focusing on the relationship between two women, a prisoner and a guard, who meet by chance on a ship some time after the war. The camp is recalled in disconnected images which undermine the willed process of forgetting. Hell is not coherent. It refuses to make sense, except as a tool of an individual conscience. Primo Levi was aware as well of the limits of recollection and analysis: "Our language lacks words to express this offence, the demolition of a man. In a moment, with almost prophetic intuition, the reality was revealed to us: we had reached the bottom. It is not possible to sink lower than this...." But Levi knew that he had to believe that "even in this place one can survive." That this was true in his case was a matter of luck, not much more.

Spielberg and Keneally's Auschwitz is made comprehensible by the coherence of its narrative. There is even, in this hell, a happy ending. As in Dante's Virgil, some people are allowed to climb out, if not to paradise, at least to safety. Even this can be endured. Survival seems a matter not of chance, but of the consequences of a *good deed*. Despite the horror, a comforting reassurance. Right at the end of his film Spielberg slips badly, as the survivors, directed towards "a city over there" by a Russian soldier, march forward to the tune of the Hebrew song 'Jerusalem the Golden'. Spielberg is probably unaware that this is a Six Day War ditty weighed down by a very particular ideological baggage. But here it is used as an artifice to mix into the line of present-day Schindler-Jews as they line up to place stones upon the real man's grave. This is a moving sequence, a Lanzmannesque invasion of the actual into the simulation. It is, ironically but perhaps unsurprisingly, the most memorable scene in the film.

In the United States these kinds of reservations cut little ice with the mass audience. *Schindler's List* is already a runaway success. The audience, accustomed to vicarious living, is responding to the Holocaust theme park. But there might remain those of us who are less moved by these inevitably ersatz images than by the bald, bare contours of Lanzmann's tormented talking heads.

I shall remember Spielberg's film as a superbly crafted work by an intelligent professional director. But I shall recall much more powerfully Jan Karski, *Shoah's* Polish courier, refusing to remember and walking out of the frame, leaving me to contemplate what horrors endure in a man's mind so fresh for over 30 years. It is that empty chair, not Spielberg's sound and fury, which raises the hair on the back of my neck. Sometimes neither images nor words, but only echoes, can prevail.

"A Man of Transactions"

....

by Terrence Rafferty
The New Yorker, Dec. 20, 1993

Steven Spielberg's "Schindler's List" is a great movie, and, like all great works, it feels both impossible and inevitable. In the opening pages of the 1982 book (of the same name) on which the film is based, the author, Thomas Keneally, tells the reader, "This is the story of the pragmatic triumph of good over evil, a triumph in eminently measurable, statistical, unsubtle terms," and then confesses to an odd sort of trepidation: "It is a risky enterprise to have to write of virtue." The writer's admission is staggering, because "Schindler's List" is a true story about the Holocaust: you would think that an artist who has taken on the task of portraying that unimaginably monstrous event wouldn't consider the representation of virtue his most daunting challenge. But the story of Oskar Schindler—a dashing and resourceful German Catholic businessman who saved over a thousand Polish Jews from almost certain annihilation—is extraordinary even by the standards of Holocaust literature, in which every kind of human behavior *except* the merely ordinary can be found. And, in a sense, Schindler's goodness really is more mysterious—tougher to account for intellectually—than the Nazis' evil, because his actions seem not to have been determined by anything resembling a conscious political, religious, or social principle. He wasn't an idealist (much less an ideologue), but he took the sort of risks that a fanatic or a willful martyr might take, and never troubled to explain himself. According to Keneally, many of the people Schindler rescued still say, "I don't know why he did it."

The triumph of the book is that Keneally's faithful, exhaustively detailed chronicle of Schindler's wartime activities never fully answers the question "Why?" and, besides, persuades us that it would be foolish to try: heroism of this magnitude is, at its heart, inexplicable. Spielberg (working from a script by Steven Zaillian) also respects the mystery of Schindler's personality, and part of what makes the film so moving is that an ambiguous, complex hero is something entirely new in this director's work. The sheer unexpectedness of Spielberg's rigorous refusal to simplify his protagonist's motives seems to connect him, in a minor but distinct way, to Schindler himself; this character is, after all, a man whose dedication and commitment to righteous action simply could not have been predicted from the evidence of his prewar life. That's the beauty of the story. What Schindler does during the years of Nazi oppression appears to constitute a kind of self-transcendence, but it's really more like an improbable self-fulfillment: in the unique, deranged circumstances of occupied Poland, his shortcomings, and even his vices, somehow turn into instruments of virtue.

Spielberg introduces Schindler with a scene of his preparations for an evening out in Kraków. Before we're shown the hero's face, we see his elegant clothes and the swastika pin that gleams in his lapel. Schindler (Liam Neeson) arrives at a swank night club filled with Nazi officials and expensively dressed women, and looks as if he were right at home. He's handsome, confident, and worldly—the very image of the man of affairs. It doesn't take him long to become the center of attention: he drinks and laughs with the Nazis, and appears to be having the time of his life. The only hint that there might be something unusual about this prosperous-looking back-slapper is provided by a handful of closeups of Schindler's watchful face in the moments just before he moves in on the Nazis. He gazes at them coldly, clinically, and it's impossible to tell whether the look in his eyes reflects deep-seated disdain or merely the pragmatic attitude of a businessman plotting his social tactics as he prepares to initiate a potentially advantageous contact. The uncertainty about the protagonist's character which Spielberg creates in this superbly directed sequence establishes the tone of the movie's treatment of Schindler, and, precarious as it is, it's precisely the right tone. Schindler, having failed at several businesses in Germany, has come to Kraków with the intention of making some easy money in the wartime economy. Poland, he feels, offers tremendous opportunities for someone like him—an energetic entrepreneur who knows how to get things done and isn't burdened by an overscrupulous sense of business ethics. The best opportunities, of course, have been created by the Reich's systematic destruction of the Jewish community, and in the film's first hour we see Schindler, apparently without qualms, buying a Jewish-owned factory for next to nothing, staffing it entirely with Jewish workers (because their labor costs far less than that of Polish Gentiles), and taking possession of a large, airy apartment vacated by a family that has been forced to move into the city's ghetto. And in these swift and sometimes darkly funny early passages Spielberg gives us glimpses of several other somewhat unsavory aspects of Schindler's character: the movie's hero, we learn, is also an enthusiastic participant in the city's black market and an inveterate philanderer. (His wife has remained in their prewar home, in Moravia, and, prudently, doesn't pay him many visits while he's in Poland.)

Schindler, nestled in a fur-collared coat, strides through this ugly world with a curious air of innocence. He's a war profiteer, but he obviously sees no harm in the way he's making his fortune. He treats the workers at his factory, which makes pots and pans for the German Army, reasonably well, and although they're basically slave labor, their employment provides them some tangible benefit: they can be considered essential to the war effort, and therefore (they hope) a little less likely to be deported to a concentration camp. Schindler is the sort of wheeler-dealer who closes even his most outrageous business propositions with a cheerful "And everybody's happy!"—and seems to actually mean it. The grotesque disparity in the degrees of "happiness" enjoyed by the Nazi occupiers and his Jewish employees doesn't appear to trouble him much; he's not gifted with a keen sense of irony. And, besides, he's just an entrepreneurial capitalist, doing what such men have always done—making money according to the conditions of whatever social system happens to obtain, without passing judgment on the system's fairness.

The hero's evolution from an unreflective profiteer to a conscious and daring rescuer of the Jews is portrayed, both in the book and in the film, with extraordinary subtlety. Keneally provides more detail, but Neeson's quietly brilliant performance makes up for the movie's elisions: this is nuanced and utterly unsentimental acting—exactly what the role requires. Schindler, who is no philosopher, never delivers the sort of high-minded speech that tells us how he made the decision to use his friendly relations with the Nazis for the purpose of resistance rather than of profit. A speech of that sort would violate the nature of Schindler's heroism, which is instinctual, unpremeditated; like a soldier in the heat of battle, he's just responding as quickly and as effectively as he can to the chaotic events around him.

In the movie, however, it's possible to identify a turning point in the hero's consciousness—not because Spielberg crudely signals a change but because he uses the resources of film so powerfully that we, in the audience, feel a profound transformation in our relation to the historical drama we're witnessing. About an hour into the film, Spielberg stages the liquidation of the Kraków ghetto, and in this turbulent and almost unbearably vivid fifteen-minute sequence the Holocaust, fifty years removed from our contemporary consciousness, suddenly becomes overwhelmingly immediate, undeniable. Spielberg, using his prodigious visual skills with an urgency and an imaginative intensity that he hasn't shown in a long time, creates images that have the force of intimate experience, the terrible clarity of your own most indelible memories. Summary executions are performed, in chillingly objective medium shots, on Kraków's beautiful streets; the narrow corridors of the ghetto's tenements become nightmarishly claustrophobic as the Jewish families rousted out of their apartments try to move quickly enough to satisfy the armed, shooting S.S. men; flashes of machine-gun fire light up the dark stairwells; abandoned suitcases litter the alleys and courtyards; soldiers fire into the walls and ceilings, to dispose of anyone who might be hiding on the other side; thousands of Jews are herded brutally through the old city, and Schindler, watching from a hilltop, tries to track the progress of a little girl in a red coat as she makes her way, alone, through the smoke-filled streets. Sights like these make us feel—viscerally, and in the most concrete terms—the obscenity of the Reich's treatment of the Jews, and the strength of our own reactions tells us that this must be the moment in which amiable Oskar Schindler begins to entertain the idea of subverting the system that has enriched him.

For the rest of the film—which runs better than three hours and doesn't seem a minute too long—Schindler's cunning manipulations of high-level Nazis play out against the background of the increasingly horrific experiences of Kraków's Jews. As the Final Solution gathers momentum, the people who survived the liquidation of the ghetto are sent to the Plaszów labor camp, and there they live under the constant threat of slow death from exhaustion or hunger, and of sudden, violent death at the hands of their captors: the camp's sadistic commandant, Amon Goeth (Ralph Fiennes), takes target practice from the balcony of his villa, picking off prisoners at random as they walk across the compound. Schindler puts his disreputable talents to good use, cozying up to the psychotic Goeth and bribing and cajoling him—one man of the world to another—into granting the businessman the most unlikely concessions. Not only is Schindler allowed to continue operating his factory, with the same workforce, but he obtains permission to turn the plant into a sub-camp and move "his" Jews onto its premises. And, late in the war, when deportations to the extermination camps are occurring at an accelerated rate, Schindler contrives to establish a new factory, in Czechoslovakia, and to have eleven hundred Jewish workers who were scheduled for transport to the camps diverted to his facility. He purchases the reprieve of each of the Jews on his list individually, out of his (rapidly dwindling) profits; and then he has to pay yet again, to liberate three hundred women who wind up, mistakenly, at Auschwitz-Birkenau. "It was Oskar's nature," Keneally writes, "to believe that you could drink with the devil and adjust the balance of evil over a snifter of cognac. It was not that he found more radical methods frightening. It was that they did not occur to him. He'd always been a man of transactions."

The irony of Schindler's methods is that his temperamental indifference to ethical niceties is precisely what makes him an effective champion of the powerless Jews he employs. If he had been a more scrupulous man, he couldn't have done what he did. An idealist would never have dreamed, in the first place, of setting up a business to profit from the misfortune of the Polish Jews; and an idealist would have been sickened to the point of incapacity at having to spend so much time drinking and schmoozing with the likes of Amon Goeth. The people who work for Schindler are lucky to be under the protection of a man who combines the recklessness of a pirate and the oily mendacity of a confidence man; a Gandhi couldn't have served them nearly so well. What's genuinely inspiring about Schindler is that in one crucial respect he did diverge, spontaneously and unquestioningly, from his instincts as "a man of transactions": when his financial interests stopped coinciding with the single, urgent interest of his workers, which was survival, he chose to dedicate himself to *their* interest. By the end of the war, he had spent so much money implementing the ever more elaborate schemes necessary to save the Jews that he was totally wiped out. From the prospective of our own rapacious times, a businessman who values his workers' lives over his own profits seems almost inconceivably noble.

What Spielberg achieves in "Schindler's List" is nearly as miraculous. (His accomplishment is less inspiring than his hero's only because art is less important than life.) It is by far the finest, fullest dramatic (i.e., non-documentary) film ever made about the Holocaust. And few American movies since the silent era have had anything approaching this picture's narrative boldness, visual audacity, and emotional directness. Throughout the film, Spielberg captures images of experiences that most of us probably thought we would never see represented adequately on the screen. There's an astonishing sequence of a "health action" at Plaszów, in which naked inmates run in circles before the eyes of camp doctors who are looking to weed out those no longer strong enough to be productive workers; the prisoners' desperation as they push themselves to the limits of their diminished capacities and then beyond is all but unendurable. And, late in the film, Spielberg's camera takes us even further, straight into the heart of darkness: we follow the women who wound up at Auschwitz-Birkenau into the showers. They've heard stories of what happens in such places; naked, shivering, their heads shaved, they crowd in; they look up at the sprinkler heads that may spray either cold water or lethal gas; the lights go out, and a collective scream rises up, a shattering, unearthly sound—you feel as if you were somehow hearing, in the space of a few seconds, the distinct, individual voice of every woman in that bleak room. It is the most terrifying sequence ever filmed.

All but a few minutes of "Schindler's List" are in black-and-white. (The cinematography, by Janusz Kaminski, is wonderfully expressive, with delicate textures and lucidly defined contrasts.) The film's monochromatic look evokes the feeling of a documentary—a feeling that is reinforced by the naturalistic style of the acting and by the use of Polish locations. (Schindler's apartment and his Kraków factory are not sets but the actual sites in which the action took place.) The black-and-white imagery also recalls the older, grander filmmaking style that Spielberg, improbably, has revived in this picture, as if it were the only style capable of doing justice to the epic scope and human richness of the story. The pictorial beauty and the honest emotionalism of his work here are worthy of D. W. Griffith, and scene after scene in "Schindler's List" has the quality that James Agee described in writing of a battle scene in "The Birth of a Nation." "It seems to me," he wrote, "to be a perfect realization of a collective dream of what the Civil War was like, as veterans might remember it fifty years later, or as children, fifty years later, might imagine it." In "Schindler's List" Steven Spielberg imagines the Holocaust with that sort of visionary clarity.

Presenting Enamelware

by David Thomson
Film Comment, March-April 1994

Schindler's List *proves again that, for Spielberg, there is a power in the world that is greater than good and greater than evil, and it is the movies. He is hardly alone in this cinéaste's theodicy.*
—Leon Wieseltier, *The New Republic,* January 24, 1994

Schindler's List is the most moving film I have ever seen—I cried more than I ever did at *The Courage of Lassie, The Glenn Miller Story, The Miracle Worker,* or *Field of Dreams.* So I went back again to get a better sense of what was moving me. On the second viewing of the film, there was only one moment from the life of "the camp" that still produced tears: the scene in which the children are trucked away to something worse and the mothers surge forward as involuntarily as a groan. (Yet some kids remain. Does only the camera see them? Or is Spielberg having his cake and eating it?) Apart from that, I watched the sufferings of the Jews with bleak composure—judging the cuts like an editor—knowing what was going to happen and what would be shown, knowing when Commander Goeth would shoot and when he would pardon. That cruel suspense only works once; or if you were an inmate at the camp.

But two other things moved me as much the second time as the first: the moment when Schindler and Stern shake hands as equals, as Schindler is about to flee; and on realizing that, for the finale in Israel, the actual survivors of Schindler's list were coming to his grave accompanied by the actors who had played their parts when nearly fifty years younger. If I think about this a little, it seems to suggest that I am more moved by some discovery of friendship, and by the imaginative coup of moviemaking—by presentation—than by what happened to the Jews. So maybe being moved is not enough?

> *One gets the impression that Spielberg, at 46, has gone through a heartbreaking, life-changing experience.*
> *When he hears it put this way, Spielberg brightens and says* "Exactly! *I have trouble saying those words but that's exactly what it is. Because when you say those words, they sound noble. When I say those words, I feel like I'm sounding pretentious. So I've not made that statement to anybody in the press, even though it's true.*"
> —Edward Guthmann, *San Francisco Chronicle,*
> December 12, 1993

Presentation: it's the trick Oskar Schindler reckons he can bring to the first deal. Wealthy Jews will put up the money in return for goods; Jews from the Krakow ghetto will supply the labor; the accountant Stern will manage the operation; while Oskar goes to the Nazi parties, buys drinks all around, and promotes the hell out of the enterprise (there is a lot of hellishness to it that needs to be voided). The business is enamelware, pots and pans for Army use.

We know Oskar can do this from the magnificent opening sequence in which he goes from being an unknown to "Why, that's Oskar Schindler!"—the words of the maître de at the nightclub (a role taken by one of the movie's producers). I say magnificent because of the authority with which it is conceived, shot, and cut—Spielberg is a master of his craft, an unsurpassed hingemaker—but more particularly because, without irony, the sequence exults in a kind of magnificence (play-acting) that is especially revered in the picture business.

The sequence reminded me of a story told about Alexander Korda, who arrived as a stranger in Hollywood with only a little money. Modus operandi? Stay at the best hotels, be seen with the most beautiful women, entertain in grand style, charge everything, but tip lavishly. Then wait for offers.

We do not know how much or how little money Schindler has at that point (later, he admits coming to town with nothing), but we are accomplices in his nerve and the film's delighted itemization of his magic: the silk suit, the swaggering tie, the cuff-links, the gold Nazi pin, the bank notes that appear in his hand beneath the waiter's nose. The rest of the world is his stooge; the German soldiery are idiots—and we are Schindler's rapt audience. He is a man of mystery (always alluring on screen), but we take pride in the smooth working of his charm. When he tells us that presentation is his game, we feel treated. There is from the outset some stealthy hint of a Scarlet Pimpernel in the making.

Schindler is tougher-minded, more grownup, than most characters in Spielberg—he even has a lovemaking scene, one so gratuitous that we cannot recognize the woman. (That's characteristic: Schindler has a camera-like readiness for all pretty women.) So many of Spielberg's characters in the past have been fully-fledged children, or nominal adults who cannot suppress the yearning to get back to childishness. That was the most damaging in *Hook*, but it was at work in the far more interesting *Close Encounters*. Still, Schindler has brought out a driven, economical, sardonic, and very precise style in Spielberg that is flawless for long passages of the movie.

I said "most of Spielberg," because there is one film that seems family to *Schindler's List: Empire of the Sun*, a commercial failure, yet—in my opinion—Spielberg's best film until now. In some ways, Schindler "explains" *Empire*: the unflinching view of a prison existence, the haphazard cruelty of its masters, and the terrible pressure to survive. The John Malkovich character in *Empire* is more ruthless and far less charming than Schindler. If Schindler presents a class act, "A" pictures, Malkovich deals in grubby B-minus movies. And the Japanese camp in *Empire* is a place of greater compromise, where survival elicits mean-mindedness, cheating, betrayal, and all the regular behavior from life outside prison. The Jews in *Schindler's List* are, without exception, decent, noble, generous, saintly, and very beautiful. They're not quite Steve Ross, the person to whom the movie is dedicated (chairman and CEO of TimeWarner who died in 1993).

There's no reason why the style and sensibility of this movie shouldn't emanate from Schindler. But that choice makes his Rick-like enigma as important a subject as what happened to the Jews. In some respects, I admire the decision, for at last Spielberg has thoroughly identified with one of his characters. We feel that he is moved. Too often in the past, his regard for central characters has been either willed and sentimental, or chilly and dispassionate. But because Schindler has captured Spielberg's imagination, the director gives him the film. Why not? It is the historic fact of Schindler's big deal that makes the Holocaust viable as a mainstream movie. That's what *Schindler's List* means to be—Oskar is a producer's dream, for he brings redemption to the ghastly scenes of exercised power.

But the style is very calculated. Spielberg has not yet found a way of doing things without congratulating himself at the same time. (That's not an attack on him. Rather, I think it's an observation about American film as a whole, where style has no higher aim than showmanship.) Especially on a second viewing, I saw too many vulgar, neat cuts on similar movements that—under the circumstances of the story—are smug and depressing.

Consider the scene in which Schindler interviews or auditions secretaries. It's a scene that makes audiences laugh; and we are desperate for relief in this story. With one nice diagonal setup we see Oskar in a chair and a succession of women at the typewriter. The setup is worthy of Lubitsch: the one real typist, a dour fatso who smokes, has Oskar glum and turned away; but a series of beauties, hunting and pecking, draw Oskar closer, until one sultry girl Friday does a very slow one-finger dance, locked in eye contact with her boss-to-be. The smack of style (or presentation) for most viewers obscures the belittling of women and secretaries. The film is on Oskar's side, so he hires all the lovely girls. It's a privilege of being the hero, and a German who employs Jews. And this is a movie about privilege.

There's one of these women with Schindler when he has his unfortunate epiphany. The couple are out riding in the hills above Krakow (it seems a rather masochistic sport) when they notice the ghetto-clearing in process. Oskar then "sees" one little girl—she is 5 or 6—walking aimlessly in the tumult of roundup, murder, and attempted escape. There is a bump in the film as it changes stock (I think), for within the black-and-white frame this child wears a coat of a drab red color, like dried blood. It matters less whether this image has been hand-colored, or colorized (I believe the latter)—at any event, the re-creation of Krakow has been intruded on by a tiny slice of *Jurassic Park* technology.

Schindler is stricken. He says nothing, yet Liam Neeson's sliced-potato face conveys the nightmare below. But does that panorama require one red coat to carry Oskar over the top of tolerance? Does he not see everything else that is going on? Or do we have to abide by the Spielbergian notion—the whimsy—that the unspeakable is only reached if it is happening to a child? Does the woman with him see the red coat? Presumably not, for she is just one of the several secretary-whores, and not really a figure in the film. If she sees red, doesn't she deserve a more privileged status? But if she sees only the whole, there is something to be said for her evident distress and her wish to go away. It is the totality that disgusts her, not the heightened gesture.

We should not forget *Jurassic Park*, probably the most influential film that opened anywhere in 1993. I'm sure Spielberg has not forgotten it. *Jurassic Park* was a sensation, and swiftly ascended to the top of the all-time top-grossing chart. It is also comically bereft of any character or purpose except that of making marvels and money: it is far worse than *E. T.* or *Jaws*, for instance. This is not to minimize the difficulty of having several "impossible" objects, dinosaurs, move as fluently and rather more intelligently than Laura Dern, Sam Neill, or Lord Richard Attenborough. Nor do I doubt the epochal significance of a film that can make unreal creatures into movie—for here is the escape for motion pictures from the last vestige of life, the lifelike. Still, if Spielberg has been undergoing a life-altering experience in the last couple of years, it did leave him time and energy for the gaping void of *Jurassic Park*.

Maybe, like Oskar, he responds best himself to heightened gesture. It intrigues me that there has been so little attention to what I suspect strikes Spielberg as a grand analogy: that a manufacturer of basic enamelware may yet save his soul with a "gift of life." To say nothing of gaining respect and winning Oscars. Schindler, as presented in the movie, is so dedicated to presentation and being hit in the eye by knockout effects. (Remember the quick wink to Stern when he cons the last German soldiers into quitting?) He loves those acted moments, and he does what he does to be a story. The most fascinating point about the picture, to my mind, is the way the real uncertainty over Oskar Schindler the man meshes with the glamorous elusiveness of Liam Neeson's chuckling showman.

Casting Neeson was the kind of touch that distinguishes Spielberg. A better-known actor would have carried too many interfering associations. Yet Neeson has hollow panache, a flat sexy look, a connoisseur's calm, untidy emotionalism with no core, and that spacious face waiting for our guess at what he is thinking. He's all seduction. Spielberg loves the mystery in Neeson's Schindler, but he's too much of a producer to trust it all the way. In the end, this Schindler sacrifices his all to be good, even to the point of a breakdown scene that is beyond Neeson and which is the most pointed failure in the picture.

How much truer it might have been if this Schindler had stayed matter-of-fact and jovial to the end, laughing off the chance of friendship with Stern (for, really, Stern isn't his type) and recollecting—as a rough joke—that the getaway car might have meant another handful of lives. But Spielberg won't permit that brusqueness with his big finish in sight. So Schindler becomes, simply, a ruined but saved man, a character such as Capra might have liked. He is driven away a wreck as much as a hero. A title tells us that, after the war, his marriage and his attempts at business failed. All Schindler had ever needed was a war.

Spielberg has made him a hero, a savior even. Yet Thomas Keneally's book confirms our doubts. No one who knew him was ever sure why Schindler acted as he did. Surely humane instincts played their part. But just as clearly Oskar was an actor who sought the admiration of fresh crowds. He wanted to be liked, so long as he was never fully known; the film is very good on his impatience as being thanked or offered particular personal respect. He seems to have wanted a gap between himself and others. He did not want to be investigated; he did not want to know himself too well.

There's another, more pragmatic explanation for what he does, not referred to by the film. Schindler purchases lives in the summer of 1944—after D-Day, at a time when no one on the German side with his wits about him could have doubted the war's outcome. Yet no one in the film mentions this; so there is no innuendo even that Schindler may have been looking to impress a new crowd. Thus, the gesture of saving lives—of converting suitcases of cash into wondrous faces, 1,100 of them—grows out of his factory-owner's roar, "They are mine," without reflection or explanation. It is a cunning transition, very effectively presented, and it may be beguiling to the director who made this and *Jurassic Park* in the same campaign and who would like to keep the two accounts separate.

But the deal doesn't bear looking into too closely. When Schindler and Stern draw up the list, there is a point at which they stop. So there were others who did not make it. Yet Stern does not shudder at the burden of having made such a list. He praises Schindler. And when those saved hurry to trains, the camera (or their eyes) does not pan away to note those less fortunate. Privilege keeps its head down and acts like part of a great story.

Spielberg is as discreet as Hollywood always prefers to be about the money. What was the going rate for one life? Nor do we sense dangers behind the simple trading arrangement. Goeth complains about the paperwork. Am I overly intimidated by five decades of the SS on screen, or weren't there sanctions against such deals? Didn't the commandant have more to fear than clerical labor? Or was the Reich really as messy and incompetent as Harry Lime's Vienna?

There is a screwup in the rescue. The train carrying the women goes to Auschwitz by mistake (and to maybe the film's most terrifying moment—yet I think, by then, we trust Spielberg to have a presenter's solution: he only enters the gas chamber because he knows he can get out—he pardons). To rectify the error, Oskar confronts the officer-in-charge (lit like classic film noir), and takes a handful of loose diamonds out of his pocket to repurchase what he already "owns." (I remember that David Selznick's father kept loose diamonds in his pocket to impress people.)

There's another implication to the deal that Spielberg prefers not to mention. If Oskar Schindler with just money could save 1,100 Jews, why were there not other deals? Why did organizations and nations not barter? As it is, Schindler's purchase amounts to a miracle. But there's really no magic to money, no matter the flourish with which it is handled. There may be much more neglect to be guilty about. Perhaps the Germans did not really care quite as much, ideologically, about the Jews as we have told ourselves.

So much real history is skirted in *Schindler's List.* Yet in the bluntest way, the movie is educational. When I first saw the film, the long line waiting to gain entrance was being ordered about by a young theater employee: "Schindler's List line up here, and then double back." It was a brazen instruction that could hardly have been shouted out repeatedly by anyone who had seen the film or knew what it described. Whatever the problems, this is brilliant American moviemaking that can leave little doubt about some basic facts.

Still, I share a feeling Leon Wieseltier voiced in *The New Republic:* "I do not doubt that the glibness of Spielberg's film (though there is nothing glib about Ben Kingsley's or Ralph Fiennes's performances) is glibness in a good cause. But Americans are quickly moved. There is something a little exhilarating about all these tears. I'd prefer a bit more stunning into silence."

That stopped me short. My tears, the first time I saw the movie, had been for Schindler and Stern in partnership, and for the picture itself, the show. Like most readers of this magazine, I'm sure, I like movies to work; I want them to be good; I want to be moved; and I want to rejoice for the filmmakers. Spielberg has always seemed a master-in-waiting, and here is a film that feels like a masterpiece.

But *Schindler's List* is a curious thing if its secret, or not so secret, effect is to celebrate Spielberg, the ways of showmen, and the power of the movies. Keneally's Schindler is so uncertain a figure. Spielberg's is so glamorous. It was only on second viewing that I realized how far Oskar's cadre of gorgeous secretaries is parallel in the very beautiful actresses who play Jewesses—the ones who strip for the gas chamber. Spielberg actually chose both teams—to make his picture pretty? to characterize the Jews? to add to the mystique of Schindler? to regard the beauties as his?

I doubt that Spielberg knows the answers, for these questions might undermine the essential confidence of a great showman—and Spielberg is perhaps the greatest, surely destined to collect Oscars to sit beside the Thalberg award given him in 1986. *Schindler's List* is fascinated by the kind of power that puts on a show. In a wonderful, Dostoyevskyan sequence, Schindler suggests to Goeth that it may be more powerful to pardon than to kill. The commandant is tempted; he becomes papal in his bathroom mirror. He spares lives. For a moment he forgives the youth who cannot remove the stains from his bath. Then he shoots at the boy from a distance—to show the fragility of pardon. Shots go to either side of the boy. Then Spielberg cuts to the figure of Stern, who shifts slightly at a third shot. We do not see its effects until the camera pans with Stern to pass the fresh corpse of the youth. The last issue of *Film Comment* remarked on this great moment, the superb mise-en-scène—but it is a use of power and suspense uncannily close to the commandant's lethal accuracy.

This is the final problem, I think, and the gravest. For there is something obscene in the most controlled narrative presentation of such scenes. No matter the pain and outrage being shown, the act of showing transcends the material and begins to alter it. There is no escaping the incriminating basis of cinema: we are only voyeurs, stuck there, helpless and impotent in the dark, witnesses to the story and the crime, but members of the communion that is made by the astonishing lucidity and management of the telling. By the show. We have to note as well as the arbitrary murder, the sound of riflefire, the tiny metallic tinkling of the shell case, the scattering of fragments, the leaping spurt of blood. We wonder how they do such things, and we become connoisseurs of enamelware.

I do not blame Spielberg. Leon Wieseltier observed that the fine and powerful black-and-white photography (by Janusz Kaminski) was too ripe, too artistic perhaps. That may be so. But if a film was to be made, photography had to be employed. Is there any image plain enough? Maybe such events should never be re-created, so that we have to judge them in the way of inspectors and spies.

I don't have the answer. In the past, I have felt that Holocaust films were "impossible," no matter how well done. But in 1993, in so many ways, Spielberg did impossible things. I would urge anyone to see *Schindler's List*—but more than once. It is worthy of Golden Globes and Oscars. There is news here for the young and ignorant. And there is all the pleasure of filmmaking craft, alas.

Some people remark on the incongruity or the jarring of its last credit—"For Steve Ross"—as if that were too mundane for so vast a subject. Yet Steve Ross was probably a Schindler in his own way. Not every viewer waits to see that credit; it comes some minutes after the story has ended. But everyone sees something I found more disconcerting—"An Amblin Entertainment." Whatever its faults and virtues, *Schindler's List* is not an ambling entertainment. But I daresay, for legal and manufacturing reasons, the logo had to be there. If the film had to be there. *Schindler's List* is a very good movie, good enough to let us realize that movies are never good enough and that they threaten to replace life. We should never forget that in its short history the medium has regularly appealed to fascists, the ideology that treasured showmanship.

"Schindler's List"
Finds Heroism Amidst Holocaust

· ·

*Cinematographer Exploits Black and White's Somber Palette
for Spielberg's World War II Drama*

by Karen Erbach
American Cinematographer magazine, Jan., 1994

Twelve years after arriving in the United States as a political refugee, Janusz Kaminski returned to Poland to photograph Steven Spielberg's stirring interpretation of *Schindler's List.* Kaminski came to Chicago in 1981 speaking only enough English to order himself eggs and toast. After enrolling in a language course, he moved on to study film at Columbia College in Chicago. He completed his education at the American Film Institute in Los Angeles as a cinematography fellow, and later served an internship with John Alonzo, ASC on *Nothing In Common.*

Kaminski seized the opportunity to shoot his first feature, *Grim Prairie Tales,* by cold-calling the production listing in the *Hollywood Reporter.* Since then he has gone on to shoot 15 features, including *Cool As Ice, Wild Flower, Class Of '61* and *The Adventures of Huck Finn.* Kaminski's longtime gaffer and friend, Mauro Fiore, also a Columbia College alumnus, flew out to Los Angeles five years ago on the hot prospect of gripping on a Roger Corman film, *Not of This Earth.* Kaminski and Fiore have worked together ever since.

Shooting for Steven Spielberg unquestionably marks an acceptance into Hollywood and catapults Kaminski into a different league. How does one make the leap from low-budget features to high-profile projects such as *Schindler's List*? Kaminski replies, "*Wild Flower* got me the job. Steven watches a lot of television and caught *Wild Flower*, which was directed by Diane Keaton, on Lifetime. The next day I received his phone call offering me the TV movie *Class Of '61*. Looking back, I think maybe that movie was a test, because later I found out he had also been considering me for *Schindler's List*."

After the completion of *Class Of '61*, Spielberg and Kaminski met again. By then Spielberg had decided to offer Kaminski his next, very personal project, *Schindler's List*. The director solicited Kaminski's thoughts about shooting in black & white, and also asked the cameraman if he was comfortable doing a film that would undoubtedly garner international publicity. Spielberg encouraged Kaminski by telling him, "You did a beautiful movie for Amblin in 22 days. It would be amazing to see your work on a 75-day shooting schedule."

And so it began. Spielberg, Kaminski and a fine international crew set out for Poland to film the inspiring and poignant story. Based on Thomas Keneally's book, *Schindler's List* is the true account of Oskar Schindler (Liam Neeson), a German Catholic industrialist whose membership in the Nazi party ironically helped more than 1,300 Jews escape extermination. A womanizer and heavy drinker, Schindler became an unlikely hero by taking over an enamelware works in Krakow and creating a benevolent and humane work camp for the Jews.

For Kaminski, the experience touched him on both personal and professional levels. "Here I am [after] 12 years in the United States, going back to the country where I was born accompanied by Steven Spielberg. I was ecstatic to be working with Steven, and yet when we began filming it brought home the sickening reality of the Holocaust. The newsreel quality of the black-and-white seemed to fade the barriers of time, making [the footage] feel like an ongoing horror that I was witnessing firsthand. I think I can speak for the whole crew when I say the experience was sobering."

Kaminski expressed an initial pride in returning home to Krakow, only to be deeply discouraged by recurring anti-Semitic remarks aimed at the cast and crew. "Although I'd like to romanticize about returning to Poland, I realized that America is really my home," he says.

Kaminski knew for a year and a half that he'd be shooting *Schindler's List*, and he used the preparation time to learn more about black & white photography by studying books from that era. "I used *A Vanished World* by Roman Vishniac as sort of my bible. Vishniac photographed Jewish settlements in the period between 1920 and 1939. I found inspiration in that book because this man, Roman Vishniac, had nothing—inferior equipment, inferior film stock and only available light—yet he managed to create really beautiful pictures with a timeless quality. When you look at the book you really don't know when the photos were taken except for giveaways like clothing and street signs and such."

Historical preparations were also important, and although the retelling of World War II genocide was part of Kaminski's education, he felt further study would only benefit his photography. "You try and get as close to the subject matter as possible," he says, "hoping that the knowledge will evoke the emotions you have about the period and you ultimately contribute to your creativity."

As the director and cinematographer were completing work on separate projects (Spielberg was directing *Jurassic Park* and Kaminski was shooting *Huck Finn*) they found time to meet and view films such as *In Cold Blood* and *The Grapes Of Wrath*. Kaminski points out that "although we discussed the styles and techniques of Conrad Hall and Gregg Toland, we were far from making creative decisions about *Schindler's List*. We primarily watched the work of others to see how style could create mood."

Once Spielberg and Kaminski were in actual preproduction, the time had come to finalize decisions, such as which film stock to use. Against studio hopes, the final print of *Schindler's List* would be black & white. The filmmakers had to decide between shooting on black & white negative or draining the hues from color negative. Spielberg wanted to colorize specific elements in certain shots, ultimately forcing the duo to utilize *some* color negative. Kaminski's big concern was whether the manipulated color would match with the black & white.

"After doing some tests we used Kodak color 5247 and 5296 to match with black-and-white 5231 and 5222, which are the only available emulsions," explains Kaminski. "We had to really fight with relatively inferior and dated film stock, basically because technology has changed but the film stock hasn't."

Kaminski worked with Don Donigi from Du Art to devise some tests. The first test Kaminski performed was to find out if a manipulated color negative could pose as black & white. "We had two cameras side by side with the lenses at the same focal length, shooting simultaneously. One camera was loaded with 5296 color negative. The other camera had 5222 black-and-white negative. Don printed the 5296 on color print stock but pulled out all the color. The black-and-white was printed on standard black-and-white stock. We set up the projectors side by side for viewing. The black-and-white had a completely different quality than the drained color negative. The black-and-white looked much more realistic, with more grain, while the color had a faint blue tint."

Since Kaminski wasn't satisfied with the look, Don Donigi conducted another test. He explains the concept and results, in layman's terms: "Black-and-white negative film is made up of silver halide and printed on silver release positive. Color is made up of silver coupled with dye. When the silver gets exposed it ignites the dye, creating color images. During the bleach and fixing process, the silver comes out of the film and all that remains is the dye. When we tried to print the color/dyed image onto black-and-white release positive it was unacceptable. This is because the print stock is orthochromatic; all you pick up is the blue information of the negative. I decided to print the color negative onto a special panchromatic high-con stock which is sensitive to all colors and used primarily for titles. Because this high-contrast stock has virtually no middle greys, I altered the process in order to extend the grey scale."

Kaminski recalls his impressions of Donigi's tests: "When I saw the results I was just blown away. They were so beautiful. From 5296 he printed it on this panchromatic stock and broadened the range. The results were amazing—no grain, no haze."

The next phase of testing involved filters. Kaminski explains how he was trying to brighten faces so that they'd appear white rather than grey: "Sometimes I'd succeed, sometimes I'd fail. I used yellow #15 and orange #21 to brighten skin tones. The principals in black-and-white are as such: if you have a red object and you apply a red filter, the red object will become lighter. Because most people's faces have a lot of orange, when you apply an orange filter, it neutralizes the orange, making the face appear lighter. With red filters you have to be careful. We used red #23 on occasion, but the faces became too bright and the lips became too dark. Lips have a lot of blue in them and red accentuates this while increasing the contrast. Another technique was to 'over-light' the faces according to my meter; when we saw the dailies, they were the perfect tone of white."

Another concern for Kaminski was how black & white film would interpret color tones. "We began the tests with make-up and wardrobe. We wanted to know how tones in wardrobe would photograph, because we weren't dealing with color as a final result. But of course, color still had to be considered.

"For example, in color film green and blue have distinct differences, but in black-and-white they read the same. This is because they have the *same tone*. But this is not the case in red and blue. The color red is not lighter than blue, but red stands out more in black-and-white because the *tone* is brighter. For this reason, tones became more important than colors. I worked with both Alan Starski, the production designer, and Anna Biedrzycka Sheppard, the costume designer, to coordinate the tones, making sure that they were either brighter or darker than skin tone."

Kaminski thought he'd solved all his problems with black & white— that is, until shooting commenced. "We began to have problems with the negative discharge of electricity that happens only with black-and-white because of the silver content in the emulsion. We would have spots on the negative that looked like little dots with arms of lightning. Sometimes we would have lines running across the top of the frame like lightning in the sky. It's very hard to avoid, and we failed. I still don't know how to avoid it. I read some comments in *American Cinematographer* by Walt Lloyd, who shot *Kafka*, [and he said] that he had the same problems. Basically, the room has to be static-free. We'd spray the room and be careful when loading or unloading to avoid any friction between the winds of emulsion. Soon we realized that a lot of the static occurred at the beginning of the roll. So we'd shoot off sixty to eighty feet at the head of every roll, providing [some room] to protect ourselves. However, there's still some footage that has static and people will see it. I don't think it's terrible—the image is not ruined—but it's unavoidable. We were shooting under harsh weather and production conditions. All those elements contribute to static discharge."

Don Donigi at Du Art reports that he hears similar stories from other cinematographers. Donigi divulged some tricks brought back from the field. One involves placing a humidifier in the camera truck and blowing air to de-ionize the environment wherever film is loaded or rewound. The most original idea was sticking a damp sponge inside the camera unit, assuring moisture.

Kaminski also confronted the logistics of shooting in a foreign country, with all of the potential problems regarding equipment and manpower. Fortunately for Kaminski, he was able to bring with him longtime collaborators, some of whom spoke Polish. "I have a crew here in Los Angeles that I've worked with for five years," he relates. "Mauro Fiore has gaffed every movie I've photographed, and we've reached a point where he can light many of the scenes without much discussion between us. Steve Tate, my first assistant, will share credit with Steve Misler, my second AC, who pulled focus on all B-camera and handheld shots. I also brought my best boy electrician, Jarak Gorozycki, whom I met at AFI and who, coincidentally, moved to America from Poland at about the same time I did. I was secure with the electrical crew chiefly because of Mauro and Jarak. I was a little worried about the foreign grip department. In general, Europeans don't use grip equipment like Americans, who are so specialized. If you want a little shadow on the wall, you've got the equipment. In Europe, if you want to create shadow you have to cut it from a piece of cardboard."

"Maura was extremely helpful," he adds. "It's easy for me to say, 'I'd like some lights here, and some there,' but he's actually the one who had to deal with the logistics and the language problems." On one occasion, after Mauro had rigged a second-story interior with Condors and many lights, Kaminski turned to him and said, "That looks nice; now let's turn everything off." Then he turned to Spielberg and said, "Steven, this looks great the way it is. We have enough daylight for two hours. Do you think two hours is sufficient time to complete the scene?" When Spielberg said that it was, the scene was shot with available light only, negating all of Mauro's efforts. Most of the time, however, Kaminski found himself using every single light that Fiore had set up and then "kissing his hand" in gratitude.

Amblin Productions got its entire lighting and camera package from Arri. Kaminski used both the Arri 535 and the brand-new Arri 535-B camera. The 535-B camera is more lightweight than the 535 because Arri did away with all the electronics. It also has additional handles for easy transport. Arri made further adjustments for Kaminski, eliminating excess weight by removing the filter box brackets and adjusting the gate for the black & white film. Kaminski used the 535 as his "A" camera and the 535-B as the "B" camera. For Steadicam work, he employed the MovieCam.

Kaminski used Zeiss prime lenses, both Superspeed and standard speed, and felt that they were perfect for this film. "Because Zeiss lenses don't have as sharp an edge as the Prios, we got a very realistic look," he says.

"In addition, the minimal focus [of the Zeisses] is greater than the Primos, which allowed us to come closer to the actors. We usually shot our close-ups at around 29mm, which is something I would never do if I wanted to glamorize. I usually use a 50mm or higher. But for this film, the 29mm seemed to provide a more realistic effect."

Kaminski arrived in Poland in January of '93, Spielberg arrived in February, and shooting commenced in March. As shooting began, Spielberg and Kaminski still hadn't discussed a specific photographic style for the film. "He gave me 100 percent free rein, which was really amazing for me," Kaminski says. "It was very exciting. Steven has always employed a certain mood, or those 'Spielberg touches,' but this movie has a completely different style than his previous films. *Schindler's List* was shot in a very crude technical manner. We were kind of aiming toward imperfection, little so-called 'flaws' that might be considered mistakes, such as handheld shots in scenes that would normally be shot on the dolly. Often we would set up the Pee Wee dolly and then have the operator, Raymond Stella, hand-hold while sitting on the dolly seat."

Kaminski saw a method in the "mistakes," an integrity that surpassed style and flash. "I approached this movie as if I had to photograph it fifty years ago, with no lights, no dolly, no tripod. How would I do it? Naturally, a lot of it would be handheld, and a lot of it would be set on the ground where the camera was not level. We weren't making dutch angles and shots like that; that was not the purpose. It was simply more real to have certain imperfections in the camera movement, or soft images. All those elements will add to the emotional side of the movie. When people go to see this movie and expect to see a Steven Spielberg blockbuster, they will find something else—a dark and unobtrusive tone. The performance that Ben Kingsley (as Itzhak Stern) gave was so subtle that very often I would not pick up on the emotional impact until later. But Spielberg was guiding this story in his own way, and the dailies projected an emotional wallop that made us all uneasy in our chairs. You also have to remember that Spielberg has wanted to make this movie for ten years. Perhaps *Jurassic Park* closes one stage of his life and *Schindler's List* represents a new one."

Despite the freedom he allowed his cameraman, Spielberg still had some definite ideas about he'd approach some of the scenes. "For instance," Kaminski recalls, "there was one scene when Nazis raid a ghetto. Steven wanted a flash effect [to simulate] machine guns firing in the hallways, but he only wanted to see the shadows of the soldiers. We placed two separate strobes at different heights, and as you look down the corridor all you see is the shadows of the soldiers created by the firing machine guns. We used a similar effect during a courtyard raid. We had a camera set outside in a courtyard and we placed seven strobe lights in various windows. On cue, we would hit each strobe, giving the illusion of a massacre inside. That intercuts with the interior, where we see Germans shooting into the furniture, into the walls, and into the ceiling. The Jews would create fake walls so that they could hide. The idea was that we would see the Germans firing into the wall and then cut back to the exterior to see the windows flashing. All the while we would see the Nazis loading exterminated victims into the trucks. Then we cut back inside the building to see blood dripping from the walls."

One example of Spielberg's colorization idea was a scene in a town square where hundreds of Jews wait for Nazi officials to decide whether or not they would receive a "blauschein," or blue stamp. The stamp would buy the Jews time by allowing them to work in branches of the Nazi industry that were essential to the war machine. Kaminski explains, "As the stamp is coming down on the document, Steven wanted the imprint to be a very faded blue. Everything else in the frame would remain black-and-white."

Spielberg also used colorization during a scene in which a little girl wearing a red dress is running through a raid. "He wanted the girl's dress colorized," Kaminski notes. "That image has something to do with how strange life can be. There is this beautiful little girl with blonde hair wearing this red dress and running through this madness, where Nazis are arresting, shooting and dragging people off the streets. The little girl just runs through the crowd and nobody bothers to stop her."

Kaminski says that surprisingly little planning went into the film, despite its broad scope. Spielberg had no storyboards, no shot lists and very often would show up on the set not knowing exactly what he would do that day. One of the tools Kaminski incorporated in order to keep up with the spontaneous energy was a small portable tape recorder, which he used to record his thoughts about lighting, problems or equipment he might need.

When scouting locations, Spielberg would sometimes get ideas on how he was going to stage a scene. Kaminski would dictate those ideas and then later transfer them to the script so that he would be better prepared. "I'd make my comments to the lab, record what I'd done and what I was trying to achieve. Then later, when I saw dailies, I could compare my notes and see if I achieved what I wanted or if I failed. It was especially useful with black & white because I was still learning the medium. And on a daily basis I would make adjustments, either through my lighting, exposure or filtration."

Kaminski offered to share some of the verbal and written notes he had made about several scenes. What follows are excerpts from the original script, along with Kaminski's thoughts on how he would light the scenes.

INT. GHETTO APT—DAY

Clothes boiling on the stove in big pots stirred by a woman in rags; sheets hanging from the lines stretched across the room over a few sticks of furniture; children with coughs; the Nussbaums staring in dismay from the doorway.

SHOOTING: "Sunset. Man shaving in front of mirror on wall. The man is not lit. The wall reads f4. I expose at f2.8. As the Nussbaums open the door, Mrs. Nussbaum reads f4. I expose at f2.8. As they walk into apartment it drops to f1.4. As they go into the other room they stand in a strong pool of light. I backlight Mr. Nussbaum at f16. Mrs. Nussbaum will be a bit darker. When he turns to the camera he is the key at 2.8. To the eye the scene looks well-balanced."

DAILIES: "The scene was very contrasty. Moody. A sense of complete poverty and desolation. Not a pretty scene. I feel like the attention will be drawn to the "realness" of the situation and not to the photography."

EXT. COUNTRYSIDE—DAY

SHOOTING: "A locked-off shot of a German staff car driving by. Dusk. Light meter shaded from sky reads f1.3, the sky reads split f2.8/4. It's getting dark and I fear underexposure."

DAILIES: "Looked good. It always amazes me how much light is actually caught even though the light meter tells me that it won't work."

Although Kaminski did his best to prepare, there are bound to be mistakes when a cinematographer doesn't have a storyboard or shot list and must deal with 100 speaking roles and 30,000 extras. Kaminski recognizes them freely: "In one instance, I had a strobing problem. It was a big dolly shot that we will not be able to use in the final cut. We were just dollying past too many objects too quickly. But sometimes you get excited and forget how technical it is to be a cinematographer. Also, I wish some faces from certain scenes shot earlier were brighter. I was exposing as if I would be exposing color emulsion and relying on what I knew the best. It was the beginning of shooting, and being insecure [at that point] you always rely on what you know the best. I mean, it'll work for the average audience, but in my opinion it was a mistake. You have to be very honest with yourself and not listen to other people when they tell you it looks great. But you learn."

When asked about some of the most difficult scenes to shoot, Kaminski sighs as he reflects back on some of the interior factory scenes or night exteriors at the camp. "I was always worried about the factories. I'd never dealt with such a scope. I was not working with high-speed color emulsion; I was working with an emulsion with an ASA of 200. As I said earlier, if you expose black-and-white with the given ASA reading, you're not going to get the results you want, so you have to overexpose by putting in a lot of light. I would rate the 200 ASA as though it were 100 ASA, which meant that some nights we had every single light working."

Kaminski describes a particularly unsettling day: "There was a scene at Birkenau, where a group of women are being lead into a transfer room. They've been stripped of their identity and deprived of their privacy. Like those women, we don't know if they're going to live or die. They've been told they'll be showered and clothed in uniforms. But as we all know, very few got what they were promised. The Nazis liked to create a facade of normalcy to avoid a panic among the prisoners. Also remember that during the transport to Auschwitz and Birkenau, these people were living for days in tightly packed cattle cars, without food or ventilation. Spielberg had some specific ideas on how to handle this scene photographically. I placed single light bulbs on the ceiling and along the walls. When the women were led into the shower room or gas chamber all the lights suddenly shut off, leaving the women in complete darkness. There were screams for 5 to 10 seconds until a strong spotlight came on and pointed toward the camera. The light outlined the nude women crowded next to each other, holding each other for comfort, not knowing whether they'll live or die. All of a sudden, the sprinklers came on and the water sprayed out. It's the most amazing scene. It's so emotional that even now, it's tough for me to hold a strong voice.

"What Steven did was to mimic Nazi sadism so that the audience, like the women, are in the dark, afraid for what could happen. It was not manipulative or sentimental. It was real. And the crew's reaction on the set was hatred—hatred for the ignorance that could do this to a group of people. But look, it's still happening in former Yugoslavia. Same stuff, fifty years later. What did we learn? nothing. That's the purpose of the movie—to remind people that it's so easy to slip into the same thing."

One of the final scenes is the liberation of the factory and Schindler's final exit. His workers present him with a ring cast from their gold teeth. Inside the ring, the Hebrew inscription reads: "Whoever saves one life saves the world."

Kaminski describes the final moments: "We see an open field with puffy clouds. Hundreds of people are coming over the horizon toward us. The next shot is in color and in Jerusalem. It's a hot, dry land. We see hundreds of people again. But this time it's the *real* remaining survivors and their relatives walking toward us."

The next shot is in a Christian cemetery in Jerusalem, and the long line of survivors stretches toward the camera. In the foreground we see Oskar Schindler's grave. Each person puts a pebble on the grave, and the little pebbles eventually become a mass of stones piled high; it's estimated that the roughly 1,300 people Schindler saved have produced close to 10,000 relatives.

"It shows what one person can do with the power that they have," Kaminski concludes.

Spielberg Strikes a Blow for Black-and-White Films

by Susan Wloszczyna, Gannett News Service
The Houston Post, Jan. 30, 1994

What's black and white and almost as extinct as silent movies? Black-and-white films. The last non-color movie to win a best-picture Academy Award was 1960's *The Apartment.* The last one even to be nominated was 1980's *Raging Bull.*

Now Steven Spielberg has redeemed the status of black and white with his Holocaust drama *Schindler's List.* The film is a harrowing reminder that shadows and light can sometimes tell a story more effectively than all the Technicolors of the rainbow.

"The photography literally becomes a character that is critical to the understanding of the film," says Richard Brown, professor of cinema studies at New York's New School for Social Research. "Black and white gives the movie weight and gravity, and suggests the filmmaker approached his difficult subject with understanding and humility."

Spielberg has likened black and white to "truth serum." And *List* has many stunning visual moments:

The white snow stained by the dark, oozing blood of slain Jews. The gray ash from incinerated bodies, floating through the city like macabre snowflakes. The garish camera flashes in the nightclub scenes.

Such images would be ill-served by color. And the black-and-white photography is made all the more powerful as it mimics the way we usually experience scenes from World War II—black-and-white newsreel footage.

What exactly can black-and-white movies achieve that color can't?

"Color shows the texture of objects. Black and white reveals the essence," says Bob Dorian, a host on cable TV's American Movie Classics. "The focus is much stronger, it gets you into the story much quicker. Roger Ebert once said that with color, you notice the fabric of a woman's dress as she enters a room. With black and white, you admire the form underneath."

Spielberg Revisited

by Stanley Kauffmann
The New Republic, January 24, 1994

If a film has genuine worth, it's more than one film. It changes with further viewings. The second time you see it, it's larger. This time you aren't "distracted" by the story, by discovering what happens next. You can concentrate on the qualities that made you want to see it again, usually acting or felicities of vision or both. (Third and later viewings—of especially fine films—have an even stranger effect: as you learn more about them, you simultaneously feel you're seeing them for the first time. This happened to me recently with *Grand Illusion* and *Citizen Kane*, each of which I've seen upward of thirty times. Though I now saw even more in them, I had a feeling of fresh arrival.)

I don't know how any times I'll see *Schindler's List,* but ever since my first viewing (*The New Republic*, December 13, 1993), I've known that I wanted to see it again, soon. For two kinds of reasons. First, personal. I'd expressed concern that people who know something about the Holocaust might find the earlier portions—ghetto enclosure and labor camps—overly familiar. Well, I know something about the Holocaust, and I wanted to examine more carefully what had happened to me, what might happen again, while watching the film. This second time, I was again so taken by Spielberg's insistent honesty, by the heightened factuality, that I saw how my familiarity *helped,* made the film a confirmation and a deepening.

Then there were sheerly cinematic reasons. I wanted to see the "second" film; and throughout, I noted subtle compositions, astringent editing, overall vigor of construction that had certainly affected me the first time—I had thought it superbly made—but now seemed even more astonishingly fine.

But with the second viewing of *Schindler's List,* some other things became clear. The film rests on two large motions of change, one within the film and one, so to speak, behind it. The first is Schindler's metamorphosis, from hustling opportunist to self-disregarding savior. Some viewers have objected that Spielberg and his screenwriter, Steven Zaillian, didn't articulate the change vividly enough; but to have done more would have been to tamper with history. Thomas Keneally, from whose book the film derives, is specific about the unspecificity:

> One of the commonest sentiments of Schindler Jews is still "I don't know why he did it." It can be said to begin with that Oskar was a gambler, was a sentimentalist who loved the transparency, the simplicity of doing good; that Oskar was by temperament an anarchist who loved to ridicule the system; and that beneath the hearty sensuality lay a capacity to be outraged by human savagery, to react to it and not to be overwhelmed. But none of this, jotted down, added up, explains the doggedness with which, in the autumn of 1944, he prepared a final haven for [the Jews who worked in his Kraków factory].

Recurrently, beginning in the middle of the film, we see Schindler being shocked beneath his poise by the blacker and blacker wolfishness of the Nazis whose party pin he wears. But never is there a Moment of Truth, together with an angelic choir on the sound track. Spielberg's artistic triumph here is that he refuses to explicate, to interfere with what is actually known. He leaves the mystery of Schindler's goodness as finally inexplicable as the mystery of the "human savagery" around him. (This, for me, is the true subject of the film.)

There's another instance of this avoidance of italics. Near the end, when Schindler assembles his 1,100 Jewish workers on his plant floor to tell them that the war is over and they are free, the German army guards, fully armed, assemble on a sort of balcony above. Schindler addresses the guards:

says he knows that they have orders to liquidate his workers; and asks them whether they want to go home as men or as murderers. After a moment's pause, one of the soldiers leaves—and is soon followed by the others. Spielberg's exquisite touch is that he never shows the face of this first soldier, no twitching, no making up his mind; after the pause we simply see the soldier pass the camera. Yes, we soon see the guards' commander wavering in decision, but he has become a character who needs finishing off. The bellwether soldier is a particle of history

The second major change is the metamorphosis of Spielberg himself. It's not possible to compare the horror itself with a film about it; still, we might venture to compare the effect of the Holocaust on Schindler with the effect of knowledge of the Holocaust on Spielberg. We know from much recent interviewing that the Holocaust has long been a presence for him (as it was with Schindler) but how he has concentrated for the most part on ingenious commerce (as did Schindler). Then (again like Schindler) the force of the horror burst through to alter him.

How is that alteration manifested? Initially, with the choice of subject. Still, the filmmaking might have been Spielberg-clever. All the cleverness was renounced. Among the new powerful austerities, including the use of black and white, two elements stand out as warrants of gravity. First, the faces. Face after Jewish face appears, most of them only once, and each of those faces is a testament. By filming in Poland, Spielberg was able to use faces engraved with knowledge, inheritors of grief, that certify and magnify his story. Though they are faces of our contemporaries, they are nonetheless faces of the past.

The best compliment to Liam Neeson, the Schindler, and Ben Kingsley, the Jewish accountant, is that they don't obtrude as actors. Their faces fit. This is also true of Embeth Davidtz, as Helena, the camp inmate selected by the Nazi commandant to be his housemaid.

Then the second element, the children. There are many, as there must be, and some of them are centered for a few moments each. They never seem to act. Spielberg has worked well with children before but always in childish matters. Here the children cannot possibly understand much, but they are convinced of *something*. Spielberg has brought these children up to the film's level of truth.

The small boy fleeing the German army's roundup of Jews in the Kraków ghetto for deportation and death, this boy who dives through the toilet seat in an outhouse, this boy who surfaces in the ordure and discovers that three other children are there already, this boy I'll remember. There's a notorious German army photo of a small Jewish boy, arms upraised, being marched out of the Warsaw ghetto by soldiers—Bergman used that photo in *Persona*. The Warsaw boy's face is in the world's memory—in reality. This Kraków boy's face, ordure-streaked—Spielberg's attempt to bear witness fifty years later—may join that earlier photo in the world's memory.

Close Encounters of the Nazi Kind

by Leon Wieseltier
The New Republic, Jan. 24, 1994

One must have a heart of stone to watch *Schindler's List* without crying; but it is also a part of Steven Spielberg's achievement to have fulfilled every director's dream, which is to make a film that will bring about a collapse of criticism. All the adulation somewhat astonishes me. What is at stake, it begins to seem, is the honor of Hollywood. Here is a big and grim movie about the biggest and grimmest subject, and its final frame says "For Steve Ross." Gravity has made peace with the grosses. Of course, gravity in Hollywood is a random force: a few years ago the American people were instructed with moral and visual eloquence that Lyndon B. Johnson conspired to murder John F. Kennedy. So we have a little luck to be thankful for. This time the subject was right for the eloquence.

But there is a sense in which the American people was owed this film. For no figure in American culture has worked harder to stupefy it, to stuff it with illusion, to deny the reality of evil, to blur the distinction between fantasy and fact, and to preach the child's view of the world than Steven Spielberg. In the years when filmmakers and poets and novelists and painters and composers were wrestling with the possibility, or the impossibility, of treating radical evil in art, Spielberg was teaching actors to sculpt mountains out of mashed potatoes in anticipation of their redemption by cuddly visitors from another planet. Oh, it was well done, and it was enchanting. But the inverse proportion between the maturity of the technology and the maturity of the worldview was so great that finally Spielberg's work came to seem like a genial cynicism, which is Hollywood's cynicism of choice.

Now the critics, almost every one of them, are demanding that we celebrate this man's late passage into adulthood as a turning point in the culture. They say that he has made a "masterpiece." Does none of them see how hale and self-regarding *Schindler's List* is? Its renunciation of color is adduced as a sign of its stringency; but the black and white of this film is riper than most color. *(The Ghetto of Madame de ...*, I thought during its first hour.) The glints and the gleams are smart. The edges of the frame are faded. (The film is designed to look like a restored print of itself.) The shadows are exquisite. The darkness of this film about darkness, in sum, is gorgeous. And its gorgeousness gives it away. For it is a sign that Spielberg has not grasped his material, that the old relation between skill and understanding still obtains.

I refer not merely to the film's mistakes. (Its Jewish mistakes are the most annoying ones: when they enter the ghetto, for example, the Jews of Kraków greet each other in Israeli Hebrew.) I refer, rather, to the complete absence from this film of any humility before its subject. This is not material, after all, that is easily mastered. Traces of difficulty, therefore, are signs of seriousness. But there are no traces of difficulty in *Schindler's List.* Very robustly Spielberg just barrels through. His camera confidently follows naked Jewish women right through the door of the "showers" at Auschwitz, which turn out to be, in this case, showers. This sadistic trick was played on a cousin of mine, who walked into, and then out of, the gas chamber at Auschwitz. I have reflected a long time on her experience, and I must say that there is a point beyond which my mind has failed to follow her. The point is the door.

The power of realism in art is owed to the continuity between the world which it makes and the world in which, and for which, it is made. For this reason, the realistic depiction of radical evil must end, if it is to stay honest, where the continuity ends. The smooth segue of Spielberg's camera from life outside the door of the gas chamber to life inside the door of the gas chamber shows that no discontinuity has been observed. No limit has been met. No rupture has reared itself. The mind of the moviemaker has not hit a bump. But there is a more egregious example of Spielberg's inausterity, of his misplaced David Leanism. In 1944, as the Red Army approached, the commandant of the concentration camp at Plaszow was ordered to open the mass graves and exhume the bodies of the thousands of Jews who were murdered during the liquidation of the ghetto in Kraków in 1943 (the liquidation of the ghetto is the most unforgettable passage in Spielberg's film) and to burn the bodies in pits. Anybody who has seen photographs or films of these fiery, open-air charnels knows that the camera has probably never recorded a sight more obscene. But here was a director, and wardrobe and makeup, poring over the tone of charred flesh, the hollowing of rotted skulls, the disposition of mangled bones, to get it right. What on earth did they think they were doing? Do they really think that they got it right?

The scene is chilling, but the scene is a facsimile; and so the greater the verisimilitude, the lesser the verisimilitude. There are facsimiles that are chilling merely for having been made. *Schindler's List* proves again that, for Spielberg, there is a power in the world that is greater than good and greater than evil, and it is the movies. He is hardly alone in this cineaste's theodicy. Thus, a few weeks after the film opened, a good and learned friend of mine remarked that it opened not a moment too soon, with "Holocaust revisionism" loose in the land. I retorted that it is wrong and abject to believe that the Holocaust needs "proving," even if *The New Yorker* recently published an essay, bizarrely called, on the magazine's cover, "Bringing Auschwitz Back to Life," in which it acclaimed the discovery of a penitent Holocaust revisionist in France of the "one single proof" that an impenitent Holocaust revisionist in France had demanded. The discussion about "Holocaust revisionism" is not a "debate" between a "view" that it happened and a "view" that it did not happen; it is a war between a truth and a disease. More to the point, Spielberg's movie does not "prove" a thing, since it is *only a movie.* In the matter of the Holocaust, too, Hollywood must not be mistaken for history. It will be a good thing if *Schindler's List* brings down the number of Americans who wonder whether the Holocaust really happened, but it will not be a great thing.

I do not doubt that the glibness of Spielberg's film (though there is nothing glib about Ben Kingsley's or Ralph Fiennes's performance) is glibness in a good cause. But Americans are quickly moved. There is something a little exhilarating about all these tears. I'd prefer a bit more stunning into silence. Americans escape easily from reality and they are not easily returned to it; and *Schindler's List* dispatches them in both directions. It transports its audience to the basest moment in history and calls it a wrap.

"Schindler's List"

by Thomas Doherty
Cineaste magazine, Vol. 20, No. 3, 1994

Connoisseurs of epochal moments of bad taste may recall the grotesque convergence climaxing the NBC-TV miniseries *Holocaust* (1978). A group of condemned Jews—huddled, naked, terrified—are herded into the gas chambers at Auschwitz. Close-up and claustrophobic, a fog of poison gas hisses down onto the innocents. The screen goes black, and, for one silent second, television evoked a searing heartbeat of pity and terror. But just a beat: in a video flash, the gas chambers of Auschwitz metamorphose into the sparkling kitchen space of a suburban American home. "What's that smell?," asks Snoopy Sniffer, harridan spokeswoman for a popular household cleanser. "Could it be something from the oven?"

Whether one burst into a cackle of nihilistic glee or sat in appalled, stupefied silence, the jump cut dislocation from Zyklon B to Easy Off Oven Cleaner expresses the emotional chasm between the past horror and the present complacency, not to say the obscenity of subsuming the unholy and unimaginable within the conventions of commerce and entertainment. That Steven Spielberg, the balladeer of suburbia, the director with twenty-twenty eyesight into the motion picture soul of America, should bridge that gulf is impressive but not unexpected. World War II has ever been at the back of his grand ambitions: the overblown comedy *1941* (1979); *Empire of the Sun* (1987); J. G. Ballard's child's-eye view of survival in a Japanese concentration camp; and *Always* (1989), a remake of the wartime weepie *A Guy Named Joe* (1943). It has also been the common source of his box office and artistic failures, perhaps because, for all his obsession with World War II, Spielberg had never taken Nazism seriously—certainly not in the Indiana Jones series, where the SS are clumsy fools befuddled by a bullwhip and Adolf Hitler is just another celebrity signing autographs. *Schindler's List* forced the confrontation. In his close encounter with spectacular evil, Spielberg has finally demanded of himself, and his audience, something more than a spellbound stare.

Adapted faithfully by Steven Zaillian from Thomas Keneally's fact-based novel, *Schindler's List* tells the remarkable and uplifting tale of Oskar Schindler, a German-Catholic industrialist who courageously and uncharacteristically rescued some 1200 Polish Jews from extermination at Auschwitz. The film arrives with the visible and temporal signs of high seriousness on the Hollywood screen: black and white cinematography and three-hour-plus running time. Forsaking the visual pleasure and contemporary perspective of color stock, the monochromatic film grain resonates with the documentary memory of the Holocaust, the stark newsreels of liberated concentration camps taken by American, British, and Soviet forces, later supplemented by captured footage from the Nazis themselves, always inveterate record keepers. Likewise, the prolonged running time is commensurate with the gravitas of the material and the esthetics of immersion in an extended, complex, and emotionally wrenching narrative.

Arriving in war-raved Krakow with an eye for the main chance, Schindler (Liam Neeson) is a born fixer for whom world war means expanding investment opportunities. On the strength of his ebullient personality and epicurean tastes in food, drink, and women, he finagles control of a metalworks factory and procures the military contracts that will make his fortune. Knowing his limitations as a hands-on executive, he leaves operational control to accountant Itzak Stern (Ben Kingsley), a member of the *Judenrat* trying desperately to keep his kinsmen alive. While Schindler ladles out beluga caviar, Hennessy's cognac, and chunks of chocolate to the Nazi officer corps, Stern runs the factory and supervises its Jewish work force. The relationship between the two men—Stern measuring Schindler, gradually trusting him, or being forced to trust him—is the interpersonal core of the film.

Schindler's upward mobility parallels the descent of Krakow's Jews. At first, he waltzes obliviously above the terror around him, singing war songs with the Nazis, comfortably occupying the fashionable apartment of an evicted Jewish family, and rutting athletically with the secretarial help. Not until the brutal liquidation of the Krakow ghetto—more recreational slaughter than forced deportation—does the genocide in progress penetrate his skull. For this lethal tableau, Spielberg unleashes a full orchestration of cinematic horror. Vignettes of instant death comprise a lush, brutal montage of point-blank killing, mass executions, and, for variety, single file execution lineups. Floor by floor, room by room, on through the night, the Nazis flush out Jews who have hidden themselves under floorboards and beds, in cubbyholes, even inside pianos. When a misstep onto a keyboard hits a sour chord, the sound of machine-gun fire rattles offscreen in response. Later, in a kind of contrapuntal accompaniment to the sputter of gunfire, music from the same piano fills the halls of the building. A Nazi soldier is playing Bach—or is it Mozart? Moving back from the action, a long shot of the ghetto skyline erupts with exploding pockets of light and sound from the apartment windows, miniature moments of death glimpsed from afar like lightning bugs.

Watching on horseback from a distant hill, Schindler surveys the carnage and seems to come to a realization. His line of sight focuses on a girl in a red coat (one of the film's few privileged uses of color), center screen, wandering among the massacre, her lone figure individualizing the mass slaughter. Early on in the film, when a one-armed worker is led into Schindler's office to thank him for saving his life, the confirmed hustler is embarrassed and angry to be saddled with moral responsibility. Now, beholding the conflagration from afar, Schindler seems to assume the responsibility he has shunned.

Little is said of Schindler's spiritual transformation from narcissist to altruist, war profiteer to angel of mercy. Just as well—even in the Keneally novel, the man's motives remain obscure, his heroism understood more as a personal gesture than a political stance or moral imperative. Spielberg's strategy is to show the action rather than probe the impulse. Save for the informational titles that signpost time and place, the weave and texture of the film is a sudden, unbidden immersion in a nightmare world. Rousted from their homes, families knead diamonds in clumps of bread to swallow them, like communion, for retrieval later. To pass medical inspection, women prick their fingers and rub the blood into their cheeks for color. Like the most compelling Holocaust literature, the tone is flat, mute, and dispassionate; death is presented matter of factly, in all its clinical, biological apathy, without shocked reaction shots or musical cues (for once, John Williams's score is an unobtrusive guide, not a thundering imperative). Since the disclosure of desperate measures and concentration camp ethnography unfolds wordlessly, the spectator must invest the narrative with the moral sense unspoken from the screen. The payoff in sympathetic participation can be heartstopping, as when a sprightly singalong tune blares out from the camp speakers and the next shot frames a huge chorus of children, hundreds of them, filling the screen and walking forward, happy lemmings ignorant of the fate awaiting them.

As in *Paradise Lost*, it is the devil who is the most magnetic character in the epic. Playing the languorous, imperious, and casually vicious SS Commandant Amon Goeth, British actor Ralph Fiennes confirms again the fascination with fascism, the way evil outperforms good as a focus for narrative interest. In his villa overlooking the labor camp at Plaszow, the fleshy Nazi entertains guests, makes love, and for diversion walks out onto his porch and shoots prisoners with a scope rifle. ("You're such a child," chides his girlfriend.) Goeth's way with murder is both malicious and capricious, businesslike and offhand. A zealous female engineer who does her work for the Nazis too well is peremptorily shot, but her advice on construction is followed. In a sequence fraught with Hitchcockian tension, a metal worker who makes hinges performs his task while a stopwatch ticks, only to find his own fate hinging on the caprice of a misfiring handgun. A dutiful true believer, Goeth may muster a certain weariness and distaste about his job of work, but never any qualms. With the Krakow ghetto an inferno in backframe, he mutters, exhausted but satisfied, that he'll be happy when the night is over.

Irresistible as an embodiment of Nazism, Goeth provokes the film's strangest scene: a sexually charged encounter between the Nazi officer and his nubile, Jewish houseservant, Helena (Embeth Davidtz). In his wine cellar, she stands forescreen, moist chemise clinging to her breasts. Goeth circles her and delivers a seductive, sinister monologue, threat and courtship, the pure Aryan contemplating a liaison with this "rat-faced" *untermensch*, who is, of course, a beautiful, tempting woman. Is he becoming human? Will his rape of this girl humanize him? If much of *Schindler's List* evokes Claude Lanzmann's *Shoah*, the wine cellar scene plays like an outtake from Liliana Cavani's *The Night Porter*.

The dramatic onslaught is so wrenching and unrelenting that the viewer may well take refuge in cinematic associations and esthetic appreciations of another sort. One notes that the meticulous recreations of the wartime ambiance extend to the smallest details, from typeface to ethnic type; that the location shooting paid off in the evocative landscape and the condensed breath of the performers in the icy air; that, yes, the casting director was smart enough to find emaciated extras of all ages. Naturally, too, the cinematic chops of one of the medium's premiere practitioners is everywhere at work. The editing of the opening sequence, which follows Schindler as he 'suits up' for a night on the town, smoothly sculpts the personality of its bon vivant hero before hammering in the final touch: a tight close-up of his swastika pin. The film's most harrowing scene is also a textbook instance of reversed expectation and parallel editing. Told to strip and herded through blackened corridors, an hysterical group of Jewish women seem set for extermination, but miraculously, these chambers really are showers and the women breathe in the water, delivered.

Other motion picture visions of the Holocaust waft through *Schindler's List*. Besides the newsreel footage of World War II, Alain Resnais's *Night and Fog* (1955) is evoked in the endless piles of luggage and human effects, Agnieszka Holland's *Europa, Europa* (1991) in the muscle-tightening tension of desperate improvisation, and (above all) Lanzmann's *Shoah* (1985), whose locomotive and snow imagery permeates the film. In dreamy slo-mo, the trademark gesture from *Shoah*—the forefinger pulled laterally across the throat as a portent of things to come (sadistic gloating said the Jews, comradely warning said the Poles)—is glimpsed from a boxcar as a cargo of victims approaches the gates of Auschwitz.

Yet the most persistent film references here derive from Spielberg's own list. Talk about the personal overriding the political: the bulk of the critical response to the first major American motion picture depicting the Holocaust has focused less on the truth of the rendering than on the artistic growth of the renderer. At long last Hollywood's aging *wunderkind* had put away the things of the child, connected with his ethnic roots, drew upon the *shtetl* not the suburbs, and came to manhood, today, with *Schindler's List*, a high serious melodrama about the most serious of topics. Set in relief against *Jurassic Park*, the director's other, presumably more characteristic public offering of 1993, the accolades couldn't hide an underlying condescension. From David Lean or Roman Polanski, an achievement like *Schindler's List* might have been expected, but from Spielberg?

Of course, this gem of rare price in an auteur's canon serves as more than the ultimate leverage on the Academy of Motion Picture Arts and Sciences. No less than the opening of the Holocaust Museum on the Washington Mall, a site heretofore preserved for memorials to the American past, *Schindler's List* is a capstone event in a process that has been called "the Americanization of the Holocaust." Edward Lutvak recently observed how, with the passage of time, the Holocaust has come to seem more and more the central event of World War II. More and more, too, Hollywood has come to seem the prism through which all history, genocidal or otherwise, is witnessed and felt. The medium that in 1945 indelibly confirmed the rumors of war now passes the information on to a new generation—with filmmakers like Spielberg the custodians of an awful legacy.

No wonder then that Spielberg's act of historical reclamation in an age in which Holocaust denial advertises itself in the pages of college newspapers has shielded the director from the usual critical qualifications. *Schindler's List* is overlong, lachrymose, and preachy in its final act; Neeson is a weak centerpiece, soft focus matinee idol photography notwithstanding; the secondary characters are a faceless chorus; and, though this is a story of endurance and survival, a Holocaust movie in which none of the sympathetic characters dies seems to miss the point of its subject (even in a boxcar on the way to Auschwitz, Ben Kingsley's character is blessed by providential Hollywood intervention, never truly at risk).

But whether Spielberg is finally getting his due or just getting undue slack, the power of the film on moviegoers is profound and undeniable: no screening in my experience has elicited so much authentic grief in the audience, not the 'good cry' of a three hankie weepie, the on-cue sniffling during a *Terms of Endearment* or *The Joy Luck Club*, but open weeping and heartbroken sobbing. *Schindler's List* is powerful but not that powerful: it's an occasion to mourn, and, no blasphemy meant, a kind of wailing wall, especially for American Jews, many of whom will bring to the soundtrack cues and visual symbols—a rabbi singing kaddish, Itzhak Perlman's mournful violin, votive candles extinguishing in a wisp of smoke—a constellation of painful memories of private loss.

Schindler's List closes with a frame-breaking coda in which the survivors of 1945 transmute cinematically into their present-day selves and descendants. In the real present now, in color, in Israel, a procession of Schindler's Jews and Spielberg's actors march by to lay a pebble on the grave of Oskar Schindler. The last mourner, standing alone at the foot of the grave in a long shot, is Liam Neeson, head bowed in reverence. One wonders why it is not the director himself at the graveside—a gesture rejected as too Hitchcockian and self-aggrandizing?—until one realizes that Spielberg's homage this time is to history, not film.

Liam Neeson Puts the Kettle On

······························

Breathes there a lass who'd say no to a wee cuppa tea with Liam Neeson? We doubt it, regardless of whether Schindler's List *turns this Irish actor into an American movie star.*

by Stephanie Mansfield
Vanity Fair magazine, December, 1993

There are two things Liam Neeson won't show me.

The first is his loft in Manhattan's SoHo. "No, no, those Filipino girls are still tied up and stuff," he says in his creamy Northern Irish brogue. As for the second, "No, no, you're *not* gonna see it," he bellows, comically covering his groin with fingers fat as breakfast bangers. Mimicking a breathless gossip reporter, he leans forward and says, "And then, Liam's partin' shot was he produced his *penis* on the table and all the stories were true!"

He laughs, crimson rising on his temples. Flushed from three glasses of Pinot Bianco and armed with the sort of sexual allure a man could be incarcerated for, he's been flirting hard with the doe-eyed waitress on the steamy patio of a Chelsea restaurant and joking about his reputation as a Big Man in Hollywood.

"I remember seeing an interview with Dana Delany, and this guy was askin' about her love life, and she said if she were in a room with James Woods and Willem Dafoe and Liam Neeson, there wouldn't be room for anathin' else. I *blewshed*. What's this about? I was sorely tempted to phone up an ex-girlfriend and say 'Have you said anathin' about our sex life?' I just *blewshed*. So if I'm ever in a room with James Woods and Willem Dafoe, we'll be kind of going ...." Here he surreptitiously appraises an imaginary figure at crotch level. Raising his brows, he sticks another cigarette into his mouth. "Checkin' each other out."

At 41, the towering Neeson (his first name is pronounced "LEE-um") is a well-respected, highly disciplined stage-trained actor with a long string of film credits, including *The Mission, Suspect, The Good Mother, Darkman, Husbands and Wives* and *Ethan Frome*. His portrayal of the dapper, hard-drinking, womanizing Oskar Schindler in Steven Spielberg's *Schindler's List* could land him on Hollywood's own shortlist of ruggedly handsome, universally appealing leading men, although the relatively low budget ($23 million), three-hour black-and-white piece is certainly a departure for both director and actor. Neeson is sanguine about the film, despite its less-than-commercial prospects. "I don't think it's gonna be a Hollywood career enhancer," he says. "The main reason being that I'm not playing an American hero. It's not Wyatt Earp."

That he is able to downplay the impact of *Schindler*—not to mention laugh about his own image as a walking Gaelic symbol cutting a swath through Dublin's pubs, London's Groucho Club and Hollywood's watering holes and soundstages—is testament to his guileless, almost malleable personality. Even onscreen, the artless landscape of his persona is evident. "He is incapable of saying a line that doesn't sound natural," says Woody Allen, who directed him in *Husbands and Wives*.

Neeson addresses all women as "darlin'," and at six-four projects a soulful innocence not uncommon in Gulliver-like creatures. Women describe him as "sensitive" and "gentle." A colleague calls Neeson a "great weeping willow of a man."

"But he's not *drippy*," says British actress Helen Mirren, who lived with Neeson in London for four years in the mid-Eighties. "He's more of an oak to me." And although Neeson "is a woman's man," says Mirren, "he doesn't *need* women. They need him, and he's very graceful with that fact. Women obviously fall for him left, right and center."

Indeed, women have played crucial roles in Neeson's journey from the grim Northern Ireland mill town of his working-class childhood—the only boy among four children—to a palm-treed and pool-equipped bungalow in the Hollywood Hills. Mirren, seven years his senior, first took him under her wing after they appeared in John Boorman's *Excalibur*, and it was Mirren who cajoled Neeson into leaving Dublin and moving into her flat in London.

Now, in London and in Hollywood, two of his agents are women, as is his publicist. His *Good Mother* costar Diane Keaton was responsible for Neeson's being cast in *Husbands and Wives,* and it was actress Natasha Richardson, daughter of Vanessa Redgrave, who last year suggested Neeson for the Broadway production of Eugene O'Neill's *Anna Christie.* It was a smash hit, with Neeson's lusty, bare-chested portrayal of merchant seaman Mat Burke garnering rave reviews and a Tony nomination. Richardson, 30, left her husband, British producer Robert Fox (brother of actors Edward and James), for her costar, who had previously had gone a-roving with such comely wenches as Julia Roberts, Sinéad O'Connor, Barbra Streisand, Brooke Shields and Jennifer Grey.

"He has a raw and open sexuality," Richardson burbled to the press. Neeson declines to discuss his affair with Richardson, other than to say "I can tell you I'm very much in love."

The actor says he finds his Celtic-gigolo image tiresome. "He's always saying to me, 'Tom, I'm tired of people writin' about my love life,'" says Neeson's friend dialect coach Tom Todoroff. "But I keep saying to him, 'Well, if you have a *different* love life and stop having these intense three-month affairs with famous actresses, they wouldn't write about it.' There's no question that Liam is in the top three percentile of charming men on earth. Women respond to it. He doesn't know he's doing it. He just really loves women. All his lights go on when he's around them."

Indeed, the boy was born without a dimmer. The previous day, at a SoHo restaurant, he had high-beamed a bosomy waitress with a waterfall of strawberry curls with the following line: "Darlin', you must be part Irish. Are you? No, well, you certainly look it." Where other men might have retreated, Neeson kept going. And why not? He'd found the most desirable woman on earth, carrying breadsticks to his table. He went on to ask about herself, her bloodlines, her great-great-grandmother. And whether or not he loved the pilgrim soul in her, he clearly appreciated her long legs.

Sitting courtside, it was like watching Jordan swish a three-pointer. At the buzzer. In overtime.

"Women have always gone potty over him," says British actor Richard Graham, another friend. "You know," says Todoroff, "he has *the* world's greatest line: *'Darlin', would you fancy comin' up for a wee cuppa tea?"* He laughs hard, recalling the numerous times Neeson has succeeded in getting the kettle on. "It sounds so cozy. And then, once inside, the door is locked." Todoroff lets out a salacious growl, imitating the actor's brogue. "'You're mine now.'"

Todoroff is constantly cautioning his friend to slow down. "He jumps into [relationships] so impetuously. It makes him nuts. At first, there's a mutual intoxication. He calls me and says 'Oh, this is it. We're talkin' about havin' kids.'" Weeks later, Todoroff says, the affair is over.

Neeson himself is candid about his pursuit of passion. "Well, the Irish are given to it," he says, looking moody all of a sudden. "You always kind of wise up. I always woke up in the morning and thought, This is wrong. The sweet sickness had passed. You know what I mean?" He does seem to possess what his countryman W.B. Yeats referred to as "a fanatic heart." Todoroff puts it less lyrically: "He's basically a really mercurial 18-year-old."

And if women tend to respond to him better than men do, the feeling is mutual. "Liam's not a man's man," says Graham. "He's very private and he's very sensitive. He just gets on better with the company of women."

"I've always loved women," admits Neeson. "I have three sisters, and they always had their girlfriends at home. Guys were boring after being in a room full of women.

"Men," he says, "are generally assholes. Women have grown in leaps and bounds over the past thirty years, and long may it continue. Men have been so shit-scared of the women's movement that they have no voice anymore. Their heroes are still the Clint Eastwood types. That's the image that makes a man a man." He draws hard on another Marlboro Light. "Take American football. 'The front line's here.' 'The battle line's here.' It's all about knocking down your fuckin' opponent. Men are really scared and confused. The only way they know how to be is to be an asshole. Anything emotional they're confronted with, it's like 'Fuck this. I'm not listening to this. I'm out the door.' They can't confront it. It's a sign of weakness.

"I was reading an article the other day, and it said in past generations men were denied. 'Don't cry. It's not manly.' The one organ they were allowed to feel was the cock!"

He grins, eyes twinkling. "Well, it *is* a weird thing to look down and go 'Jesus, what is this thing?' It is strange, you know, this tackle hanging there. I'm one of those that got off on confession. I remember saying to a priest once that I had committed the sin of Onan, which is masturbation. Oh, my God, I'll never forget it. This priest just tore strips off me. He said, 'You'll have no confidence by the age of 21. And no willpower.' I really just shriveled up and thought, Fuck, I've committed a big one now. I remember leaving the confessional, and people were gathering in the pews for Mass that evening. I felt like it was six miles to walk down that aisle past these biddies. It was terrifying. So I thought, I'm not touchin' my dick ever again. That's it."

He laughs loudly, the lines in his broad forehead crinkling. His nose is wide and crooked, having been broken in the ring during his youth back in Ballymena, a gritty Protestant stronghold near Belfast. Neeson's congeniality belies a tightly coiled inner self. "There's a side to him that's a real loner," says Mirren. "There's a part of Liam that one will never penetrate."

The fierce determination that motivated him to move from London to Los Angeles took its toll; he landed in the hospital six years ago with diverticulitis and had to have 40 percent of his colon removed. It was, he says, from holding all the pain, rejection and fear inside. The difficulty of trying to find the right projects, the expectations dashed, the opportunities lost, the yearning for "a wee bit of clout" and the Hollywood sweepstakes that pit him against younger, equally ambitious stars have resulted in a certain jadedness. "I have a love-hate relationship with this business. I swing from one extreme to the other, from absolutely loving it to 'Get me *out* of this fucking thing. This is stupid. I don't understand why I want to be an actor.' I'm not saying this to make myself sound complex. It's a dilemma. It's also a business, and you're a product."

He asks his agency, CAA, to send him everything that's out there, every script making the rounds. "Eighty percent of it is dross. Absolute regurgitated bullshit."

And as for the social scene, "it's so fascist. You order a glass of wine at lunch and people go ...." He affects a disapproving stare. "And the conversations are either about what they ate that morning or how far they ran. 'Four miles this morning. Yesterday I could only manage three.' 'Oh, really? What was wrong?' 'I think it was that mashed yeast I ate at breakfast.' Fuck me! Get a life, will ya? And the women out there! They all look the same. And they say 'I'm 26. I'm too old.' It's terrifying. It's so easy to become cynical out there.

"People always ask me 'Wasn't it great to work with Clint Eastwood?'

[Neeson had a small role in *The Dead Pool*.] I was kind of goin' 'Yeah, it was great.' Afterward, I thought, It wasn't great. It was like clockin' in to a factory. He was in his dubbing studio [finishing *Bird*] in his head. He's a lovely man, but it was like 'Come on, say the lines. Hit the marks.' We probably said five words to each other."

And although Richard Graham says the "always very ambitious" Neeson "enjoys the success but can see what's bullshit," the actors has, in fact, learned to play the game.

He laughs ruefully. "If I'm asked by some director or producer to meet with them, sometimes I like to ask 'Why do you think I'm right for this?' And they say 'Well, you've got this quality; you're *vulnerable*.' And they say 'What did you think of the script?'" He pauses for effect. "I say 'I liked it because there's this *vulnerable* quality to this guy.' You know, the bills have to be paid. Everybody does it."

But with the role of Oskar Schindler, it was different.

Neeson did a test for Spielberg in September 1992, then heard nothing. "I knew he was seeing other people, and he was quite right to." The director was apparently concerned that Neeson didn't have the bulk to carry off the role. Schindler, a German Catholic businessman who saved 1,300 Jews from death camps by employing them in his suburban-Kraków enamelware factory, was a charismatic, slightly cynical bear of a man and an unlikely hero: a burly bon vivant and member of the Nazi Party with a weakness for women. An Olympic-class boozer who profited from the war, he nevertheless managed to rescue his "list" of workers, some of whom later supported him financially when he fell on hard times. Schindler, who died in 1974, was honored by the Israeli government at Yad Vashem, the Holocaust memorial in Jerusalem.

The film, based on Thomas Keneally's best-seller, took more than a decade to bring to the screen, partly because of problems with the script. Screenwriter Kurt Luedtke (*Absence of Malice, Out of Africa*) spent four years on the project and turned in only thirty pages. Eventually, Steven Zaillian (*Awakenings, Searching for Bobby Fischer*) was brought in, and he completed a working script. It was Spielberg's passion for the story that kept the project alive.

Neeson kept hearing that Spielberg was undecided, so he went off to New York and did *Anna Christie*. Suddenly, the actor was red-hot. His dingy dressing room spilled over nightly with Champagne-sipping admirers, including Francis Ford Coppola, Gregory Peck and Paul Newman. The night Spielberg and his wife, Kate Capshaw, saw the play, they brought Capshaw's mother backstage. Mrs. Capshaw was so moved by the performance that she was in tears. Neeson put his strong arms around her and gave her a bear hug. Walking out, Capshaw told her husband, "That's exactly what Schindler would have done."

Neeson got the part within a couple of weeks, not only because of his sheer physicality but also, Spielberg has said, because Neeson shares with Herr Schindler a certain "naive optimism," as well as "a wonderful cigarettes-and-cognac voice." Observers have noted other similarities between the two. But even broaching the subject is an insult to the actor's considerable talent. Neeson laughs softly. "I think if Steven had said, 'Well, I'm giving you this part because I think you're a womanizer and you're a big drinker, I would have said, 'You can go fuck yourself. I'm going back to do a play.'"

The Neesons of Ballymena, Barney and Kitty, were as opposite as husband and wife could be. He was quiet and self-effacing, while she—warm, vibrant, with a love of music, people and good "crack" (as the Irish call colorful yarns)—was filled with life and fire. He worked as a custodian in a Catholic girls' school; she was the school cook. Together, they had four children in four years: Elizabeth, Bernadette, William John and Rosaleen. The boy was called Liam for short, after a revered local priest. The family lived in a Housing Trust project. "It was a tiny house," recalls Helen Mirren, who went for a visit years later. "It was really minute. You can't believe they could all squeeze into it."

"My father had a gentle, dreamy disposition," says Bernadette, now a teacher in Worthing, England, outside of Brighton. Barney Neeson's father had owned a pub "and he saw the indignities of drink. My mother, too. So we had a temperate household." Neeson says his father's only indulgence was a weekly poker game with the parish priests. "I'd hear him come back at four in the mornin', having lost five pounds. My mom would get upset over that." (Barney Neeson died several years ago of a heart attack.)

Kitty was very protective of her quiet, slight son. "My mother worried that he studied too much," recalls Bernadette. "But I envied him his discipline. He was an exemplary student and the sort of boy who was not a bully. I used to fight some of his battles for him."

To help Liam gain self-confidence, Barney Neeson suggested his son try boxing at the local Boys Club. "The boy needs to be able to defend himself," he told his wife. Liam was good at it, and eventually became Irish youth heavyweight champion before realizing he didn't have the killer instinct necessary to go pro.

His early self-discipline seemed to abandon him once he got to Queens College in Belfast, where he dropped out after a depressing year. He then enrolled in a teachers' training college in Newcastle upon Tyne, where, he says, he plagiarized a paper and was gently persuaded to leave. But by then, he had discovered amateur dramatics. In 1975, on a dare, he called up the Lyric Players Theatre in Belfast and won a part over the telephone based on his description of his physique. It was a happy time for the young man, who slept on friends' floors, drove a forklift for a brewery in the afternoon and went to rehearsals at night. Two years later, he moved to Dublin and joined the troupe at the Abbey Theatre, where he was eventually spotted by director John Boorman, who cast him in *Excalibur*. Mirren, a star of the 1981 film, was instantly enchanted by Neeson's "Irishness." "It's an immense sense of discipline," she says, "very family-oriented; there's a gentleness and civility, as well as graciousness."

Friends of the actress's were not surprised by the affair. "At first, it was 'Who's Helen's new boy toy?'" recalls one London friend. "Liam was a lovely, gentle giant whom no one took seriously."

"Helen liked him and believed in him immediately," says Maggie Parker, Mirren's London agent. "She took him around, and people got to meet him. She wanted to promote him."

Neeson credits Mirren with introducing him to a sophisticated new world: She knew London and Paris and secured him entré into Britain's theatrical inner circles. His career flourished; he managed to get roles in several BBC television productions and was tapped for supporting roles in *The Bounty*, with Mel Gibson, and *The Mission*, with Robert De Niro and Jeremy Irons.

Ultimately, due to their separate work schedules, the relationship came to an end. "Liam was living in my house," says the actress. "All of our friends were my friends. It was time for him to spread his wings. It was painful, but we both recognized it was time for him to move on, to gain independence."

Neeson began making plans to leave for America. Always a risktaker, he packed his bags in January in 1987 and flew to L.A. with a few names in his pocket and six weeks' worth of rent. He did seven films in two years, including the scene-stealing turn as a deaf-mute in *Suspect* and the aging rock star in the low-budget Justine Bateman vehicle *Satisfaction,* which costarred the then-unknown Julia Roberts. Neeson claims to have never seen the film.

"It wasn't a pleasant experience," recalls director Joan Freeman, "and there were people who were not happy with him. It was stifling, creatively. And he doesn't like to be stifled. He probably felt very underappreciated. But there was one good thing: He met Julia through it."

Roberts and Neeson lived together a short while. She subsequently went off to make *Steel Magnolias* and fell in love with costar Dylan McDermott. Neeson is said to have been heartbroken. "He got very sick over that," recalls Todoroff. "He was hurting big time."

Film projects such as *Darkman, Shining Through* and *Leap of Faith* were also a disappointment. So last spring, hanging fire on Spielberg's decision, the actor decided to return to the stage. "Then they come chasin' you, you know? It's like Zen philosophy. If you go grabbin' after somethin', it will always be one step ahead of you. Once you step back, it will come to you."

Neeson is sitting on the patio of a downtown restaurant. When we parted the day before, he left looking agonized. "I feel you wantin' to know more about relationships and stuff," he said. "I hate that. I really do. It's all fuckin' water under the bridge."

Now he stares at his hands, twisting a gold signet ring that once belonged to his father, and sighs. "I like ...." He is searching for the right word. "Vagueness." He kicks back, laughing hard. "Yes, that's it. *Vaaaague.*"

A young hostess with waist-length auburn hair and Cleopatra eyes hovers behind his chair. He has done the "darlin'" routine with her, and she is captivated. After she leaves, the actor leans over his wineglass and frowns. "I get maudlin from time to time."

If, as Helen Mirren says, Neeson needs "a strong hand," he may have found it in Natasha Richardson. Her marriage to Robert Fox was the union of two theatrical dynasties. But when she fell for Neeson, during rehearsals for *Anna Christie,* she fell hard. The two vacationed in Thailand two months ago and are planning more projects together.

London was somewhat shocked by the affair. "A lot of people thought she behaved very badly," says a journalist friend, who describes Richardson as "a charismatic girl and a cool customer. She's got verve and ambition, and she's very self-possessed."

Other friends believe the pairing makes perfect sense. "If there's anyone on earth who's got the right stuff, who's got what it takes for Liam, Natasha's one of those few people," says Mirren, who has known the actress for years.

Whether the sweet sickness will pass, as it is wont to do, is debatable. But the irresistible Irishman is momentarily caught by the bonny hostess, who follows him out the door to the sidewalk.

"If I weren't in love," he confides under his breath, "I'd be back here in twenty minutes."

Fiennes Sits on the Brink of Major Stardom

....

by Lisa Anderson
The Chicago Tribune, Feb. 10, 1994

It's his eyes that you remember. A peculiarly piercing shade of blue-gray, arctic-clear, set in a gauntly handsome face, they could be the eyes of a poet or a mass murderer.

But sitting across from him, over a frothy cup of cappuccino at a little hearthside table in his suite at the Lowell Hotel, one has little doubt that these are eyes soon to blaze from the covers of millions of glossy magazines yet to be printed.

Few people know his name, and if they do, they probably don't know how to say it, but Ralph Fiennes (pronounced Rafe Fines) is clearly teetering on the slippery brink of major movie stardom.

Everyone seems to think so. Vanity Fair has dubbed him "The biggest movie star you've never heard of." London's Telegraph magazine, fairly bursting with unabashed chauvinism, has confidently marked him as the "Next Big Thing." More than once, he has been compared to the young Laurence Olivier.

Pleased with success

Fiennes, a 31-year-old whose off-camera shyness is as powerful as his on-camera presence, finds this all pleasing, if rather discomfiting.

"What should I say?" he murmurs with an embarrassed shrug as he takes an offered compliment on his performance in Steven Spielberg's monumental Holocaust effort, *Schindler's List.*

More important, however, critics are saying the right sort of things. As the psychotic, chillingly boyish S.S. officer Amon Goeth, the bon vivant barbarian who runs Poland's Plaszow concentration camp in *Schindler's List,* Fiennes already has picked up a slew of kudos, handily snagging the best-supporting actor awards from the New York Film Critics, the National Society of Film Critics and the Boston Film Critics. He's just been nominated for the best supporting actor Oscar for his role, so an Academy Award may well be in his immediate future.

Not bad for a country-born lad from rural Suffolk, England, who has been seen in only two other films: *Wuthering Heights* (1991) and *The Baby of Macon* (1992).

An intense man not given to easy smiles and soberly dressed in a well-cut olive green suit and starched white shirt, Fiennes gives a Hamlet-like sigh, leans forward on the table and rakes long fingers through his shock of brown hair. He rubs his face and suddenly looks up and acknowledges his good fortune with a shy grin.

'The bad angel'

In that moment, there is a glimpse of one side of Nazi commandant Goeth, a hedonist and sadist who delighted in randomly shooting passing prisoners from the balcony of his concentration camp quarters with the unthinking verve of a little boy pulling the wings off a butterfly.

That is what Fiennes and Spielberg wanted to depict, he says. "We both agreed that it was very important to avoid the cliché, the typical Nazi. He had to have depth, he had to be human, he had to have his vulnerable side to him."

As such, the middle-class, Austrian Catholic Goeth plays a kind of dark doppelganger to Oskar Schindler, a man from a similar background, who starts out as a war profiteer and ends up as the savior of his Jewish workers. Fiennes says Spielberg called them "the good angel and the bad angel."

The image of childish cruelty is particularly apt, Fiennes says. "Surely all these perpetrators of violence were extending quite a natural childhood delight in squashing the insect against the windowpane. It's that sort of thing," he says.

"In someone who's off-center and unhappy as Amon Goeth, that kind of kick, that kind of buzz, that sense of power gives him a sense of self-worth, and he knows who he is when he's being violent. It's just an extension of that childhood urge. He hasn't absorbed any moral sensibilities, really."

Newsweek, which called Fiennes' "the film's most compelling performance," said his Goeth depicts "evil in all its banality, all its primal ferocity." But, says Fiennes, Goeth was not evil incarnate. "No, you can't say that. He's just this guy who's gone wrong," he says, which he finds somehow even more frightening.

Weighty preparations

Scarier still, Fiennes says, was the preparation for the role, which included adding 25 pounds to his normally lanky 5-foot-11-inch, 150-pound frame.

"It was scary and not very pleasant. It's not good for you to do that, to force your body into a shape it's not naturally meant to be," says Fiennes.

"In actual fact, Goeth was very tall, and he was vast. He didn't just have a big belly, he had a big everything. In the photographs, he got very obese at the time he was at his most brutal. He lost it all and got diabetes after the war. He was hung in 1946," says Fiennes, who researched his character through documentaries on the period, interviews with camp survivors and books about the Holocaust, including Thomas Keneally's 1982 book upon which the film is based.

Fiennes, in effect, became a different person for this role. "It helped a lot. Not just the weight, but experiencing the sort of psychological effect of being overweight, being unfit. And I allowed myself to smoke and drink. I don't usually smoke. Just sort of not treating yourself very well, it's sort of an ambivalent feeling of self-disgust but at the same time a sort of pleasure in it. I found that useful for the role."

Fiennes got the role after Spielberg saw him as Heathcliff in *Wuthering Heights,* his film debut, and as T.E. Lawrence in a 1992 TV program, *A Dangerous Man: Lawrence after Arabia.* It was all rather lucky because Fiennes had not made his TV debut, with a bit part in the British miniseries *Prime Suspect,* until 1991.

In fact, for years Fiennes planned to be a painter. The oldest of six children born in seven years, Fiennes is the son of a Suffolk farmer-turned-landscape photographer, Mark Fiennes, and his novelist wife, Jini, who wrote successfully under the name Jennifer Lash.

Moving with his family to Ireland and then to Wiltshire in England, Fiennes led a peripatetic but cultured life.

"My mother had always encouraged an interest in literature and drama," he says. "The whole family would listen to Shakespeare-type records or go to see Laurence Olivier in *Henry V.* All of us, not just me, but all of the family had an awareness of drama and theater. And I suppose I had always latently thought I'd like to act."

It was in 1981, during his year as a student at the Chelsea School of Art, that he decided to become an actor.

After art school he joined an amateur youth company, "just so I'd be getting up there and doing it," he says. "And that gave me the confidence to audition at the main drama schools in London." That in turn won him a place at the Royal Academy of Dramatic Art, which he joined in January 1983.

Barely five years later, after a round of regional theater, he joined the prestigious Royal Shakespeare Company, where he garnered critical acclaim for his roles as Troilus in *Troilus and Cressida,* Edmund in *King Lear* and Berowne in *Love's Labour's Lost.*

Reticent about his personal life, Fiennes will say only that he is married, to actress Alex Kingston four months ago, and has no children.

When moviegoers next see Fiennes on the screen, it will be in Robert Redford's upcoming film *Quiz Show,* about the 1950s TV quiz-show cheating scandals. In it, Fiennes plays popular TV panelist Charles van Doren.

Fiennes, who has played an American once before, in the Royal Shakespeare Company's 1989 production of *The Man Who Came to Dinner,* describes his colonial accent as a sort of "educated, Waspy kind of American."

Say something in American, he is urged.

"No," he says politely, narrowing his pale eyes in a sidelong, Goeth-like glance that brooks no contest.

Actors Look Back at
Moments with Steven Spielberg

by Karen Thomas, Gannett News Service
The Houston Post, March 22, 1994

The man to be at the Academy Awards this year was Steven Spielberg, whose command of movie-making has hit a popular and critical high with the box office spectacular *Jurassic Park* and the Holocaust epic *Schindler's List*.

His past visions have earned 59 nominations and 14 wins, but until this year the only Academy Award Spielberg himself had taken home is a special career-achievement award in 1986.

Spielberg, 46, has touched many in Hollywood during his career. Some of them share their movie-set anecdotes:

Dennis Weaver: Spielberg was a 23-year-old unknown when he directed 1971's *Duel*, a TV movie pitting Weaver against a malevolent 18-wheeler. "I had never worked with more than two cameras on a film and we went out to shoot the final scene where the truck goes over the cliff—and Steven had five cameras out there to shoot that one scene. I thought, 'Boy, this young fellow really has moxie.'"

Richard Dreyfuss: Spielberg was 27 when he directed *Jaws* in 1975 and sent the world scurrying back to its beach blanket.

"We found ourselves at the artificial lake in back of Universal, having to stay awake for a number of hours while the lights were set up for water. And Steven and I just sat around telling stories to one another. And he began to tell me the story of the film *Jaws* that he might have made," recalls Dreyfuss.

"In the course of this evening, Steven told me how he could have shot *Jaws* and (Spielberg) could have come out the star. And he specifically told me scene by scene, placing cameras here, shooting long lenses here ... and I'm not versed in that craft, but I got the picture."

John Lithgow: While directing early 1980s blockbusters like *E. T.* and *Raiders of the Lost Ark*, Spielberg was also producing films, including *Twilight Zone—The Movie* in 1983 and *Harry and the Hendersons* in 1987.

"If he dropped by the set, nobody would know; it was unannounced (but) you would notice something in the air—everybody was a little bit energized," says Lithgow. "Then you'd see him, crouching in the corner somewhere with a baseball cap on. He was like that quote from Shakespeare: 'A little touch of Harry in the night.' .... That always happens with executives, but with Steven, he was also always one of the gang."

Oprah Winfrey: With a handful of blockbusters under his belt, Spielberg worked with movie newcomers in 1985 for *The Color Purple*.

"Every day I worked with Steven Spielberg I was terrified because I was trying to figure out how to act while I was acting," says Winfrey.

Among her film offenses: looking right at the camera. Spielberg had to keep telling her, "'Don't look at the camera, let the camera find you.' I thought he was going to fire me that day. But he didn't."

John Goodman: Goodman recalls a complicated scene from Spielberg's first romantic comedy, 1989's *Always*, in which "the set looked like a hive with very expensive toys."

"Steven and I were sitting on a film truck waiting for them to set up, and as we sat there, there was a lull. And he just looked at me and said, 'Jeez, I just love making movies.' It's just frozen in my mind. I'll never forget it."

Robin Williams: To play Spielberg's forever-young Peter Pan in 1991's *Hook*, the abundantly hairy Williams was concerned, "I said, "You don't want me, I'm furry.' And he said, 'That can be arranged. You'll shave. We'll get Nair.'"

Laura Dern: "There's nothing like Steven Spielberg making the sounds of dinosaurs," says his *Jurassic Park* star. Once Spielberg shouted "action," Dern says he roared into a megaphone, mimicking dinosaur sounds. "At times it brought horror and at times laughter," she says.

Spielberg takes his movie-making seriously; he's "professional and adult," says Dern, "yet he would know more than any 6-year-old why it was fun and amazing."

Seriously Spielberg

....

*With "Schindler's List," Steven Spielberg shattered his own image—
an image he admits he helped create—as a P.T. Barnum of
American movies. How could he have made "Jurassic Park" and
"Schindler's List" in the same year? And where will he go from here?
The industry and Spielberg himself are waiting to find out.*

By Stephen Schiff
The New Yorker, March 21, 1994

At the Consumer Electronics Show in Las Vegas a couple of months
ago, Steven Spielberg looked like someone who hadn't grown into his
brother's clothes. His jeans were baggy, and so was his salmon-colored
sweatshirt; he wore a baseball cap that said "Brown University" on it (because his seventeen-year-old stepdaughter, Jessica, had just been admitted
there), and the gray streaks in his beard might have struck one as improbable. He was being squired about by Lew Wasserman, the dapper chairman of MCA, and Sidney Sheinberg, the company's president. And around
them blinked several lesser lights, mostly officials of Panasonic, which, like
MCA, is owned by the giant Japanese conglomerate Matsushita. The cav-
erns of the Las Vegas Convention Center were filled with squawking video
games, stereos, wide-screen televisions, and scary-looking motion simula-
tors, and Spielberg strode among them all with his hands clasped behind his
back, like General Patton. For him, this was conquered territory: everywhere one looked, there were variations on themes from his movies "Juras-

sic Park," "Raiders of the Lost Ark," "E.T.," "Close Encounters of the Third Kind," even "Jaws." As he strolled, techies goggled at him, snapped pictures, aimed camcorders, and thrust little control panels and joysticks into his hands: "Play this one, Steven!" "Steven, you'll love this. It'd make a great movie!" Wasserman and Sheinberg, two of the most powerful men in Hollywood, hung behind like courtiers, attending to his needs and directing his gaze to whatever shiny gewgaw might amuse him, and every so often Spielberg would throw out a question about something juicy like ROM capacity or interactions per minute, and new minions would appear at his side with answers. As he played with a video game that traced the berserk journey of a runaway truck on a sere and distant planet, I overheard a pimply young techie murmur, "Look, it's God." His companion craned his neck, caught sight of Spielberg. "Hey, you're right," he said. "God."

There are limits to the dominion of a techie god. But when you turn on the television or go to the movies, when you play a video game or enter an amusement park or a shopping mall, there it all is: the Spielberg vision, imitated, replicated, and recycled—the upturned faces awaiting miracles, the otherworldly white backlighting, the here-comes-the-shark music, the mischievous but golden-hearted suburban children, the toys that fidget and romp by themselves, the Indiana Jones jungles and deserts and hats. That Spielberg is the most commercially successful movie director in history, with four of the top ten all-time box-office hits, is widely recognized; less so is the enormous influence that his vision has had on all the other visions the entertainment industry purveys. For better or worse, Spielberg's graphic vocabulary has engulfed our own. When car manufacturers want to seduce us, when moviemakers want to scare us, when political candidates want to persuade us, the visual language they employ is often Spielbergese—one of the few languages that this intensely fragmented society holds in common. We all respond to the image of "a place called Hope" when it's lit like a Spielberg idyll; we understand what we're being told about a soda can when it arrives in a Spielberg spaceship; we get the joke when an approaching basketball star shakes the earth like a Spielberg dinosaur. The way Steven Spielberg sees the world has become the way the world is communicated back to us every day.

Still, prophets are without honor in their own country, and in Hollywood, a town famous for its vindictiveness and Schadenfreude, the supernal glow around Steven Spielberg had, by the beginning of last year, begun to fade. The word was that industry people hated him for his wealth, his sharp business practices, his happy-go-lucky-kid demeanor. The memory of the dreamlike "E.T. the Extra-Terrestrial," which had become the most successful film in history, was a decade old, and Spielberg had slipped up several times since that movie's release: with "The Color Purple," his unconvincing first foray into the world of grownup cinema; with "Empire of the Sun" and the wildly overblown "Always," a pair of flops also aimed at adults; with "Indiana Jones and the Temple of Doom," which some thought too sadistic to be any fun; with "Indiana Jones and the Last Crusade," which some thought too tepid to be any fun; and finally with "Hook," his lumbering Peter Pan saga, which cost more than any other movie he had ever made, and which practically no one much liked—including Spielberg. Throughout the eighties, Spielberg's films often seemed like imitation Spielberg films, only preachier. Even in the summer of 1993, after the release of the dinosaur picture "Jurassic Park," which swiftly replaced "E.T." as the largest-grossing film in history, Spielberg could still be shrugged off by his less charitable contemporaries much the way that they had always shrugged him off: as a kind of adolescent savant doomed to accomplish nothing beyond Spielberg movies—in other words, boys'-book fantasies, light shows, theme-park rides. You could be smug about a filmmaker like that, even if he was richer and more powerful and more famous than you, because the gap between his technological gifts and his artistic maturity seemed almost comical; his limitations were clear.

But that was before the release of his masterpiece about the Holocaust, "Schindler's List," a work of restraint, intelligence, and unusual sensitivity, and the finest fiction feature ever made about the century's greatest evil. Adapted from Thomas Keneally's superb book about Oskar Schindler, a Nazi businessman who began by employing Jews in his Kraków factory and wound up saving eleven hundred of them from the death camps, "Schindler's List" is the sort of film that fashions of taste and politics won't soon dislodge; it will take its place in cultural history and remain there. And for Spielberg it has had the effect of a giant bar mitzvah, a rite of passage. Prince Hal has become Henry V; the dauphin has emerged a king.

"I had to grow into that," Spielberg told me recently. "It took me years before I was really ready to make 'Schindler's List.' I had a lot of projects on my shelves that were of a political nature and had 'social deed' written all over them—even had 'politically correct' stamped on top of them. And I didn't make those films, because I was censoring that part of me by saying to myself, 'That's not what the public will accept from you. What they will accept from you is thrills, chills, spills, and awe and wonder and that sort of thing.' I was afraid people would say, as some of them did say about both 'Empire of the Sun' and 'The Color Purple,' you know, 'Oh, it's the wrong shoe size. And it's the wrong style. What's he doing? Who does he wanna be like? Who's he trying to become—Woody? Or is he trying to become David Lean? Is he trying to become Marty Scorsese? Who does he think he is?' And I listened to that criticism. It gets to you. I certainly felt that everybody had sent me the message loud and clear that I was, you know, bad casting. I was a kid for life. And I almost slept in the bed they made—no, I made the bed for myself. But when I wanted to wake up and do something different many people tried to get me to go back to bed. 'Go to your room. And don't come out until it's something my kids will love, young man.'"

Yet, paradoxically, Spielberg's coming of age has been celebrated nowhere more ardently than in Hollywood—cynical, envious Hollywood, the community that has for so long denied the neighborhood rich kid its highest accolade, the Academy Award.

Anyone who has spent any time there lately will have noticed that it has become voguish for the movie industry's prominent players to display a disdainful indifference to the films they make. The formulation that runs, "It's only a movie; it's not a cure for cancer," has been popular, even when the movie in question was budgeted at a cost precisely suitable to a cure for cancer. So the mood was right for "Schindler's List," which not only was a very great film, but seemed itself to be a kind of worthy cause. Still, there have been worthy-cause films before, and the impact of "Schindler's List" has outstripped nearly all of them, because, to so many people in the movie business, it seems an inexplicable phenomenon. Hollywood understands talent, but it is baffled by genius; it understands appearances, but it is baffled by substance. Spielberg's genius is all the more bewildering because he gives very little outward sign of having any. In a town obsessed with surfaces, Spielberg wears goofy clothes, collects goofy art (he has twenty-five Norman Rockwell paintings), makes wide-eyed, goofy conversation, and maintains a personal style that is unpretentious to a fault. It has been almost preposterous that this awkward prodigy—not a child of Holocaust survivors, not previously steeped in the literature, not even terribly Jewish—

has turned his famously gaudy light on this darkest and most difficult of subjects and come back with a masterpiece. In the end, Hollywood couldn't dismiss it, couldn't resent it, could barely even digest it. Instead, people there fell back in flabbergasted awe, sputtering wildly, the way they often do at fund-raisers and award ceremonies.

"I think 'Schindler's List' will wind up being so much more important than a movie," Jeffrey Katzenberg, who runs the Walt Disney film studios, told me. "It will affect how people on this planet think and act. At a moment in time, it is going to remind us about the dark side, and do it in a way in which, whenever that little green monster is lurking somewhere, this movie is going to press it down again. I don't want to burden the movie too much, but I think it will bring peace on earth, good will to men. Enough of the right people will see it that it will actually set the course of world affairs. Steven is a national treasure. I'm breakin' my neck lookin' up at this guy."

Whether or not "Schindler's List" really is Santa Claus, the tooth fairy, and Dag Hammarskjöld rolled into one, a number of Spielberg's friends think that making the film has transformed him, or, rather, that it marks the latest and largest advance in a seasoning process that began around 1985, when he had his first child, Max—whose mother is his first wife, the actress Amy Irving—and has developed throughout his second marriage, to the actress Kate Capshaw. Spielberg has become more outgoing lately, more clubbable, more capable of intimacy. "I don't think Steven's had this many friends in his life since I've known him," Capshaw says. "He's got real buddies—he's never had that." These days he hangs out, often with prominent show-biz figures who more or less answer the same description: child-men, many of whom have settled down with take-charge, family-oriented, often relatively unglamorous wives, to raise children of their own—Robin Williams, Dustin Hoffman, Tom Hanks, Robert Zemeckis, Jeffrey Katzenberg, Martin Short. Together, these grown-up kids form a benign aristocracy, very different from the one that once dominated Hollywood—not dangerous, not druggy, not sexy, not wild. Their boyhoods are etched in their faces. These aren't the guys who passed their youths rat-packing around the neighborhood and getting into mischief; these were the wimpy guys, the nerds who spent their days in the vicinity of Mom, alone in the sandbox or playing in their room, developing the inner world that would one day conquer the outer one.

"The thing about Steven is he's still the A.V. guy in junior high school," Tom Hanks says. "You know, the guy who brings the movie projectors around and knows how to thread them, and all that kind of stuff. And I was the same way. So when we go out and do 'guy' things, it's not like we're out, you know, parasailing. We're not spearfishing, or anything like that. We're out just talking about a bunch of stuff and waiting to pick up our kids. We were out walking around on Friday, and a young girl approached him, and she said, 'I just had to tell you,' and she talked to him about 'Schindler's List.' And within forty-five seconds this girl had emotionally come undone, because she was saying, 'My Nana used to tell me stories,' and she had connected this movie to her grandma. And Steven, as best he could, reassured her. He put his hand on her shoulder and said, 'I made this movie so that people like yourself would realize ...'—something that was very appropriate and not very astute. And then she collected herself and she went off. And then we walked across the street, and Steven came emotionally undone. It took him a while to collect himself. And I assume it was because, just as that girl was not prepared for the power of what she had seen Steven do, Steven hasn't been quite prepared for the emotional power of what he has done."

Now, though, he is not doing much of anything—at least, not by Spielberg standards. True, his MCA-based company, Amblin Entertainment, is producing several feature films, some animation, some TV. And Spielberg himself is dabbling in extracurricular activities—designing rides for the Universal theme park in Orlando, for instance, and investing, with Katzenberg, in a new restaurant chain called Dive, which will sell submarine sandwiches. But, for the first time in his career, Spielberg doesn't know what his next directorial project will be. There are those who, like the Warner Bros. president, Terry Semel, believe that Spielberg will now direct an adaptation of the Robert James Waller best-seller "The Bridges of Madison County," which Amblin is producing. But Semel may be disappointed.

"I have no idea what to do next," Spielberg says. "And, more important, I don't care. And that's what allowed me to go to that Consumer Electronics Show in Las Vegas. I mean I would never have done that—I would have been so driven to do the next project. So I feel I can treat myself to some time off. Right now there's nothing that's inspired me, nothing that makes me want to work in '94 at all. I'm not really interested in making money. That's always come as the result of success, but it's not been my goal, and I've had a very tough time proving that to people. I've never been in it for the money; I was in it for the physical pleasure of film-making. It's a physical pleasure being on a set, making a movie, you know—taking images out of your imagination and making them three-dimensional and solid. It's magic."

Spielberg is a fast talker, and the way he stammers and burbles, swallowing some of the words, makes the impression of boyishness even more pronounced: he's like an excitable prepubescent, his hormones zinging, his thoughts scooting by so fast that his mouth can't trap enough language to express them. Beneath the round Armani glasses and the patriarchal beard, Spielberg has the face of the forty-six-year-old man he is; there are deep creases in his neck now, and a genuine gravity in his heavy-lidded eyes. But he is also squirmy and coltish: he bites his fingernails; he twiddles his thumbs. Energy leaks out of him everywhere.

"Maybe when I made 'Indy Two' and 'Indy Three' were the two times I could have been motivated by making money, by an easy slide into home plate," he says. "And if I do a sequel to 'Jurassic Park,' that would be an easy choice. I have no embarrassment in saying that with 'Jurassic' I was really just trying to make a good sequel to 'Jaws.' On land. It's shameless—I can tell you that now. But these days I'd rather make the more difficult choices. I just was so challenged by 'Schindler's List' and so fulfilled by it and so disturbed by it. It so shook up my life, in a good way, that I think I got a little taste of what a lot of other directors have existed on all through their careers—people like Altman, people like Kazan, even people like Preston Sturges, who made fiercely independent films. I suddenly saw what some of the tug was to the real filmmakers, who are always drawn to the subject matter because it's dangerous. I made 'Schindler's List' thinking that if it did entertain, then I would have failed. It was important to me not to set out to please. Because I always had."

Of course, the almost unmentionable secret of "Schindler's List" is that it does entertain: that part of its greatness comes from the fact that it moves swiftly and energetically, that it has storytelling confidence and flair, that it provides pain but also catharsis—that it is not, in short, a lecture but a work of art. I ask Spielberg whether, in the past, his propensity for pleasing an audience had interfered with his pleasing himself. "Yes, definitely," he replies. "It was like believing your own publicity. Everybody kept trying to equate my name with how much money the movie made on opening weekend or in the long run, as opposed to how good the movie was. So if I could stay successful and my movies made money I could stay Steven Spielberg. I would be allowed to keep my name. And I've always had an urge to please the audience, to please people other than myself. I never thought about compromising my own self-respect. I was beyond self-respect. I was into putting on a great show and sitting back and enjoying the audience participation. I felt more like P. T. Barnum that John Ford, for a lot of my career. And I wasn't ashamed of that. I've always thought that filling every seat in every theater in America was the ultimate vindication and validation. And the thought of pleasing myself only came to me recently."

As we talk, Spielberg is showing me around Amblin, a moviemaking haven like no other in Hollywood. Built in 1983, this place is perhaps the most visible emblem of Spielberg's power: twenty-five thousand square feet of offices, editing rooms, and conference rooms, with a palatial day-care center, a screening room (with popcorn-and-candy counter), a full-scale gym, a video-game room, a restaurant-size kitchen, and a separate building for directors called Movies While You Wait. The style is Santa Fe pueblo, and though the bricks are genuine baked adobe, the whole complex manages to look kitschy and unreal, like a movie set—or the world's fanciest Taco Bell. It sits in a remote and unnaturally quiet corner of the Universal lot (the corner nearest Warner Bros., for Warners and Universal are the two studios Spielberg generally works with), and its oasislike atmosphere is enhanced by lawns, palm trees, and a small Japanese garden: bubbling brook, fake-looking boulders, even a school of koi, the colorful Japanese fish, which Spielberg likes to capture on videotape—he sets their hungry gaping to Puccini, so that they appear to be singing "Madame Butterfly." Nothing here is higher than two stories, because Spielberg has a phobia about elevators (though that hasn't stopped him from keeping an apartment in the upper reaches of New York's Trump Tower), and Spielberg's own office sits above a sunny courtyard; walking there, you feel as though you were padding from the pool back to your room at some Mexican resort hotel. Although Spielberg has been known to be steely in his business dealings and sometimes insensitive about dispensing gratitude, the denizens of Amblin appear to be happy campers.

"I began wanting to make people happy from the beginning of my life," Spielberg says. "As a kid, I had puppet shows—I wanted people to like my puppet shows when I was eight years old. My first film was a movie

I made when I was twelve, for the Boy Scouts, and I think if I had made a different kind of film, if that film had been, maybe, a study of raindrops coming out of a gutter and forming a puddle in your back yard, I think if I had shown that film to the Boy Scouts and they had sat there and said, 'Wow, that's really beautiful, really interesting. Look at the patterns in the water. Look at the interesting camera angle'—I mean, if I had done that, I might have been a different kind of filmmaker. Or if I had made a story about two people in conflict and trying to work out their differences—which I certainly wouldn't have done at twelve years old—and the same Boy Scout troop scratching the little peach fuzz on their chins had said, 'Boy, that had a lot of depth,' I might have become Marty Scorsese. But instead the Boy Scouts cheered and applauded and laughed at what I did, and I really wanted to do that, to please again."

Of course, he may want to please again now, especially when, as is virtually certain, his latest film receives the Best Picture and Best Director Oscars (an eventuality he is too superstitious to talk about but has long coveted). And it occurs to me that his reluctance to take on a new directorial project may be tinged with fear. In making "Schindler's List," Spielberg threw away all the usual contrivances of his trade—his reliance on drawing storyboards to map out complex shots, his cranes and zoom lenses—and went against his propensity for excess and overemphasis. The movie is inspired; it looks and feels as though it had been directed in a kind of fever, and fevers are difficult to conjure on demand. Spielberg may not know quite how he made "Schindler's List." He may not know where the muscles that built it are, or how to find them again, and that could make him hesitate a very long time before plunging into something fresh., Besides, what *can* he direct now without tumbling from his new Olympus? Surely not "The Bridges of Madison County."

On the screen, what has always made Spielberg Spielberg is his peculiar combination of technical mastery and playfulness. As a director, he had all the heavy artillery of a Major Motion Picture Maker like David Lean, or a master of spectacle like Cecil B. De Mille: he could manipulate vast landscapes and tremendous crowds; he could fill the screen with intricately choreographed activity; he could make a camera fly across immense expanses and deliver intimacy along with the grandeur. No one since Hitchcock has been better at visual storytelling, at making images—rather than dialogue or explanation—convey the narrative. And no one since Orson

Welles has understood so deeply how to stage a shot, how to shift the viewer's eye from foreground to background, how to shuttle characters and incidents in and out of the frame at precisely the right moment, how to add information unobtrusively. Watching his elegant tracking shots— of an enormous archeological dig in "Raiders of the Lost Ark," for instance, or of a posh house party in Shanghai in "Empire of the Sun"—one absorbs the sort of sweep and detail a nineteenth-century novelist might pack into a long, magisterial chapter. And yet the viewer never loses sight of the character who is guiding him through the scene—never becomes aware of the camera's dexterity, never spots the holes that are being opened up at just the right moment for just the right line of dialogue, never loses the urgent pressure of the plot against one's back. No technical challenge appears to be beyond Spielberg. In his cumbersome Second World War comedy, "1941," he used miniatures to stage dogfights and submarine attacks with a deftness that few practitioners of that technology had ever imagined possible. He made platoons of cars seem to flirt and shimmy in his first feature, "The Sugarland Express"; he staged two of the sassiest, most high-spirited musical numbers ever seen on film in "1941" and "Indiana Jones and the Temple of Doom"; he created the most convincing and sympathetic outerspace creature in movie history in "E.T." and built dinosaurs that looked as real as house cats in "Jurassic Park."

But perhaps what has most charmed the fans of Steven Spielberg (and what most surprised them when he made "Schindler's List") is how lightly he has worn his gifts. Has anyone else ever deployed so much know-how in the service of mere play? The better Spielberg movies are jokey and spry: long passages in them have a refreshingly tossed-off, improvisatory feel, and his approach to pleasing an audience teeters between wowing us and tickling us. When Spielberg arrived, in the middle of the seventies, his films were like a balm. Amid the sourness of a culture so recently bullied by Vietnam, Watergate, and recession, here was a filmmaker who soft-pedaled his obvious power, who could scare the living daylights out of you or thrill you to the marrow but always grounded his vision in the reassuring bedrock of suburbia—of brand names we recognized and jokes we knew. If George Lucas's "Star Wars" films imagined an extraordinary world and peopled it with ordinary characters, Spielberg began with the ordinary and then revealed its astonishments. That felt like a generous gesture; and it was generosity, above all, that marked Spielberg's movies. He seemed to know in his bones what his audiences expected, and he always delivered more—more danger, more thrills, more wonder, more light.

And he was generous in another way as well. For every macho blowhard crushing a beer can, like the Robert Shaw character in "Jaws," Spielberg provided a likable doofus crushing a Styrofoam cup, like Richard Dreyfuss. His movies made it O.K. not to be remarkable by telling us that we already were. In that sense, "Schindler's List" itself is not so much a departure as a deepening of a central Spielberg theme, for the story of Schindler is not the story of a born hero, like Raoul Wallenberg, but the story of a common— even a base—man. Just as Richard Dreyfuss is "chosen" for transformation by the aliens in "Close Encounters," just as Christian Bale is chosen by John Malkovich in "Empire of the Sun" and young Henry Thomas by E.T., so Oskar Schindler is chosen, in a sense—whereas a more outstanding and therefore more scrupulous or obtrusive man might not have been. Before the war, the movie tells us, Schindler had been something of a ne'er-do-well; after the war, he was a failure. And yet under the right circumstances he becomes a saviour. It is only the presence of monstrous evil that makes Schindler a good man—and, finally, an exceptional one.

Spielberg, of course, rather resembles these ordinary characters of his. And as you race with him through his day it is not necessarily apparent that he is in command of an empire. Amblin has about forty-five employees, nine of whom report directly to Spielberg. There is a TV division (run by the veteran television executive Tony Thomopoulos); a merchandising division; an animation department, with offices in London and at Warner Bros. in Los Angeles; and a motion-picture division, with three development executives and their staffs. For the most part, Spielberg leaves the television and merchandising departments alone, but he's deeply involved in the animation, which, unlike most of the TV and movie production, has not just Amblin's name on it but his own. "It's just selfish," he says. "I get a real pleasure out of animation and less pleasure out of doing TV shows and looking at dinosaur toys."

The movie division, meanwhile, has been leaderless since the departure of Amblin's president, Kathleen Kennedy, early last year. (She left to start her own production company with her husband, Spielberg's sometime producer Frank Marshall.) But in May the screenwriter and producer Walter Parkes will become Amblin's president, and his wife, the producer Laurie MacDonald, will become his executive vice-president.

"Walter has extremely good taste as a producer and as a writer," Spielberg says. "And I really wanted Amblin to be more writer-driven. I think the weak link of some of our produced movies has been in the screenplays, and I think it's partly because in recent years we've had a tendency not to stay with one writer for a long enough time. If a writer flamed out, we would just give up on him and go to another writer.

"Here's an example. 'Schindler's List' went through many, many stages of development, but I always stuck with Steve Zaillian, and Steve stayed on the project even when he and I both thought the best thing for 'Schindler's List' was for me to go south and Steve to go north. I liked Steve's screenplay, but I wanted the story to be less vertical—less a character story of just Oskar Schindler, and more of a horizontal approach, taking in the Holocaust as the raison d'être of the whole project. What I really wanted to see was the relationship between Oskar Schindler—the German point of view—and Itzhak Stern—the Jewish point of view. And I wanted to invoke more of the actual stories of the victims—the Dresners, the Nussbaums, the Rosners. At first, Steve resisted, but then we went to Poland together, and the plane ride back was cathartic. We went over the script page by page, and Steve was having a second vision. So, even when Steve was stubborn and resistant to change and I threatened to bring somebody else on, we went through all those sorts of marital strife, but we succeeded with each other. And I wouldn't have succeeded if I had switched and gone to somebody else."

Zaillian says, "I had made a rule for myself that any scene that didn't involve Schindler wasn't in there. Schindler didn't have to be in the scene—the scene just had to have some effect on him. But there are now some scenes that resulted from our work together that don't do that. The biggest change when Spielberg got involved was the liquidation-of-the-ghetto sequence, which in my original script was about two or three pages, and which finally ended up to be about thirty pages. Spielberg said, 'I want to follow everybody we've met up to this point through this sequence.' So that was something that changed in a big way. And then, as we got closer to filming, one of the survivors might talk to Spielberg about something or there might be something in the book that he particularly responded to, and that would go in. I think his changes were good. The thing is, when he reads something he sees it visually. I mean, there are three hundred and fifty-nine scenes in this movie, and every one of them has to have a visual idea. And from my very brief experience of having directed one film, 'Searching for Bobby Fischer,' I know that after a certain point you run out of ideas. And he didn't. His great strength is really in being able to visually interpret a script."

It is a sunny Tuesday during the week before the earthquake, and Spielberg and I are on our way to a "punch-up" session for "Casper the Friendly Ghost," which Amblin is adapting from the Harvey Comics series. The movie was written by Sherri Stoner and Deanna Oliver, veterans of the Warner bros. animation group, but Spielberg is putting the screenplay through a process more common to sitcom production than to film—a roundtable. In this one, Stoner and Oliver join eight other writers to go over the script, adding new gags and polishing old ones. Spielberg first tried this technique on an Amblin production of "The Flintstones" (whose director, Brian Levant, has been drafted to run the roundtable); the resultant dispute over "Flintstones" writing credits has become a bit of a nightmare. But as we enter the conference room the atmosphere is jolly: the assembled company is singing, practically in unison, "We had joy, we had fun, we had seasons in the sun." Spielberg pretends shock. "I turn my back for five minutes, and now it's a musical?" he says.

The matter at hand is a scene in which a ghost enters the mouth of a sleeping middle-aged man; the man wakes up, looks in the mirror, and sees his face metamorphosing into other faces before his eyes. But the scene's particulars are growing fuzzy, and Spielberg, sitting in a chair a few feet away from the conference table, calls out, "Don't lose the good stuff, you guys! Remember, I committed to the script four drafts ago."

"So what was the good stuff then?" somebody yells.

Spielberg grins and shakes his head. Then he turns to me. "What I prefer to do is let them create all this," he says, "and then they give me pages to read, and I come in with my comments. They're mainly logic comments. I'm a little bit fastidious about that, because when you do fantasy it has to be based on common logic. When my kids see movies, they'll buy anything if it sort of makes sense. But if they're confused they get pulled out of the movie. You know, when I was seven years old it used to piss me off in serials when in Week 14 the car would go over the cliff and it would blow up and in Week 15 you see a shot you didn't see in Week 14—the hero jumping out of the car before it went over the cliff and blew up. I was pissed off that they cheated like that. They tell you the truth in Week 14 and lie to you the next week."

"Sort of like being engaged," an eavesdropping writer adds.

"Steven? Could I ask you something?" It's Sherri Stoner. "O.K., we've got him waking up after the ghost enters him and then he looks in the mirror."

"Yeah," Spielberg says. "And what he sees is that he's Mel Gibson, or whatever movie star will let his face be used for seven seconds. At a billion dollars a second." General laughter. "And then he says, 'Lookin' good.' And listen, you guys. Now you have the ghost entering through the guy's ear. It's gotta be through his mouth. You have to have the guy snoring, and have him enter through the mouth. Ear's no good. Mouth's much better."

"O.K.," Stoner says. "So then after he turns into Mel Gibson we want him to turn into, like, a monster face, right? And then he screams?"

"No, no," Spielberg says. "See, it's much funnier if he sees three different faces, including a monster face, and he *doesn't* scream. He's just looking at them and making little comments. And then he sees his own face. And that's when he screams. *That's* funny."

"So what's the best monster face?" Stoner says.

"I thought Mike Ditka was next," another writer says.

"Well, he could go from Mel Gibson to Mike Ditka," Spielberg says. "The problem with Mike Ditka is my wife thinks *he's* handsome, too."

Another writer: "Rodney Dangerfield."

"To go from Mel Gibson to Rodney Dangerfield is interesting," Spielberg says. "And then a monster, like someone like Wolfman. And then he sees his own face and he screams. That's the broad arc."

"How about Jerry Lewis?" Deanna Oliver says. "Jerry Lewis is a lot scarier than Rodney Dangerfield."

As if on cue, all ten writers unleash their Jerry Lewis imitations, crossing their eyes and screaming the word "Lady!" over and over again.

"Come on, come on," Brian Levant yells. "Let's focus."

As the dust settles, an older writer named Lenny Ripps turns to me. "'Schindler's' would have been a lot funnier if we'd done it this way," he says.

If you ask Spielberg where his ideas come from, he pleads ignorance. "Those images aren't coming from any place in my head," he says. "I guess it's just something that happens. I can't explain it, and I would be fooling everybody to say that I have a lot of self-control over what I do. Basically, I don't. I don't have a lot of experience in really talking and really dealing with my life in an analytical way. I just kind of live it. A true artist works from someplace inside himself that he is not capable of confronting when he's having breakfast. When I'm having breakfast, I read the cereal box. I read the top, the sides, the front, the back, and the bottom, just like I did when I was a kid."

He admits to watching too much television—"I junk out on bad TV movies," he says—and he has an insatiable passion for video games. Sometimes he plays them by modem with Robin Williams, who lives in San Francisco. Sometimes he just plays by himself. He plays after the kids go to bed, and on weekends, and sometimes on movie sets.

"He has little hand things," Dustin Hoffman says. "On 'Hook,' while they were lighting, he shut everybody out, and he sat on the camera dolly and he played those—what are they, Game Boy? And then for a while he was getting all the flight information from L.A. International Airport, so he's sitting on the dolly and he's listening to the pilots. And he's doing that *while* he's playing Game Boy."

Here he is at lunch with Janusz Kaminski, the Polish-born cinematographer who directed the extraordinary black-and-white photography of "Schindler's List." Kaminski is not the brooding artiste one might expect. He is a whimsical thirty-four-year-old moon-faced character with prodigious dimples, and he has spent much of the morning hanging outside Spielberg's office saying things like "This Holly Hunter—maybe I meet her. I like very much. She is wonderful girl." But now we are eating fish at a restaurant in the Universal CityWalk mall, and he and Spielberg have been reminiscing about filming "Schindler's List" in Poland. Spielberg suddenly changes the subject. "You know what you should try, Janusz?" he says. "I did this last night—it was amazing. You take a piece of Saran Wrap and put it over a flashlight, and wrinkle the Saran Wrap up. What I do is, I do shadow shows with my hands for my kids. I lie in bed with my kids—we have a white ceiling—and I put a flashlight pitched between my legs and I do these shows where my hands are huge on the ceiling. I do T. rexes attacking lawyers—I do everything. They really enjoy that. And then last night I had put the flashlight down, and it happened to be next to some Hanukkah wrapping that was clear like cellophane. And I saw the pattern against the wall with the flashlight. I thought it was fantastic, so I grabbed the cellophane, put it on the flashlight, and began making patterns on the walls. And it was amazing—it's like ocean waves on your wall. I don't know how you use it, but it was *amazing!*"

Can we understand how amazing? Perhaps not. Even Kaminski, who is nearly as boyish as Spielberg, looks a little puzzled beneath his grin. But then that has always been Spielberg's problem, ever since the beginning— the simultaneous urgency and impossibility of communicating what it is he sees. You can feel it in the oddly repetitive way he explains himself to an interviewer, stating and restating, doubling back on his sentences, laboriously spelling things out, so that everything is perfectly clear. His films, too, are, above all, emphatic. His signature storytelling devices insist that we get the point: the thunderous John Williams music; the famous reaction shots that cue the audience to feel fear or wonder; the brilliant light that Spielberg shines in our eyes, forcing our attention, hiding things or revealing them or enrobing them in awe. The entrance of a hero is announced by framing him in a doorway, silhouetted against the light, the camera looking reverently up at him, even rushing in to greet him. At its best, this sort of thing comes across as bounty; at its worst, as egregious overkill. Except for "Schindler's List," Spielberg's movies are based on the power of more.

He is harsh with his film crews, even ruthless, and for similar reasons— he's impatient with them when they don't deliver what he thinks he has communicated. "Oftentimes he's thinking so far ahead that he doesn't want to waste the time explaining to anybody what he's trying to do," Kathleen Kennedy, who ran Amblin from 1983 until last year, says. "He needs people around who will just do it, and not question—be there and just execute, and not try to understand every little detail—because he's on the fly. When we were doing the big airplane sequence in 'Raiders of the Lost Ark,' where they have the fistfight under the wing—that whole time from when Indiana Jones runs out to the wing until the airplane explodes is about a hundred and twenty cuts. They can only go together one way. And he knew already in his mind exactly what every single shot would be. And he just *sees* all of that. And what happens is he gets impatient, because once he sees it he doesn't want to lose what he sees."

He is also, it is said, an unusually tough businessman, a ferocious, canny, and obsessively secretive negotiator, and not a terribly generous one. Although Spielberg has long been the wealthiest director in America— and, indeed, one of the wealthiest men in the entertainment business (*Forbes* estimates his earnings over the last two years at seventy-two million dollars)—even his sister Anne Spielberg, who co-wrote and co-produced the movie "Big" and has several projects brewing at Amblin, says,

"He's a very tough bargainer. He's a hard man to deal with on those things. There are times I'd be tempted to take things other places, where I know that I would get a better deal."

Spielberg is still a demon negotiator, but when he developed his close friendship with Steve Ross, the late chairman of Time Warner, his pockets began to open. "After I met Steve," Spielberg says, "I went from being a miser to a philanthropist, because I knew him, because that's what he showed me to do. I was just never spending any money. I gave nothing to causes that were important to me. And when I met Steve, I just observed the pleasure that he drew from his own private philanthropy. And it was total pleasure. And it was private, anonymous giving. So most everything I do is anonymous. I have my name on a couple of buildings, because in a way that's a fund-raiser. But eighty per cent of what I do is anonymous. And I get so much pleasure from that—it's one of the things that Steve Ross opened my heart to."

Ross, Spielberg has said, was like a father to him, and for Spielberg that designation carries considerable emotional freight. One can sense it in his films, which are full of yearning for home and family, and especially for fathers—departed fathers (as in "E.T.," "Empire of the Sun," and "Indiana Jones and the Last Crusade"), failed fathers ("The Sugerland Express," "Hook," the grandfather in "Jurassic Park"), fathers who become distant, evil, or unrecognizable ("Close Encounters," "Indiana Jones and the Temple of Doom," "The Color Purple"), and fathers who return to save the day ("Jaws," "Jurassic Park," "Hook"). Even "Schindler's List" can be viewed as a story of patriarchy—of Schindler, an irresponsible child-man who must become father enough to protect his immense "family" from the enormity that will otherwise destroy it. In Spielberg's movies, fatherhood has a mystical shimmer.

His relationship with his own father, though, was rather bumpy. Arnold Spielberg was a computer pioneer and something of a workaholic; Steven's mother, Leah, was a former concert pianist. The marriage was never a very happy one, and the Spielbergs finally split up in 1966, when their son was eighteen. "My dad was of that World War Two ethic," Spielberg says. "He brought home the bacon, and my mom cooked it, and we ate it. I went to my dad with things, but he was always analytical. I was more passionate in my approach to any question, and so we always clashed. I was yearning for drama."

The boyhood of Steven Spielberg has been recounted so often that it has become a minor American legend, a myth for the age of the triumphant dweeb: how the pencil-necked Jew at a suburban Gentile school won over the local bully by starring him in his films, how dissecting frogs made him sick in biology class (and inspired a classic scene in "E.T."), how gawky young Steve purposely lost a road race so a retarded boy could beat him, how the cruelties visited upon him by his smooth Wasp classmates drove him into the arms of his art. His sister Anne, who is two years his junior, recalls some of it a little differently. "He had more friends than he remembers having," she says. "I don't think he realized the crushes that some girls had on him. Some of my friends had major crushes on him. If you looked at a picture of him then, you'd say, Yes, there's a nerd. There's the crewcut, the flattop, there are the ears. There's the skinny body. But he really had an incredible personality. He could make people do things. He made everything he was going to do sound like you wished you were a part of it."

That gift served him well from the time he began making 8-mm. movies in his Scottsdale garage at least until 1969, when Sidney Sheinberg, then the head of Universal's television department, saw Spielberg's rather saccharine short film "Amblin'" and signed him to a seven-year contract as a TV director. The producer Richard Zanuck, who with his partner, David Brown, gave Spielberg his first stab at a feature film, remembers much the same quality. The movie they made together was "The Sugarland Express," and Spielberg was only twenty-four when he started shooting it. Zanuck says, "I was thinking, Well, let's take it easy. Let's get the kid acclimated to this big-time stuff. But when I got out there the first day he was about ready to get this first shot, and it was the most elaborate fucking thing I've ever seen in my life. I mean tricky: all-in-one shots, the camera going and stopping, people going in and out. But he had such confidence in the way he was handling it. Here he was, a young little punk kid, with a lot of seasoned crew around, a major actress"—Goldie Hawn—"on hand, and instead of starting with something easy, he picked a very complicated thing that required all kinds of very intricate timing. And it worked incredibly well—and not only from a technical standpoint, but the performances were very good. I knew right then and there, without any doubt, that this guy probably knew more at that age about the mechanics of working out a shot than anybody alive at that time, no matter how many pictures they'd made. He took to it like—you know, like he was born with a knowledge of cinema. And he never ceased to amaze me from that day on."

Although "The Sugarland Express" was a box-office flop, Zanuck and Brown immediately hired Spielberg to direct another picture—"Jaws." The project was star-crossed from the beginning. On the third day of shooting, the mechanical shark sank. By the time it could be made functional, the movie was a hundred days behind schedule and more than a hundred per cent over budget. "I was panicked," Spielberg says. "I was out of my mind with fear—not of being replaced, even though people were trying to fire me, but of letting everybody down. I was twenty-six, and even though I actually felt like a veteran by that time, nobody else felt that way about me. I looked younger than twenty-six. I looked seventeen, and I had acne, and that doesn't help instill confidence in seasoned crews."

In the end, of course, "Jaws" proved to be a terrific movie, a cheeky, unpredictable thriller that set the tone for a generation of cheeky, rather more predictable thrillers—and became, at the time, the highest-grossing film in history. Spielberg collected three million dollars, which in 1975 was enough to make him very rich—even Hollywood rich. But he was also movie-obsessed, to the exclusion of everything else; like his father before him, he didn't have a life. Although the memoirs of Julia Phillips, the co-producer of "Close Encounters," mention his dating such Hollywood tigresses as Victoria Principal and Sarah Miles, Spielberg says, "I didn't stop to notice if women were interested in me, or if there was a party that I might have been invited to. I didn't ever take the time to revel in the glory of a successful or money-making film. I didn't stop to enjoy. By the time 'Jaws' was in theaters, I was already deeply into production on 'Close Encounters,' and by the time 'Close Encounters' was released I was deeply into production on '1941,' and before '1941' was over I was severely into preproduction on 'Raiders of the Lost Ark.' So I never had a chance to sit down and pat myself on the back or spend my money or date or go on vacations in Europe. I just haven't done that, and I just haven't done that because I put my moviemaking ahead of some of the results. I thought that if I stopped I would never get started again, that I would lose the momentum."

The momentum? The ability to make hits? To keep the ideas coming?

"No, the momentum of being interested in working. I was afraid that if I stopped I would be punished for enjoying my success by losing my interest in working. Like I feel right now. If I felt ten years ago what I'm feeling today, I would panic. I would really panic. I wouldn't know how to handle these feelings."

But Spielberg appears to have socialized more than he remembers, and in 1976 he met Amy Irving, the daughter of the actress Priscilla Pointer and the actor-director Jules Irving, who was one of the founding directors of the Lincoln Center Repertory Theatre. Spielberg was immediately smitten. He and Irving carried on a tempestuous and troubled relationship, breaking up around the time she made the 1980 film "Honeysuckle Rose" with Willie Nelson, and finally reuniting dramatically in 1983, when Spielberg flew to India to scout locations for "Indiana Jones and the Temple of Doom." Irving, who had been filming "The Far Pavilions" there, surprised him at the airport. They were married in 1985, and Max was born the same year, but the marriage was stormy almost from the start.

"I like Amy a lot," Spielberg's old friend Matthew Robbins says. But, he adds, "when Steven decided to marry her I was very worried. It was no fun to go over there, because there was an electric tension in the air. It was competitive as to whose dining table this is, whose career we're gonna talk about, or whether he even approved of what she was interested in—her friends and her actor life. He really was uncomfortable. The child in Spielberg believed so thoroughly in the possibility of perfect marriage, the institution of marriage, the Norman Rockwell turkey on the table, everyone's head bowed in prayer—all this stuff. And Amy was sort of a glittering prize, smart as hell, gifted, and beautiful, but definitely edgy and provocative and competitive. She would not provide him any ease. There was nothing to go home to that was cozy." Spielberg and Irving remain good friends (Irving now lives with the Brazilian film director Bruno Barreto), but they divorced in 1989. Irving's settlement was reported to have been a recordbreaker—though she has denied rumors that it was in the neighborhood of a hundred million dollars.

During the ups and downs, there had been other women, and one of them was Kate Capshaw. Spielberg had met her in 1983, when she auditioned for the role she eventually won in "Indiana Jones and the Temple of Doom," and though friends say that for him their early relationship was essentially a fling, Capshaw was resolute from the start. "I think it was just the way he smelled," she says. "He smelled like my family. It was a smell of familiarity. I'm speaking not just metaphorically but olfactorily. They say that once a woman takes a whiff of her infant you can blindfold her and march twenty babies in front of her and she'll pick hers, and that's how it felt to me. I felt like I was blindfolded and took a smell and said, 'This is the guy.'"

Capshaw giggles a lot when she talks, and indulges in girlish squeals; her hair is sometimes reddish brown and sometimes blond, her eyes are a keen, pale blue, and, though she has a fetching sexy-pixie air, one senses a will of steel beneath the wiles. She is not a sophisticate or a fashion nut, and she doesn't pretend to be. Today she is wearing coveralls over a leotard, and we are tramping around Spielberg's verdant Pacific Palisades neighborhood with their youngest child, a very blond two-year-old boy named Sawyer, tucked in a stroller. Clearly, she has taken Spielberg in hand, managing the house here and another in East Hampton and the five kids (one each from previous marriages, two from their own, one adopted). They have been married for two years and have lived together for four. And the winning of Spielberg was a long campaign. Capshaw even converted from Methodism to Judaism, a move widely thought to have been contrived as the final snare. Both Spielberg and Capshaw deny any ulterior motive, of course, and Capshaw says, "When I converted, Steven was delighted, but then all the people in his family who were supposed to fall to their knees in exultation didn't say a word, because they so wanted me to know that it didn't matter to them."

Capshaw says she had long been drawn to Judaism; she liked its emphasis on the family. "We were watching 'Indiana Jones and the Temple of Doom' the other night on television," she says. "And I turned to Steven and I said, 'What happened to my career after that movie?' He said, 'You weren't supposed to have a career. You were supposed to be with me.' And it's true." She peers at me for a moment, and perhaps she reads some consternation in my face. "Oh, I absolutely feel that way," she says. "I think you have to have a great deal of ambition—these careers of our A-list ladies don't happen by accident. And if they do they don't sustain. And I didn't do the things you have to do. My focus was on Steven and a large family."

Just now, their three-year-old daughter, Sasha, is running around the Spielberg living room naked, wearing a plastic knights-of-the-Round-Table helmet, brandishing a rubbery sword, and screaming at the top of her lungs. Her father is standing by the fireplace, and he is on the telephone with Robin Williams. "I've only been playing Syndicate," Spielberg is saying, "and it's much harder to play. They put a lot more graphic design into some of the bullets. And I haven't got far enough into it yet, but I hear there's air cover. And there's also supply drops and there's also air strikes. We only played two countries, and I got my ass whipped in the second country. So I've got another seventy-five countries to go. So you want to do a mission today? O.K. Let's do it. Let's do one mission."

The house we are in is huge, white, airy, and Mediterranean in style, and it sits on five and a half acres of palm trees and gardens, along with several large outbuildings—a screening room, an office, a guesthouse. Douglas Fairbanks, Jr., once lived here, and so did David O. Selznick when he was making "Gone with the Wind," and Cary Grant when he was married to Barbara Hutton. Spielberg has renovated much of it, but parts of the original structure remain. On one living-room wall is a small Modigliani, and, on the adjacent wall, a big, luminous Monet. Under that is a table, which, like most of the other furniture in the house, is in the Arts and Crafts style (much of it by Gustav Stickley), and on the table are three scripts under glass: originals of "Citizen Kane," "Casablanca," and Orson Welles' radio broadcast "The War of the Worlds." Everywhere else you look there are Norman Rockwell paintings.

There is a mystery here, and it is, finally, the mystery that makes "Schindler's List" so hard to fathom. What is on the screen is overwhelming—tremendously moving; insightful about the nature of evil and even the nature of goodness. And yet here is the man who made it, an overgrown boy in a baseball cap, with a sweet, happy wife and five lovely kids and, behind him, a childhood whose sufferings were so much milder and more banal than the sufferings that popular mythology insists that an artist must undergo. Here he is, playing video games.

I remember something Kathleen Kennedy told me: "Steven has trouble with a level of intimacy. He gets close to people to a point, and then it begins to break down, because I don't think Steven is always comfortable communicating his feelings. His inability to trust very many people creates a certain amount of personal loneliness for him. But I also think it comes from just wanting to be by himself and be close to some creative, inanimate world he can live within, rather than deal with the real world and real people. I've sometimes witnessed him doing this thing: I see him withdrawing, and he's going into a place where he's more comfortable. He goes to that place, and it is completely devoid of other people and other pressures—it's almost Zen-like. And he comes out with extraordinary things.

He goes there just like a monk. And he doesn't even know what it is."

What it is, perhaps, is a kind of sandbox, and, once he is in it, everything is mutable—subject only to the laws of play. Spielberg understands those laws instinctively, and he can apply them to anything. Whatever subject you throw at him, large or small, great or mean—the Holocaust or Casper the Friendly Ghost—is taken back into the sandbox and played with until he has made it marvellous.

Play is a kind of manipulation, and Spielberg is an unusually deft manipulator. Richard Dreyfuss likes to tell a story about a long night near the end of the shooting of "Jaws," during which Spielberg kept Dreyfuss wide awake by going through the movie scene by scene and explaining how else he might have shot it—how it might have been, for instance, an art film, a film that would call attention to Spielberg's own directorial technique instead of to where the shark might pop up next. Spielberg's talent is protean, overlush: he can tell your story better than you can, and then tell it a different way, better still. When he is producing, he flits from project to project like some pollinating insect, sinking proboscis-deep into the fantasy at hand, and then going on to the next.

But, of course, there *is* a difference between Casper and the Holocaust, and even between his other great films—"Jaws," "Close Encounters," "E.T."—and "Schindler's List." It is too easy to say that the difference lies in the subject matter. Rather, the difference lies in the quality of emotion that Spielberg brings to it. "Schindler's List" is angry. And the anger in it, one feels, is not like the other Spielberg emotions. The terror in "Jaws," the wonder in "Close Encounters," even the longing for love in "E.T."—all those things come, in some way, from the boy playing in his sandbox; they are beautifully manipulated, but manipulated all the same. The anger in "Schindler's Life" is not. It feels earned and vital; it feels as though it took even Spielberg by surprise.

And it leaves him in a difficult situation. For if you talk with him, watch him work, observe the way he lives, you know that he still resides in the sandbox—and that it is going to take something very unusual to make him rise from it again.

He knows it, too. "I'm kind of in a pickle," he says. "And I'm looking forward to not getting out of it for a long time."

Holocaust Drama is a Spielberg Triumph

by James Verniere
The Boston Herald, Dec. 15, 1993

With "Schindler's List," Steven Spielberg delivers a dazzling and completely unprecedented one-two punch. Last summer, he brought us "Jurassic Park," the most profitable film in history. Now, he gives us "Schindler's List," a searing, real-life Holocaust drama that will help silence the argument that he's all surface and no depth. Most admirable of all, "Schindler's List" is an amazing demonstration of restraint by the master of emotional overkill.

Based on the 1982 book by Australian novelist Thomas Keneally, this three-hour-plus, black-and-white film tells the story of Oskar Schindler (Liam Neeson), a Czech-born German who risks his life to save more than 1,100 Jews during World War II.

When we first meet Schindler in 1939 in a high-class Krakow nightclub, Spielberg's camera deliberately emphasizes Neeson's Olympian shoulders and movie-star profile. A type of *bon vivant* and war profiteer-in-training, Neeson's Schindler is a gorgeous male animal on the prowl, and if he had not been a real person, someone would have had to invent him.

After greasing the Nazi hierarchy with Cognac, Champagne, caviar and chocolates, Schindler succeeds in setting up an enamelware factory in Krakow, where he develops a paternal relationship with its Jewish slave-labor force. His closest contact is with Itzhak Stern (Ben Kingsley), a dignified Jewish leader who can barely control his grief or disguise the loathing he feels in the presence of any German, even Schindler.

But Schindler really is different. When the Jews are routed from the Krakow Ghetto in 1943 and transported to nearby Plaszow Camp, they come under command of *Untersturmfuhrer* Amon Goeth (the amazing Ralph Fiennes). A sadistic killer with dead eyes and a lupine face, Amon paves his camp's road with Jewish tombstones and shoots prisoners at random from his balcony. But Schindler refuses to let "his Jews" out of his grasp, even if it means wrestling with Satan himself. In a scene that reeks of danger, Schindler charms even Goeth, persuading him that he needs his "skilled workers" to help the war effort.

This is where Spielberg establishes a link between Oskar and Amon, a useful insight in a film conspicuously lacking in motivation, although it runs the risk of generating sympathy for the devil. Like Keneally, Spielberg sees Oskar and Amon as mirror images, pure sensualists interested only in what makes them feel good. By some accident of fate, Oskar discovers saving lives gives him his greatest thrill, which perhaps explains why he would later spend a fortune to ransom his workers' lives. Conversely, Amon gets his kicks only by killing and brutalizing. Both men, however, are finally enigmas.

Notably, at no point in his development does Schindler lose his carnal appetites. He is never a saint. He drinks, smokes and eats to excess and has no qualms about cheating on his wife (Caroline Goodall), although Spielberg does omit one of Schindler's more spectacular indiscretions: We do not get to see Oskar's nude swim with a blond SS maiden. A kind of Eastern European Gary Cooper, Neeson's Schindler is a master of seduction, a man whose personal style is pure Hollywood *chutzpah*, and this is easily Neeson's finest performance.

If the film lacks psychological depth, it makes up for it in technical virtuosity and in its careful handling of this chapter of the Holocaust. Spielberg's images, which can be ponderous and self-congratulatory, don't call as much attention to themselves as they usually do. For once, he lets them speak for themselves, and occasionally he achieves a kind of baleful poetry. In one scene, ghetto tenements are lit from within by blasts of gun-fire like giant, blinking Christmas ornaments. Later a sudden, blanketing snow squall turns out to be a shower of human ash.

"Schindler's List" is not for the faint of heart. The Nazis here are not the cartoon villains of the "Raiders of the Lost Ark" films. Viewers will sympathize with the terror of families stripped of everything and shipped to their deaths. Spielberg does not turn away from Auschwitz's smokestacks or shower rooms. Most pathetic of all, perhaps, is the sight of naked men and women running for their lives in order to persuade Nazi "doctors" they can still be useful as slaves.

Because Keneally's book is based on actual records and testimony of surviving *Schindlerjuden,* it is not a work of fiction, but a historical novel. Perhaps this is why Spielberg has reined himself in so effectively. He respects the sources too much.

Except for a misguided, present-day scene at the very end and a farewell speech by Schindler that is entirely out of character, "Schindler's List" is Spielberg's long-awaited dramatic triumph. It is not only a major addition to the body of work about the Holocaust, it is also an undeniably great movie.

Spielberg's "List"
A Commanding Holocaust Film

by John Hartl
The Seattle Times, Dec. 15, 1993

Movies about the Holocaust were once overwhelmingly grim and oppressive.

That has changed in recent years with the release of a series of more hopeful fact-based films about resistance and survival under the Nazis: "Escape from Sobibor," "Lodz Ghetto," "Europa, Europa," "Weapons of the Spirit" and last year's revelatory documentary, "The Restless Conscience: Resistance to Hitler Within Germany, 1933-1945."

The most visible and ambitious of these, Steven Spielberg's adaptation of Thomas Keneally's 1982 novel, "Schindler's List," was recently endorsed by President Clinton, as he responded to a heckler who claimed that the president had done little about the AIDS crisis.

"It's about a non-Jew who as a member of the Nazi Party saved over 1,000 Jews by his personal efforts in World War II from the Holocaust," said the president. "The reason I ask you to go see the movie is you will see portrait after portrait of the painful difference between people who have no hope and have no rage left and people who still have hope and still have rage. I'd rather that man be in here screaming at me than having given up altogether."

Presidential movie endorsements can be scary and self-serving (Reagan and "Rambo," Nixon and "Patton" come to mind), but this one seems quite spontaneous, appropriate—and deserved.

In a severe, uncompromising manner that none of his previous films has approached, Spielberg has captured the terror of the Nazi reign as well as the determination and resourcefulness of those who resisted. He has created one of the most shocking movies yet made about the Holocaust (there were several walkouts at the screening I attended) and one of the most inspiring. It opens today.

Violence Difficult to Watch

The savage scenes of random, cruel slaughter in the Polish ghetto and concentration camps are difficult to watch. Determined Spielberg critics may find it just was hard to handle the final turn toward sentiment. But there's nothing cloying or false about these closing moments (or John Williams' atypical subdued score). The emotions are earned.

The story of Oskar Schindler, a Catholic businessman who exploited Krakow Jews, then became their friend and protector, seems ready-made as narrative and character study. He kept hundreds in his factory and out of the camps while challenging and manipulating an especially vicious and childish S.S. officer. The characterization of Schindler is one reason the movie is so involving. During the 195 minutes the story takes to unfold, Schindler undergoes a subtle transformation, from hedonistic exploiter of slave labor to savior with a mission and finally to hero in hiding.

In this key role, Liam Neeson uses his watchful eyes to size up dangerous situations, to guess how far he can go with charm, bribery, bluffing and delaying tactics. You don't always know what Schindler is thinking, or what he is willing to risk, but Neeson successfully demonstrates that everyone's a bit at sea in the chaotic world Spielberg so vividly evokes. It's just that Schindler, who's a bit of a gambler, seems more in command than others.

As the S.S. officer Amon Goeth, Ralph Fiennes is simultaneously terrifying and riveting. His performance here is so effective that it's likely to cause nightmares. The character is introduced as a paunchy, overindulged brat, but he's an unpredictable adult brat with murderous power and a snaky sensuality—a Third Reich Caligula.

The other key part is Schindler's Jewish accountant, played with self-effacing brilliance by Ben Kingsley, who gives the movie just the touch of warmth and sanity it needs. Powerless as his character is, he becomes a kind of touchstone, the one person who tries to make sense of ongoing, unmanageable disaster. When his life is endangered, the audience feels threatened.

While Steven Zaillian's skillful screenplay relies heavily on these three to carry the story, there are many vignettes, many scenes about people who did not survive. Children hide in makeshift toilets, a construction expert is cynically shot for suggesting a necessary change, refugees swallow jewels, doctors calmly administer poison to their threatened Jewish patients. More than any previous non-documentary Holocaust movie, this one convinces through the accumulation of such detail.

Effective Cinematography

The decision to film most of "Schindler's List" in black-and-white was a sound one. Spielberg and his cinematographer, Janusz Kaminski, are particularly effective at using monochrome to capture a mood of oppression: the humiliation of the Jews in the streets, the sudden worthlessness of conventional wealth and status, the realization that "it's not just old-fashioned Jew-hating; it's policy now."

Some have questioned whether we need another Holocaust film, whether we must go through this once more, whether those who were born long after 1945 need to be exposed to this material. As long as the existence of the Holocaust can be seriously debated, as long as "cultural revolutions" and "ethnic cleansing" continue to be a fact of 20th century life, the answer is yes.

Spielberg Tells a Powerful Holocaust Tale

by Louis B. Parks
Houston Chronicle, Dec. 15, 1993

Steven Spielberg may not be Oscar's orphan much longer. "Schindler's List" is a great movie and a tremendous directorial achievement.

It finally should win him that elusive Academy Award.

The long-awaited epic about the real-life Nazi who saved more than 1,100 Jews from Hitler's Holocaust opens today, and it caps an amazing year, even for Spielberg. First he made the century's most profitable film in "Jurassic Park". Now he has topped that feat artistically with "Schindler's List."

The film is emotionally powerful—finding humanity in an inhumane situation—and truly horrific. It is Spielberg's finest work.

"Schindler's List" has already won the Los Angeles Film Critics Association award for 1993's best picture, making it a leading contender for an Oscar next spring. Spielberg has to be in the running for best director.

It's odd to use the word entertaining on a work so gut-wrenching. This is no preachy, dry film on An Important Subject. It's compelling and absorbing—personal, grab-your-throat, make-you-cry, applaud-the-credits filmmaking.

But Spielberg has put art and feeling before commercial interests. He even elected to work in black and white. He wanted to evoke the 1940s period and avoid the usual glamour of movie violence and blood.

Liam Neeson ("Shining Through") stars as Oskar Schindler, a Nazi Party member who arrives in Krakow, Poland, shortly after the Nazi army crushes Polish resistance in 1939, at the start of World War II.

Schindler hopes to find the business success that has eluded him. In Krakow he can get lots of cheap labor. If he uses Jews, they will cost him almost nothing. Jews are not allowed to have money, and Schindler merely pays German officials for each one he wants.

As he ingratiates himself to the local military commanders, the charming Schindler seems oblivious to the Jewish plight. He neither hates nor likes Jews; they merely represent good business opportunity. He even lives in a house the Nazis have stolen from a Jewish family. (There is some evidence Schindler tried to find the family and pay them.)

Schindler has no business skills, so he hires a Jewish accountant, Itzhak Stern, played wonderfully by Ben Kingsley ("Gandhi"). Stern is first frightened, then wary of Schindler. After announcing (as the law requires) that he is Jewish, he declines the job offer. Schindler insists, and Stern cautiously agrees.

It will be the smartest choice of his life. Soon he is Schindler's right-hand man, but it will be months before he trusts the friendly German. Together they set about hiring Jews, Stern cleverly forging work documents to get intellectuals, old people, women and children into the factory, even though they have no manual skills.

Over the next five years, the Jewish plight in Krakow goes from horrible to almost certain death. This is driven home to Schindler not only through the endless casual killing he sees, but in the increasingly matter-of-fact attitude of the German officers.

After Schindler kisses a Jewish slave-laborer in front of officers at his birthday party, a Nazi warns him not to be concerned about any Jew. "They have no future. That's not just good old Jew-hating talk," he explains quietly. "It's official policy."

Eventually, the ghetto-imprisoned Jews are rounded up. Most are massacred in a detailed scene of nightmare horror. The rest are moved into a work camp, where many will be killed before the time comes for them to be shipped to the death camps for extermination.

Only those on Schindler's work roles survive. But Schindler seems unaware of this until a girl begs him to get her parents into his factory. Everyone knows your factory is a haven, she tells him.

From then on, he is transformed from passive rescuer to obsessed savior. He begins spending his new fortune bribing as many Nazi officials as he can to buy more and more lives. Often he must rebuy them again and again. The Nazis take notice and don't like it. But they do like the money.

When the war goes badly for the Germans, the Krakow camp is closed and all the Jews left are sent to death camps. If any are to survive, it will take all Schindler's money and several miracles.

At three hours, there is not a dull moment in "Schindler's List," with its scenes of suspense, heroics, sheer terror and breathe-again relief.

The afterimages cling, and some are painful:

Amon Goeth, the camp commandant, sitting shirtless on his balcony, casually shooting workers who move too slowly. A clerk, listing items taken from the Jews, suddenly opening a package of gold teeth. A child trying to hide by dropping through the seat holes in the camp outhouses, only to find too many other children already hidden among the filth.

There is blunt, brutal ugliness that's hard to sit through: countless men and women shot in the head; a row of prisoners lined up so a soldier can see how many bodies his rifle will fire through; small children killed—though Spielberg has said he couldn't film the worst atrocities against children.

The violence was so realistic that I occasionally looked away. A few people left the auditorium.

In addition to the violence, there is language not usually heard in a Spielberg film. The film contains sexual nudity, as well as mass nudity during camp inspections.

Why go to such a film? There is the argument that if we do not learn from history, we are destined to repeat it. But this is not a history lesson. It is one of the most moving, involving films ever. Few moments in film are as moving or hopeful as the final scenes.

There have been countless powerful documentaries about the Holocaust, but in focusing on a few affected people, "Schindler's List" makes real the terror of life under daily threat of torture, humiliation and imminent death. It proves the brave and righteous efforts of one good person can counter a massive amount of evil.

This is Spielberg like we've never seen him. He is still the master entertainer, telling a hypnotic story with compassion and hope. But this time he does so without the calculated commercial cuteness that has softened everything he's done since "Jaws," undercutting the power of "The Color Purple" and "Empire of the Sun." In its place is a gritty, dark realism.

Neeson is good as Schindler, allowing us to see the indifference slowly turn to awareness, shock and then dedication. He never plays him as saint.

But the film is almost stolen by Kingsley, whose character is a composite of several Jews who worked for Schindler. Though his expression is always guarded, we can clearly read suspicion, fear, relief and, on rare occasions, delight. It's a terrific performance.

14. *Oskar Schindler (gesturing) at a party with local SS officials. At parties like this one, Schindler bribed the SS in order to receive vital information about imminent deportations. Krakow, Poland, April 28, 1942.*

15. *Amon Goeth, standing on a balcony overlooking the Plaszow concentration camp, ready to shoot a passing prisoner.*

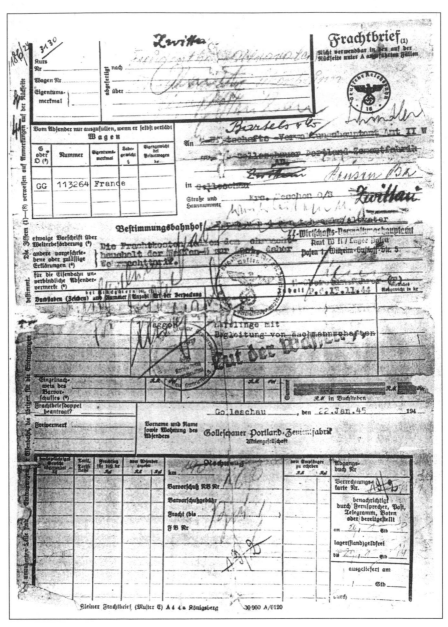

16. *Front and back of the* Deutsche Reichsbahn *(German Railroad System)* *waybill for the "Frozen Train" of death camp inmates rescued by Oskar and* *Emilie Schindler and the* Schindlerjuden. *Oskar Schindler gave a copy of the* *waybill to Herbert Steinhouse, probably in 1949.*

Stempel der Umlade- oder Zugwechselbahnhöfe

Schön...

2 L L -20--8583

erbero

2 L L - -8 -121 8

22.1. 3 - 1685

A Dieser Frachtbrief darf nicht verwendet werden bei Sendun... n mit Angabe des Lieferwerts oder mit einer Nachnahme, bei Sendungen, die einer Zoll- oder sonstigen verwaltungsbehör... chen Behandlung unterliegen, sowie bei Sendungen, bei denen der Absender dem Frachtbrief eine Anlage bei... ab... ... en der Raum für die Inhaltsangabe nicht ausreicht. In allen diesen Fällen darf nur der große Frachtbrief (Doppelblatt) benutzt werden.

B Anmerkungen

(1) Für den Frachtvertrag gelten die Eisenbahn-Verkehrsordnung und die in Betracht kommenden Tarife.
(2) Die Verwendung eines gedeckten Wagens ist mit „G", eines offenen Wagens mit „O" anzugeben.
(3) Eine Vorschrift über Weiterbeförderung kommt nur in Frage, wenn das Gut mit einem anderen Verkehrsmittel (z. B. Kraftwagen) weiterbefördert werden soll (z. B. „mit Kraftwagen weiter nach . . . .").
(4) Hier... einzutragen:
     Anerkenntnis über Fehlen oder Mängel der Verpackung, etwaige Vorschriften des Absenders, z. B. „bahnlagernd", „bahnamtlich verwiegen", „Entladestelle . . ." und andere vorgeschriebene oder zulässige Erklärungen.
(5) Auf diese Zeile oder auf das freie Feld der Rückseite können für die Eisenbahn unverbindliche kurze Vermerke, die die Sendung betreffen, nachträglich eingetragen werden, z. B. „Im Auftrag des RR", „zur Verfügung des RR".
(6) Auch bei Wagenladungen können die für Stückgüter vorgeschriebenen Angaben gemacht werden.
(7) Stückgüter sind mit den Anschriften des Absenders und Empfängers, Buchstaben (3-ichen) und Nummer, Tag der Ausgabe, Versand- und Bestimmungsbahnhof zu bezeichnen. Beklebezettel der Anhänger müssen den amtlichen Mustern entsprechen.
(8) Hier kann der Gesamtbetrag des Barvorschusses für den Empfänger im einzelnen berechnet werden. Verbindlich für die Eisenbahn ist nur die Eintragung im schraffierten Feld.

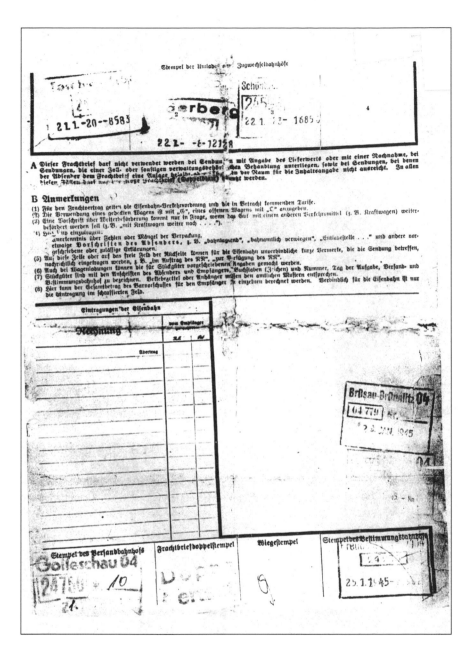

Eintragungen der Eisenbahn

Nachnung | vom Empfänger

Übertrag

Brüsau-Brünnlitz 04
04 779
2 3. JAN. 1945

Stempel des Versandbahnhofs | Frachtbriefdoppelstempel | Wiegestempel | Stempel des Bestimmungsbahnhofs

Goileschau 04 | | | 25.1.1945-

17. *Oskar Schindler (center, behind flowers) at a party with local Nazi officials.*

18. *Itzhak Stern (left) and Oskar Schindler at the first Schindlerjuden reunion, Paris, 1949. They had not seen each other since the end of the war in 1945.*

19. *Oskar Schindler in conversation in Herbert Steinhouse's office at the American Joint Distribution Committee, Paris, 1949, just after the first post-war party of the Schindlerjuden.*

20. *Schindler (second from right) at the first Schindlerjuden reunion, Paris, 1949. The others in the photo had been workers in his factory.*

21. *"Sto Lat! A hundred years may he live!" Early 1949. The Schindlerjuden in Paris hadn't seen Oskar Schindler in almost four years. According to Herbert Steinhouse, who witnessed the scene, Schindler was turning away because he was embarrassed by the accolades and was close to tears.*

22. *Oskar Schindler at the 1949 Paris Schindlerjuden reunion. The woman had been a nightclub dancer and ended up by accident in Schindler's factory, where she survived the war.*

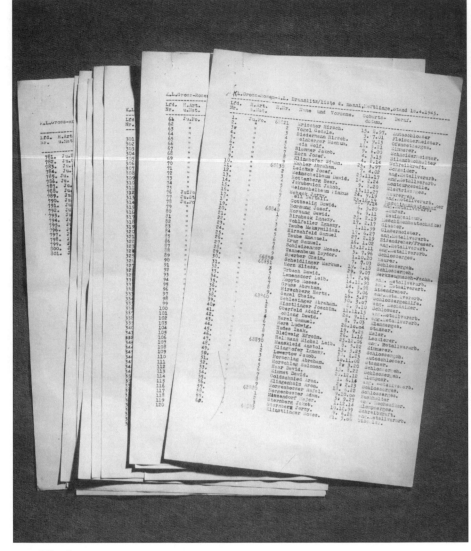

23. *The List.*

The Paradox of a Candle

by Scott Rosenberg
San Francisco Examiner, Dec. 15, 1993

The very first image to appear on the screen of "Schindler's List" is a hand lighting a candle. For a brief moment—the only one in Steven Spielberg's three-hour chronicle of the Holocaust—the picture is aglow with color. Then the screen, like the story it is about to record, fades to monochrome—sometimes murkily gray, sometimes marked by extreme contrasts of light and darkness.

It is a Shabbat candle, we eventually learn, lit by the hand of a rabbi in a most improbable place—a German-owned factory in Central Europe during the bleakest days of the Second World War. The epigraph to "Schindler's List" is a Talmudic saying—"Whoever saves one life saves the world entire"—reflecting upon the deed the film records: the unlikely, persistent and ultimately successful efforts of a Nazi businessman named Oskar Schindler to rescue his employees, 1,100 Jews, from the exterminating maelstrom that would swallow 6 million others.

Placing those two numbers side by side, it is perhaps more natural to despair than to be roused to action. The enormity of the disaster, and the relative modesty of Schindler's benefaction, gives immediate pause. The concept of a "good German"—someone who worked among atrocities with a sane human being's full awareness of their atrociousness—is fraught with paradox: How could one be content saving so few, knowing so many were doomed? How, on the other hand, could one not save as many as one could manage?

If you think of the opening of "Schindler's List" in that light, the candle brings to mind the famous eulogy Adlai Stevenson offered for Eleanor Roosevelt: "She would rather light a candle than curse the darkness." Somehow Schindler found it in himself to kindle a small light at a time when the darkness was everywhere and in a place where matches were few.

Light is precious in the nightmare world of "Schindler's List," which is mostly set in or near Krakow, in Nazi-occupied Poland. The film traces the gradual extinguishing of hope among this region's Jewish population—from the bureaucratic indignities of the first days of the occupation, to the establishment of a cramped ghetto, to the emptying of the ghetto into forced-labor camps, to the emptying of the work camps into the extermination centers.

Amid this general calamity, one small, specific group of Jews, separated from the flood of victims by provident chance, finds a savior. To their amazement, the Nazi who owns the pot and pan factory they work in keeps rescuing them from the death machine. As it gets more ruthless, he gets more determined.

Neither Spielberg's film—nor the Thomas Keneally book it's based on, a "novel" scrupulously based on historical fact—can explain why. Schindler starts off as an opportunistic war profiteer, a carpetbagging industrialist who sees a great future in free Jewish labor and does his best to befriend the politicians, bureaucrats and SS generals whose help he needs. Only gradually, as he gets to know his workers and becomes a witness to appalling crimes, does he begin thinking in terms of saving lives instead of making money.

There's no precise turning point, but both Keneally and Spielberg zero in on the 1943 liquidation of the Krakow ghetto as one transformative moment. The war is going well for Schindler (Liam Neeson), and he and his wife are out riding on the hills overlooking the crowded ghetto. From their perch they see the SS men's door-to-door, street-by-street hunt, punctuated by the rattle of suitcases dumped in courtyards and the point-blank firing of guns at defenseless people's heads. A little girl dressed in red catches Schindler's eye (Spielberg, in a poignant yet understated touch, makes her stand out from the crowd by tinting her palely in, as if water-colored by hand). He is later to notice her in the work-camp yard—and, still later, as a corpse in a wheelbarrow.

Somehow, unlike most of the Gentiles around him, Schindler comes to see the Jews as fellow human beings instead of a hated enemy, threatening "other" or a problem in need of a "final solution." Once that happens, inevitably, he stops using the Jews to pile up his fortune, and instead begins using his fortune to stockpile Jews in a safe refuge.

It's not easy, particularly after the ghetto is emptied and the Jewish workers are herded into Plaszow. This forced labor camp is presided over by a psychotic SS officer named Amon Goeth (Ralph Fiennes), who takes sharp aim at randomly chosen prisoners from the balcony of his "villa."

When the Russian Front collapses and the camp must be closed, Schindler arranges to move his factory, now making both mess-kits and munitions (duds only, he secretly ensures), to his hometown on the German-Czech border. With the help of his right-hand man, Jewish accountant Itzhak Stern (Ben Kingsley), he compiles a typed list of the more than a thousand "highly skilled workers" who must be separated from the doomed trainloads and rerouted to his new plant.

They're all vital to the war effort, he maintains. When a skeptical Nazi officer asks why he needs the children, he invents a lie: Only their hands are small enough to polish the insides of shells. In the film's climactic rescue, after a trainload of the women on his list is mistakenly sent to Auschwitz, he even manages to bribe the concentration-camp commandant and win their release.

"Schindler's List" is efficient and thorough in chronicling suffering—it's a true-to-life horror film sans special effects. The black-and-white photography and hand-held shots contribute to a documentary feel, and so does the avoidance of familiar faces in the casting. The film works hard to keep the "Schindlerjuden," Schindler's Jews, from being faceless victims, and though at times it risks coming off as an epic-length string of anecdotes, it largely succeeds in weaving its separate stories into a cogent whole.

Still, after so many exhaustive Holocaust films, "Schindler' List" would probably be unwatchable—a rehash of overfamiliar torments—if it weren't for the film's fascinating delineation of the character of Schindler himself. "Oskar," Keneally writes, "had the characteristic salesman's gift of treating men he abhorred as if they were spiritual brothers." Neeson's calculated, mesmerizing performance vividly captures that gift.

Schindler can never be mistaken for a saint, and "Schindler's List," thankfully, makes little effort to canonize him. With one eye on his co-gnac and another on his women (there seems to be a different beautiful mistress beside him in every other scene), he's too much the high-living tycoon for any Nazi to suspect his "Jew-loving" until it's too late.

In both the bonhomie he showers on the Germans—particularly the monstrous Goeth—and the slow-to-erode reserve with which he meets the Jews, Neeson slowly lets you in on Schindler's complicated game. Then—in amazing scenes like the one in which he literally gambles for the life of a pretty Jewish housemaid (Embeth Davidtz) who has had the bad luck to attract Goeth's attentions—he shows you just how much of the game is an improvised bluff.

There is no pat explanation for why the war, which brought forth so much evil from so many, evoked the good in Schindler. To his credit, Spielberg does not try to offer any. Schindler's story, at any rate, has brought out the good in the director, who has so habitually mistaken sentimentality for emotion that a Holocaust film seemed well outside his range. One feared a Spielberg-directed "Schindler" would be like a cello sonata played on a calliope.

The issue was not that Spielberg might somehow bring his warm-glow-of-childhood approach to this material; no one—certainly not an intelligent, skilled entertainer—would make the mistake of trying to view Auschwitz through the candied glaze that marred the most significant previous "adult" movie by Spielberg, "The Color Purple." But you couldn't help wondering whether years of making dazzling cartoons might have left the director incapable of taking the kind of self-denying approach this subject demands.

"Schindler's List"—a thoughtful, rigorous and thereby moving piece of work—puts such questions to rest. Spielberg's greatest feat here is to resist the urge to imprint his own sensibility on the film, and instead to give the ordeals it depicts the aesthetic and emotional space they require. (Only in the final scenes do traces of Spielberg treacle leak in, but by then it's too late to wreck the film's achievement.)

We can leave the director's rediscovery of his Judaism, which surely ought to be his own private affair, to the gossip columns. What's far more important is his rediscovery, after these long years since "E.T.," of the human core of his talent.

"Schindler's List" Follows a Man's Trek to Heroism

Spielberg Masters Subtlety in Film

by Roger Ebert
The Chicago Sun-Times, Dec. 15, 1993

Oskar Schindler would have been an easier man to understand if he'd been a conventional hero, fighting for his beliefs. The fact that he was flawed—a drinker, a gambler, a womanizer, driven by greed and a lust for high living—makes his life an enigma.

Here is a man who saw his chance at the beginning of World War II and moved to Nazi-occupied Poland to open a factory and employ Jews at starvation wages. His goal was to become a millionaire. By the end of the war, he had risked his life and spent his fortune to save those Jews and had defrauded the Nazis for months with a munitions factory that never produced a single usable shell.

Why did he change? What happened to turn him from a victimizer into a humanitarian? It is to the great credit of Steven Spielberg that his film "Schindler's List" does not even attempt to answer that question. Any possible answer would be too simple, an insult to the mystery of Schindler's life. The Holocaust was a vast evil engine set whirling by racism and madness. Schindler outsmarted it, in his own little corner of the war, but he seems to have had no plan, to have improvised out of impulses that remained unclear even to himself. In this movie, the best he has ever made, Spielberg treats the fact of the Holocaust and the miracle of Schindler's feat without the easy formulas of fiction.

The movie is 184 minutes long, and like all great movies, it seems too short. It begins with Schindler (Liam Neeson), a tall, strong man with an intimidating physical presence. He dresses expensively and frequents nightclubs, buying caviar and champagne for Nazi officers and their girls, and he likes to get his picture taken with the top brass. He wears a Nazi party emblem proudly in his buttonhole. He has impeccable black market contacts, and he's able to find nylons, cigarettes, brandy: He is the right man to know. The authorities are happy to help him open a factory to build enameled cooking utensils that army kitchens can use. He is happy to hire Jews because their wages are lower, and Schindler will get richer that way.

Schindler's genius is in bribing, scheming, conning. He knows nothing about running a factory and finds Itzhak Stern (Ben Kingsley), a Jewish accountant, to handle that side of things. Stern moves through the streets of Krakow, hiring Jews for Schindler. Because the factory is a protected war industry, a job there may guarantee longer life.

The relationship between Schindler and Stern is developed by Spielberg with enormous subtlety. At the beginning of the war, Schindler wants only to make money, and at the end he wants only to save "his" Jews. We know that Stern understands this. But there is no moment when Schindler and Stern bluntly state what is happening, perhaps because to say certain things aloud could result in death.

This subtlety is Spielberg's strength all through the film. His screenplay, by Steven Zaillian, based on the novel by Keneally, isn't based on contrived melodrama. Instead, Spielberg relies on a series of incidents, seen clearly and without artificial manipulation, and by witnessing those incidents we understand what little can be known about Schindler and his scheme.

We also see the Holocaust in a vivid and terrible way. Spielberg gives us a Nazi prison camp commandant named Goeth (Ralph Fiennes) who is a study in the stupidity of evil. From the verandah of his "villa," overlooking the prison yard, he shoots Jews for target practice. (Schindler is able to talk him out of this custom with an appeal to his vanity so obvious it is almost an insult.) Goeth is one of those weak hypocrites who upholds an ideal but makes himself an exception to it; he preaches the death of the Jews, and then chooses a pretty one named Helen Hirsch (Embeth Davidtz) to be his maid and falls in love with her. He does not find it monstrous that her people are becoming exterminated, and she is spared on his affectionate whim. He sees his personal needs as more important than right or wrong, life or death. Studying him, we realize that Nazism depended on people able to think like Jeffrey Dahmer.

Shooting in black and white on many of the actual locations of the events in the story (including Schindler's original factory and even the gates of Auschwitz), Spielberg shows Schindler dealing with the madness of the Nazi system. He bribes, he wheedles, he bluffs, he escapes discovery by the skin of his teeth. In the movie's most audacious sequence, when a trainload of his employees is mistakenly routed to Auschwitz, he walks into the death camp himself and brazenly talks the authorities out of their victims, snatching them from death and putting them back on the train.

What is most amazing about this film is how completely Spielberg serves his story. The movie is brilliantly acted, written, directed and seen. Individual scenes are masterpieces of art direction, cinematography, special effects, crowd control. Yet Spielberg, the stylist whose films often have gloried in shots we are intended to notice and remember, disappears into his work. Neeson, Kingsley and the other actors are devoid of acting flourishes. There is a single-mindedness to the enterprise that is awesome.

At the end of the film, there is a sequence of overwhelming emotional impact, involving the actual people who were saved. We learn that "Schindler's Jews" and their descendants today number about 6,000 and that the Jewish population of Poland is 4,000. The lesson would seem to be that Schindler did more than a whole nation to spare its Jews. That would be too simple. The film's message is that one man did *something*, while in the face of the Holocaust others were paralyzed. Perhaps it took a Schindler, enigmatic and reckless, without a plan, heedless of risk, a con man, to do what he did. No rational man with a sensible plan would have gotten as far.

The French author Flaubert once wrote that he disliked *Uncle Tom's Cabin* because the author was constantly preaching against slavery. "Does one have to make observations about slavery?" he asked. "Depict it; that's enough." And then he added, "An author in his book must be like God in the universe, present everywhere and visible nowhere." That would describe Spielberg, the author of this film. He depicts the evil of the Holocaust, and he tells an incredible story of how it was robbed of some of its intended victims. He does so without the tricks of his trade, the directorial and dramatic contrivances that would inspire the usual melodramatic payoffs. Spielberg is not visible in this film. But his restraint and passion are present in every shot.

Spielberg Triumphs with His Forceful Epic of the Holocaust's Unlikely Hero

by Susan Stark
The Detroit News, Dec. 25, 1993

Once in a very great while, a movie insinuates itself so deeply into your consciousness that it offers not vicarious experience but instead, direct experience. Steven Spielberg's heartfelt, monumental *Schindler's List* is such a movie.

An epic of the Holocaust, a three-hour drama crammed with emotionally telegraphic detail taken from life, this is the picture that marks Spielberg's coming of age as an artist. His film version of Thomas Keneally's *Schindler's List* takes as intimate and confrontational a look at the Nazi beast as any document in the vast literature of the Holocaust.

Oskar Schindler, played mostly from the eyes by Liam Neeson, was a stylish but unsettled German businessman who came to Cracow just after Hitler's forces mowed down the Poles. Schindler saw that there was big money to be made from the war effort and promptly launched himself as a profiteer in pots and pans.

He persuaded the few Jews in the city who still had money to finance his business. The many Jews in the city thrown out of work, including dozens of highly educated professionals, became his die makers, machinists, metal polishers. A Jewish accountant, played as a model of controlled desperation by Ben Kingsley, ran the business and tracked the elaborate scheme of payoffs and kickbacks that sustained it.

And Schindler? He contributed what he himself defines in the film as "panache"; in a happier time and place, he'd have been a PR guy in a shantung suit.

What makes Schindler's story compelling and hauntingly ironic is that by trying to do well, he wound up doing good.

Between 1939 and 1945, this bounder, this hedonist, this ambulatory study in aimlessness and mediocrity slipped into heroism. As the Third Reich's unrelenting Nazi campaign against the Jews moved from vicious to bestial, Schindler found ways to protect his Jewish workers by hoodwinking and paying Amon Goeth (say Gert), the SS boss at the notorious Plaszow work camp near Cracow.

With dead eyes and a nasal, droning voice, newcomer Ralph Fiennes (say Fines) makes the handsome, sadistic, terrifying mercurial Goeth a mesmerizing figure. He hand-picks a tremulous wisp of a young Jewish woman named Helen Hirsch, heart-breakingly well played by Embeth Davidtz, to be his house maid. Like Helen, you quickly learn to dread the very sight of Amon Goeth.

Yet your eyes stay glued to Fiennes every time he shows up on camera. The performance is plain hypnotic; it amounts to a brutally precise account of a manic-depressive disaster waiting to happen.

Eventually, more than 1,000 Jews escaped death at Goeth's hand (or order) by living and working in Schindler's factory. Those who had their name on Schindler's list were thought to be engaged in what the Nazis considered "essential work"; theoretically, that meant work for the war effort. In the case of Schindler's pots and pans factory, the "essential work" ruse reached farcical proportions by 1942, but Schindler's skill at maintaining it grew in proportion to the Nazi threat.

Oskar Schindler certainly didn't set out to be a hero, nor was heroism thrust upon him. Yet somehow, gradually, he was transformed from profiteer to protector by the unimaginably hideous and dehumanizing spectacle around him. Like the book, the film allows Schindler's transformation a real measure of mystery.

You'll see moments of recognition in Schindler's eyes, moments that suggest an altruistic twinge or a quiver of conscience, but there's no being struck down by a blinding light in this story. That, finally, is what makes it both unusually accessible and unusually compelling. Oskar Schindler wasn't anywhere near larger than life. Indeed, he falls in on the puny side of life. Yet he fulfilled the Talmudic precept more than 1,000 times over: Who saves one life, saves the world entire.

Spielberg's approach, and that of the dynamic, purposeful script furnished by Steven Zaillian, is almost exclusively anecdotal. The result is a film with momentum to match its lucidity. It expeditiously sets the scene, introduces the primary characters, and tracks their shared drama in evocative detail as things go from cruel to worse.

Without exception, Spielberg moves directly to the heart of the matter. *Schindler's List* is a mercilessly and, finally, sublimely confrontational film. That's new for Spielberg. That's also an imperative in telling a story like this one. It's either unsparing or worthless. Spielberg goes for unsparing.

When a new contingent of Jewish men, women and children arrive at Plaszow, the camera takes in the entire camp yard. At gun point, the Jews are ordered to strip and to run around naked in front of the camp bosses who, at a glance, decide which new arrivals are fit to work and which are not. Then Spielberg pulls the camera closer, humanizing one prisoner after another in excruciatingly precise terms: hollowed buttocks, stooped back, withered breasts, terrified eyes, stringy hands.

The most brilliant example of his unsparing approach occurs much earlier in the film. A Nazi goon gets orders to shoot an elderly, one-armed Jewish man, apparently for shoveling snow too slowly. The camera moves from a long shot of the street scene to within inches of the dead man's head as his life's blood stains the snow.

That anecdote speaks poignantly about the entire film and on two fronts.

First, it orients you to the Nazi mentality by bringing you to understand that the old man wasn't shot for his slowness; he was shot for the good Nazi sport of it, the fun of it.

Second, it demonstrates that Spielberg's handling of black and white is every bit the match of the greats who worked before the appearance of color film. That old man's blood on the snow is red as red can be, even though this is a black and white film. The magic is all in the lighting and the careful screening for both color and texture of the materials being photographed.

Spielberg moves to full color for the coda, a contemporary gathering at Schindler's grave of the surviving *Schindlerjuden* (Schindler's Jews, as they came to call themselves) and the actors who play them. Spielberg also begins with color, albeit spare, for the lighting of the Sabbath candles behind the opening titles.

During the course of the film, he very judiciously tints portions of a handful of images, to stupendous emotional effect in the case of a red coat on a little girl who appears in two separate crowd scenes. Yet finally, this is a film in fastidiously evaluated black and white and it is gravely, hauntingly impressive at that.

When the measure of Spielberg's work to date is taken, three pictures will be cited as essential.

First, *Jaws*, which established his prodigious gift as a shot maker. Second, *E.T.,* the playful but exquisitely imagined and realized work of a visionary. Third, *Schindler's List*, an urgent call to memory that completes the maturation process launched with *The Color Purple*.

Understand this about Steven Spielberg: He might have spent a lifetime reworking fanciful themes like those of *E.T.* and *Jurassic Park* and counted himself professionally blessed like no film maker before or since.

Instead, at midcareer, he chose to tackle Alice Walker's *The Color Purple*, a novel loaded with political, racial and sexual land mines, and to make exactly the film he wanted to make from that book. Now, he steps up to the daunting challenge of Keneally's *Schindler's List*, a novel from life filled with comparable perils for a film maker.

Without question, it will come to be seen as a feature film companion piece to *Shoah*, Claude Lanzmann's landmark documentary of the Holocaust. The two pieces share a passion for precise detail and, most importantly, a profound moral gravity.

As movie, as memory, as experience, Spielberg's *Schindler's List* stands as the most rare and valuable kind of opportunity. Seize it.

Extras in the Shadows

······························

by Frank Rich
The New York Times, Jan. 2, 1994

Negative words about "Schindler's List," Steven Spielberg's Holocaust movie, are verboten in polite company. Everyone from President Clinton to the nation's movie critics has called it a masterpiece, with some enthusiasts pointedly reassuring readers that, at 3 hours 5 minutes, the film is not a moment too long. "Schindler's List" is the culture's new Messiah: the antidote to the terrifying 1993 Roper Organization poll in which 22 percent of the American public expressed doubt that the Nazi extermination of the Jews actually happened.

So why, I asked myself, did this particular American Jew find "Schindler's List" more often numbing than moving? And why am I skeptical that Holocaust ignoramuses will even see it, let alone be swayed by it?

The problem is not that Mr. Spielberg, a giant talent, has made an inept, insincere or vulgar film. "Schindler's List" is not "The Color Yellow." Its only fabulously cheesy scene is a finale in which the righteous German war profiteer Oskar Schindler (played by Liam Neeson) gives a sentimental speech to the Jewish factory workers he saved, and they look up at him awestruck, as if he were the levitating mother ship in "Close Encounters of the Third Kind." Other sequences are stunning, especially the horrific passages of hand-held, pseudo-documentary camera work that depict the liquidation of the Cracow ghetto and the gas chambers at Auschwitz.

What's missing from 'Schindler's List'

••••••••••••••••••••••

But if such atrocities are made exceptionally vivid by the director's cinematic brilliance, their emotional power is muted by the anonymity of the film's Jews. Mr. Spielberg has found hundreds of evocative faces to populate his simulated Holocaust, but their souls are skin-deep. The only major Jewish character in the script, Schindler's accountant (Ben Kingsley), is a type—"king of the Jewish wimps," as one of the movie's few tough critics, Ilene Rosenzweig of the Jewish newspaper The Forward has put it. The others, who have the generic feel of composites, are as forgettable as the chorus in a touring company of "Fiddler on the Roof," or, for that matter, the human dino-fodder of "Jurassic Park." They blur into abstraction, becoming another depersonalized statistic of mass death. Since Schindler is also presented as a psychological blank, no wonder the unhinged Nazi commandant (Ralph Fiennes) runs away with the movie.

I cried at Mr. Spielberg's graphic depiction of genocide anyway. Weaker Holocaust dramatizations than this one have pushed my buttons. Like anyone who is Jewish, knows Jews or simply knows history, I can automatically flesh out the human ciphers in "Schindler's List" with characters and associations of my own. This may be the case for much of the large and, I imagine, heavily Jewish audiences who have made the movie a hit so far, in major American cities where remedial education about the Holocaust is less needed than any place this side of Israel.

But what happens when "Schindler's List" is released in the great American malls, not to mention other countries, where Jews are sparse? Will teenagers check it out? Will audiences who have never heard of "Shoah" or "Europa, Europa?" They might do so more readily if Mr. Spielberg's movie were not self-indulgently overlong—by a good hour. (This same syndrome afflicted Spike Lee's "Malcolm X," which ended up preaching mainly to the converted.) The film might also more effectively draw indifferent audiences into its historical nightmare if the Jews on screen were as individual and intimately dramatized as Anne Frank or even Meryl Streep's Sophie.

What is most worrisome about the wild overpraise of "Schindler's List" is the complacency it invites. The hype is already taking on a life of its own, wrapping the movie and the Holocaust in a neat, uplifting Hollywood ending that allows everyone to sleep easier. As this comforting litany has it, some 1,100 Jews on Schindler's list did survive, after all; the Nazi sadist did get his just deserts; Schindler's heroic example may inspire others to resist future Nazis; a hit movie will eternally preserve the Holocaust in the world's memory.

And there's a happy ending for Mr. Spielberg, too: Having come of age as a Jew, he may get a prize greater than a fountain pen—the Oscar he has so long and unjustly been denied.

"Schindler's List" is good news for everyone, it seems, except its shad owy and often nameless extras, the six million dead.

Spielberg Finds a New Light in the Darkness

······················

by Michael H. Price
Fort Worth Star-Telegram, Jan. 7, 1994

Hollywood, a kingdom established by immigrant Jewry as a refuge from an intolerant society, dealt so tentatively and cartoonishly with the Nazi menace in its 1940s heyday that even many red-blooded gung-ho American civilians came to wonder how real the threat could be. Here was a world problem that was nothing to laugh at, and here was an American film industry responding with ridicule at best.

The Holocaust, in which Hitler's Third Reich methodically slaughtered Jews and other misfits in a deliberate attempt at genocide, scarcely has been mentioned in popular cinema until recent years. Claude Lanzmann's epic documentary film "Shoah" (1985) opened many avenues, and it probably would not have come into being if not for the trail-blazing influence of Art Spiegelman's magnificent and eccentric book on one family's Holocaust legacy, "Maus," which was begun during the 1970s and continues to generate chapters.

But "Maus" is unfilmable (so Spiegelman himself insists), and "Shoah" is a nine-hour investment of grueling emotional concentration. After these essential studies of the Holocaust, the essential such film proves now to be Steven Spielberg's "Schindler's List," a formidable drama from an unlikely source.

It is a brilliant film, the first screen drama in which the Holocaust emerges as a sweeping force comparable with the way in which "Gone With the Wind" (1939) portrays the Civil War or John Ford's magnificent "The Hurricane" (1937) portrays the tempest of the title.

German industrialist/playboy Oskar Schindler (played by Liam Neeson in a job that must land an Academy Award) is of lesser importance, as is his list, that roster of marked-for-death Jews whom Schindler conspires to save from the Reich's death camps. All move before the Holocaust, their lives shaped by a campaign of evil that grows beyond the control of any one human mastermind.

It was Schindler's conceit that he could overrule the Holocaust by subterfuge, and indeed he tempered its vile sting more than somewhat. Neeson plays the fellow less as a savior than as a gambler, one whose unlikely heroism is an outgrowth more of daring than of any humanitarian spirit.

Spielberg, working from the 1982 book by Thomas Keneally and a screenplay by Steven Zaillian, packs an overwhelming lot of story into the 195 minutes' running time (which seems briefer) and keeps things at a devoutly intimate level. The master of impersonal narrative, whose "Jurassic Park" feels distant even when its dinosaurs are in your face, Spielberg takes so achingly personal a tack here that his work seems almost the accomplishment of someone else.

But no—there are enough "Spielbergian" set pieces and incidental touches (the bursts of beauty amidst squalor, the gimmicky color sequences in an otherwise black-and-white film, the most melodic scenic compositions and camera movements) to keep Schindler accessible to those who believe that the best Spielberg is the perky Spielberg of the "E.T." and "Indiana Jones" romps.

Neeson is hardly the only dramatic presence here, but he is the spine of a cast that also includes Ben Kingsley, as a co-conspirator; Ralph Fiennes, as an example of pestilence incarnate; and "Army of Darkness" leading lady Embeth Davidtz, as a captive whose fate is kept naggingly in suspense.

The random danger of this crooked piece of time is what the film most memorably portrays, however—its utter absence of safety emphasized by the stark cinematography.

Redemption Amid Tragedy

"Schindler's List" Tells of a Saving Decency in Hitler's Mad World

by Frank Gabrenya
The Columbus, Ohio, *Dispatch*, Jan. 14, 1994

All the praise you have heard for *Schindler's List* is justified.

Steven Spielberg's magnificent film about a German who saved 1,200 Polish Jews from the Nazi gas chambers is starkly realistic and deeply tragic. Yet it ultimately is redemptive in a muted way that leaves viewers drained but reassured that mankind isn't entirely mad.

For much of the three-hour film, that redemption seems impossible. Spielberg re-creates the nightmare of the Nazi occupation of Krakow after the fall of Poland in 1939, the liquidation of the Jewish ghetto, the agonies of the work camp of Plaszow and the hideous approach of Hitler's "final solution" in the ovens of Auschwitz.

Told against this grim background is the true story of Oskar Schindler, an Austrian-born German entrepreneur who went to Krakow to exploit cheap Jewish labor and make his fortune. During the next five years, what he witnessed slowly turned Schindler from selfish profiteer to selfless savior of people branded for extermination.

Spielberg has managed to project his childlike spirit onto one of the darkest chapters of history without cheapening the tragedy. In both form and content, his film is the work of a master director reaching maturity.

Visually, *Schindler's List* imitates the murky documentaries that witnessed the horror of World War II, even using non-shaded titles that sometimes vanish against white backgrounds. Shot in subdued black and white amid the mud and slush where it happened, Spielberg's movie looks and feels frighteningly real.

Spielberg has said that he prepared for the film by throwing out most of his standard toys, such as cranes and dollies, and depending on hand-held cameras. Even more important, he has avoided the hyper-editing that suited *Raiders of the Lost Ark* but torpedoed more serious efforts, such as *Empire of the Sun*.

As splendidly photographed as the movie is, every shot seems composed to deliver information, not to show off. Without the artifacts of melodrama, the many executions seem more savage and arbitrary. Even a small blotch of color—the red coat of a young Jewish girl running from SS troops—is more symbol than novelty.

Without compelling characters, *Schindler's List* might be just another empty triumph of style (see *Jurassic Park*). But the core of the film is a classic tug of war for the soul of an uncommitted man.

When Schindler arrives in Krakow and sets up his enamel factory to turn out field mess kits for the German army, he is what he claims to be: a shameless profiteer exploiting the political situation. Although Thomas Keneally's docu-novel, on which the movie is based, speculates that Schindler already was sickened by Nazi methods when he reached Poland, the Schindler of the movie is an apolitical opportunist who seems devoid of sympathies.

Played as an imposing presence by Liam Neeson, Schindler is a master flatterer who knows how to bribe the Nazi lowerarchy of petty officials. He is a hedonist and womanizer whose most formidable skill is holding his liquor.

Schindler's conscience is pulled in opposite directions by Itzhak Stern, the Jewish accountant who runs his factory, and by Amon Goeth, the brutal Nazi commandant who spreads terror in Plaszow.

Stern, played with subtle cunning by Ben Kingsley, orchestrates the safe haven of the factory without Schindler's knowledge, converting scholars and artists into workers with "essential" skills. He senses the goodness in Schindler but must proceed cautiously. How far could a Polish Jew trust any German?

Goeth, brilliantly brought to sadistic life by British actor Ralph Fiennes (pronounced Rafe Fines), is a bleary-eyed thug who specializes in casual brutality. For pre-breakfast sport each day, he shoots idle workers from the balcony of his bedroom with a high-powered rifle.

Goeth is more terrifying than all the Darth Vaders or merciless Mings of movie lore. Compounding his instability is his dark attraction for Helen Hirsch (Embeth Davidtz), the Jewish woman he keeps as cook, maid and object of abuse.

Steven Zaillian's perceptive script suggests that Schindler, who is Goeth's drinking buddy as part of Schindler's bribery system, might absorb some of Goeth's evil but for the gentle tugging of Stern.

Schindler's transformation is eventual and believable; in no scene does a light bulb suddenly come on above his conscience. At first, he tries to convince Goeth that the random killings are bad for business. As the war winds down, and the Nazis increase the operation of the ovens, he takes action to save his Jews, known to this day as the *Schindlerjuden.*

The film is full of unforgettable scenes: the liquidation of the ghetto and the return visit by the Nazis at night to smoke out Jews still hiding in the walls; the frenzied attempts of women to prick their fingers and smear blood on their cheeks to appear healthier when the sick are being sent off to the gas chambers; the moment of stark terror when a train full of Schindler women, misrouted through a clerical error, pulls into Auschwitz in the middle of a snow-driven night.

The acting is superb, the pacing excellent; and even John Williams' conventional score, highlighted by Itzhak Perlman's solo violin, doesn't detract from the central drama.

When news arrives that the war is over, no one in the film or the audience cheers. A few have been saved, but too many have died. Still, in the genocidal world of *Schindler's List,* a few constitute a miracle.

Spielberg's grim epic is an experience that will haunt for weeks, possibly forever.

Part Four

The Holocaust —
Issues, Implications

After the Survivors

....

by Jonathan Alter
Newsweek, Dec. 20, 1993

"Who, after all, speaks today of the annihilation of the Armenians?"
Adolf Hitler is said to have asked in 1939, referring to the more than 1
million Armenians slaughtered by Ottoman Turks as World War I began.
Hitler was then already planning his own crime. But in betting that the
world would also forget his extermination of European Jewry, the führer
himself forgot something he once understood—the importance of the
century's greatest new medium: moving pictures. The man who grasped the
power of Leni Riefenstahl's "Triumph of the Will" should have anticipated
that another gifted filmmaker might some day immortalize his deed on
celluloid.

Now, just as the eyewitnesses have begun to die off, that day has come.
Steven Spielberg's masterpiece is more than just another serious film that
will win a bunch of Academy Awards. "Schindler's List" inserts the audience
squarely inside the crime of the century, and by doing so, it enlarges the
potential of the medium itself—to teach as well as entertain, to evoke history as much as fantasy, to prepare us for our own context of violence.

Mail bombs sent by neo-Nazis last week blew off the fingers of the
mayor of Vienna. "Ethnic cleansing" continues in Bosnia. A Hollywood
movie—even one that the president of the United States "implores" the
public to see—can't stop that. But the reach of film today is greater than

Joseph Goebbels could have possibly dreamed. Across the world, movie-goers believe Oliver Stone's myths about the Kennedy assassination. If there's any justice, these same millions will now believe Spielberg's truths about the concentration camps. The message of "Schindler's List" comes from the Talmud: *Whoever saves one life, saves the world entire.* All it takes is one. In the darkness of the theater, in East Timor or Croatia or Burundi, may sit just one Oskar Schindler, waiting to be reborn.

This is the connection between Spielberg, Schindler and Leopold Page (Pfefferberg in his earlier life), the survivor most responsible for bringing the story to life. Page owned a luggage shop in Beverly Hills and for 30 years he told the story of Schindler to any writer or movie type who walked into his store. Finally, in 1980, Australian novelist Thomas Keneally was waiting for his credit card to clear and heard Page's tale. He listened, and his extensively researched novel became the basis of the film. "A human being—a single person—can change the world. That's what I've been trying to do since 1945 when I promised Schindler I would tell everyone about his story," Page says. Schindler Changed Page who changed Keneally who changed Spielberg who changed ... who?

During screenings, the movie frequently sparked comparisons to "Gone With the Wind," though it lacks any romance. There are technical reasons for its timelessness: it's a period piece, shot in black and white, and stylized like a 1930s classic. But the larger accomplishment is that Spielberg has brought history and film into rough but proper alignment. For years, memories of the Civil War were passed down from grandpa to the rest of the family. Then grandpa finally died, and "Gone With the Wind" took up the Homeric burden of passing the epic along. The same will soon be true for the Holocaust and "Schindler's List." When literal memory ends, cultural memory can begin.

Some people believe too much has been made of the Holocaust. They haven't seen the latest polls. In a survey of Americans, The Roper Organization found last spring that some 22 percent of respondents said it seemed "possible" that "the Nazi extermination of the Jews never happened." Another 12 percent said they didn't know. (The numbers in a similar poll were much more encouraging in Great Britain.) The explanation isn't so much anti-Semitism as ignorance. More than 50 percent of high-school students didn't know what the word "Holocaust" means. A quarter of all adults didn't even know that it was in Germany that the Nazis first came to power.

They must have missed those "Hogan's Heroes" reruns.

Of course the same ignorance applies to much of American history, and nobody seems worried that, say, the survivors of Pearl Harbor are dying. But there aren't "scholars" popping up to deny that Pearl Harbor was bombed. Without new testaments every generation, the hate virus grows stronger and attaches itself more firmly to despised peoples everywhere. As the eyewitnesses to this and the century's other genocides pass on, the gap must be filled in the only way possible—by art with the power to transform.

Hollywood isn't often about art, and the commercialism embodied by Spielberg would seem a peculiar mix with the sanctuaries of history. Indeed, the World Jewish Congress would not allow Spielberg to film at Auschwitz, explaining that it was sacred ground, a graveyard. He was restricted to an area outside the gates. Little did those Jewish leaders know that the director was building his own memorial, which will last as long as any bricks and mortar. That's why the presence of Spielberg and his actors inside the Washington, D.C., Holocaust Memorial Museum seemed strangely fitting last month. A ceremony honoring Schindler pointed up how much the museum and the movie have in common. With their eye for human detail, they each transfix, overwhelm, linger. Most of all, they universalize, by conveying how easily the world slipped into madness. Yesterday, the Jews. Tomorrow, anyone. The Holocaust Museum, open only since April [1993], is so much more popular than expected that it is turning away visitors on weekends, and more than 60 percent of the nearly 1 million who have already made the tour are non-Jews.

'How is one to tell a tale that cannot be — but must be — told?' Elie Wiesel has written

This bodes well for "Schindler's List." The film is much more proudly Jewish than other Holocaust movies, but it is built around the story of a German Christian. That broadens access to the story and sharpens the central moral question: What would you have done? One of the great ironies of postwar American cinema is that such an idea, so potentially rich in artistic inspiration, has been extraordinarily difficult to evoke in film. The evil is so immense—and thus so prone to trivialization—that the normal approach has been to back off from confronting it directly.

"How is one to tell a tale that cannot be—but must be—told? I don't know." Elie Wiesel has written. Wiesel, Primo Levi and other survivors bear witness on paper, but filmmakers have usually either chipped off tangential pieces of the story or worked as documentarians. For all the hundreds of movies employing World War II themes, the strange truth is that until now no major feature film has unflinchingly faced the horror of the Holocaust itself.

"The Pawnbroker" and "Sophie's Choice" beautifully mined the displaced sorrow of survivors in the years after the war, as did "Enemies, A Love Story." "The Diary of Anne Frank" and the TV movie "Playing for Time" focused on the character of one woman doomed by history. "The Night Porter" nihilistically exploited the story for its sadism. All were disturbing but lacked the direct descent to hell depicted by Spielberg. They also lacked the redemptive uplift of Liam Neeson's protagonist. Somehow, "Schindler's List" manages to be simultaneously more overpowering and less depressing than anything on this subject attempted by Hollywood before.

Among documentaries, Alain Resnais's "Night and Fog," Claude Lanzmann's "Shoah" and Marcel Ophuls's "The Sorrow and the Pity," "The Memory of Justice" and "Hotel Terminus" all brilliantly used either archival footage or, more effectively, personal memories. The directors served as heroic historians, preserving scores of firsthand accounts while the witnesses were still alive. Yet as movie experiences, they can feel numbing and forbidding, certainly for mass audiences. To someone who hasn't seen it, "Schindler's List" sounds as if it's in the same category. It certainly seems like a movie made by a European auteur ("It is impossible that these are the same blokes who made 'E.T.'," says Keneally). But it compels in its own, entirely fresh way.

The only other frontal approach outside the art houses came in 1978 when NBC aired the miniseries "Holocaust.' This served an extremely valuable educational function for the historically ignorant, especially when it was shown in Germany. But the plight of the Jews came off mostly as just another sentimentalized disease-of-the-week show, torqued up for sweeps. The series managed to diminish the horror even as it melodramatized it. Only "The Killing Fields," which was about the destruction of Cambodians, not Jews, approaches "Schindler's List" in authentically conveying the texture of genocide.

One of the ways that Spielberg negotiates the dangers inherent in the material is to meld old-fashioned storytelling with the documentary style. But he manages this without seeming deceptive or cheap, perhaps because he never intercuts archival film, as Oliver Stone does. At the very end, when the actual, now elderly Schindler's Jews gather at his grave in Israel, the "true" story intrudes, but this is mostly just to remind us that Oskar Schindler is not Indiana Jones but someone who lived.

Because he's painting with reality, Spielberg resists personalizing the Jewish victims too much. He's been criticized, wrongly, for this. The horror is actually more authentic for its impersonal nature. If characters we knew well were killed, the murders would be most heart-wrenching, perhaps—but less palpably real. An even greater challenge was to rip the Nazis free of their clichés. This is accomplished by emphasizing officious bureaucrats who are the embodiment of Hannah Arendt's "banality of evil"— and by Ralph Fiennes's warped commandant, Amon Goeth. His depravity in the film is no exaggeration. "I knew Goeth," says Anna Duklauer Perl, a survivor with no connection to the book or movie. "One day he hung a friend of mine just because he had once been rich. He was the devil."

Plenty of Amon Goeths live on today—in Bosnia, among other places. Spielberg says he made the film in part for that reason. But invoking the Holocaust in modern-day policy discussions has always been perilous. Does it minimize the particularity of the war against the Jews? Does it superimpose differing circumstances on top of each other? Or is it that deepest of moral questions circling back toward us again?

Shortly after he saw the film, I asked President Clinton whether it made him rethink his Bosnia policy. After condemning the "crazy" and "terrible" ethnic hatreds in the region, he answered; "I really think it's different. I don't think you can make a case that it is the same thing and to the same degree that drove us into World War II." (Actually, it was Pearl Harbor, not violence against civilians, that drew us into the war.) "On the other hand," the president continued, "the most troubling thing to me about 'Schindler's List' was being reminded that we turned away boatloads of Jews.... And so, we are now engaged in the longest humanitarian airlift in American history in Bosnia. We have, I think, helped to forestall anything worse happening in Sarajevo. [The film] didn't make me think we should have put huge numbers of soldiers on the ground to try to stop them. It did make me think we cannot afford to be totally disengaged."

The president cannot move more aggressively in Bosnia because, quite simply, the American people do not want him to. Changing that view—if indeed, it should be changed—is mostly a matter of his political leadership. But it is also in the realm of art and memory. Shortly before he committed suicide, Primo Levi wrote:

"For us [the survivors] to speak with the young becomes ever more difficult. We see it as a duty and, at the same time, as a risk: the risk of appearing anachronistic, of not being listened to. We must be listened to: above and beyond our personal experiences, we have collectively witnessed a fundamental, unexpected event.... It took place in the teeth of all forecasts; it happened in Europe; incredibly, it happened that an entire civilized people ... followed a buffoon whose figure today inspires laughter, and yet Adolf Hitler was obeyed and his praises were sung right up to the catastrophe. It happened, therefore it can happen again: this is the core of what we have to say."

That is the core of what Steven Spielberg has to say in "Schindler's List." And it is the core of what the rest of us have to see.

The Uniqueness of the Holocaust

*A Professor at Cornell University Argues that the
Nazi Attack on the Jews Was the Only True Genocide in History*

by Liz McMillen
The Chronicle of Higher Education, June 22, 1994

Elie Wiesel is usually credited with introducing the term "Holocaust" to describe the destruction of the Jews by the Nazis. Nowadays, though, people speak of the American Indian holocaust, the Armenian holocaust, and the "real holocaust" of black slavery.

While each of those events was brutal and horrific, none equaled the Nazi attempt to eradicate the Jews of Europe, says Stephen T. Katz, a professor at Cornell University. The Holocaust was the only true genocide in history, he says, the only systematic attempt to kill all members of a group of people simply because they had been born. It was unique.

This is a simple argument, but it is taking Mr. Katz three massive volumes, a mastery of scholarly documentation in 11 languages, and thousands of notes to make it.

The Holocaust in Historical Context is Mr. Katz's Herculean effort to prove definitively that the Holocaust was a singular event in human history. The study is being published by Oxford University Press.

In the first volume, which was released in May, Mr. Katz examines mass murders and brutalities that have been compared with the Holocaust, beginning with slavery in ancient Greece and Rome and continuing with the

European witch craze and persecution of religious heretics and homosexuals.

In later volumes, he will study executions under Stalin, mass deaths under the Khmer Rouge in Cambodia, violence in contemporary African countries, and the structure of the Holocaust. Along the way, he ponders the nature of genocide.

And Mr. Katz is not even a historian. Trained as a philosopher, he is a professor of Jewish history and religion at Cornell whose earlier work focused on comparative mysticism and Jewish philosophy. He says he came to study the Holocaust "quite by accident."

Invited to give a lecture at the University of Notre Dame in 1981, Mr. Katz planned to speak about the Holocaust, thinking that it would have universal interest. "My prejudice was that it was another example of violence against Jews, another example of violence against *people*," he says. "It had no distinctiveness for me.

"I worked on this for six months, and I eventually came to the realization that I was doing something dishonest," he continues. "I was ignoring evidence or explaining away the data."

'Thousands of Pages'

He set to work on a "small" book comparing the Holocaust with other examples of violence and mass murder throughout history. "Before I knew it, it was 10 years later and I had generated thousands of pages of manuscript," he says.

The Holocaust in Historical Context is a reply to those who deny that the atrocities of the Holocaust ever happened. It is also meant as a corrective to the loose rewriting of history that in Mr. Katz's view turns slave owners into death-camp operators and Inquisitors into the Nazi SS.

While such parallels may be emotionally satisfying, they are not accurate, he maintains. "This is a new field, only 40 years old," he says. "What I found is that emotion has substituted for scholarship. People are not doing the comparative work. They know their own tragedy, and they really want to advance their common agenda. We didn't have neutral observers."

Although the uniqueness of the Holocaust argument isn't new—Yehuda Bauer, Lucy Dawidowicz, and Israel Gutman have made the same case—several scholars say that Mr. Katz has made the position virtually incontrovertible. "It's never been demonstrated with the scholarly rigor it has here," says Alan L. Berger, an associate professor of religion at Syracuse University. "From now on, people will not venture into the field of Holocaust studies without using his book as a point of reference."

'Employing this definition we can begin to recognize that Assyrian, Babylonian, Persian, Hellenistic, Roman, and Crusade policy was cruel, but not every cruelty is genocide.'

Jacob Neusner, a professor of religious studies at the University of South Florida, has reviewed *The Holocaust in Historical Context* for a forthcoming issue of the *AJS Review*, the journal of the Association for Jewish Studies. "The Holocaust has found its philosophical historian, the uniqueness of the Holocaust, its first fully articulated and compelling presentation," Mr. Neusner writes. "Steven T. Katz has written the best work of historical interpretation of the Holocaust in any language, the largest in conception, the most majestic in vision, the most careful and thoughtful in execution, above all, philosophically the best, most rigorously argued."

Although some people are bound to be offended by Mr. Katz's project, he says he doesn't want to deny or minimize the suffering of any group. "Even if people disagree with me, the nature of the notes will raise the level of discussion," he says. "This book will force people into a new seriousness, to master the material better than I have."

And to those who would argue that treating the Holocaust as unique somehow amounts to "special pleading" for the Jews, Mr. Katz has a ready reply: "Being turned into ashes over Central Europe is not a privilege," he says. "I thought very carefully about how I use the term 'unique.' I never use the term in a moral sense."

Mr. Katz's comparisons are not based on numbers of people who suffered—either absolute or percentages—since, for example, more people died in Stalin's *gulags* than did Jews in the Holocaust. Nor is it based on a scale of evil or cruelty, since how would one quantify suffering?

The key difference between the Holocaust and other historical examples is what Mr. Katz calls intentionality, Hitler's plan to rid the world of the Jewish population. Although some may argue that the notion of intention is ambiguous, Mr. Katz points out that it is a standard and meaningful legal concept.

"Employing this definition we can begin to recognize that Assyrian, Babylonian, Persian, Hellenistic, Roman, and Crusade policy was cruel, but not every cruelty is genocide," he writes. "That Hun, Muslim, Mughal, Imperial Japanese, Mongol, and conquistador behavior was tyrannical, but not every tyranny is genocide. That slavery—ancient, Caribbean, and American—is an abomination, but not every abomination is genocide."

Dozens of sources for each case

Mr. Katz read widely for each case study he built, consulting dozens of historical, philosophical, archaeological, and theological sources. He considers the loss of life in Mexico and South America following the arrival of the Europeans in the 15th century "very probably the greatest demographic disaster in history." Yet for all its terror and death, the depopulation of the New World was largely an unintended tragedy, he writes. Disease, not malice, was the main killer of the Indians.

Mr. Katz also differs with some scholars by claiming that Nazi policy toward Jews was not an outgrowth of Christian thought toward the Jews. Despite its crimes against the Jewish people, and there were many, Mr. Katz writes, the Roman Catholic Church never condoned a policy of physical "Judeocide."

"The Jews survived 1,600 years of Christianity," Mr. Katz explains. "They almost didn't survive four years of World War II. Something different must have happened."

Recent events in Bosnia and Rwanda have forced Mr. Katz to revise some chapters in the second volume. He doesn't consider either a case of true genocide. "What you have in Bosnia is a population transfer supported by violence," he says. "Neither side has a program to destroy the other down to the last Muslin or the last Croat."

'Intent is missing'

As for Rwanda, where members of the majority Hutu tribe have killed tens of thousands of the minority Tutsi tribe, Mr. Katz sees the conflict as tribal warfare. "It's about tribal domination, not genocidal purpose," he says. "Each tribe wants to assert its self-interest. There again, the intent is very clearly missing."

Even without the latest revisions, putting Mr. Katz's study to a huge undertaking. One university press passed on th its length and complexity. Mr. Katz has written some 7,000 manuscript pages for the three volumes, with more than 3,000 pages of footnotes. The first volume, totaling 702 pages, took an entire year to copy-edit and another year to produce. "They asked me questions about every umlaut," he says.

Mr. Katz's prodigious reading became something of a joke for his editor, Claude Conyers, editorial director of the academic reference division at Oxford. "I would tell him, 'Don't read any more books. We can't add any more,'" Mr. Conyers says. "His compulsion to add and call people's attention to something—that's an admirable quality in a scholar.

"I think this is a staggering work of scholarship," Mr. Conyers adds. "That it could come from one man is even more staggering."

'I've been obsessed'

The extensive documentation—on some pages, there are more lines of notes than text—is necessary because emotions run so high on the subject of the Holocaust, Mr. Katz says. He also wanted to satisfy both the specialists in particular fields of study as well as scholars of the Holocaust.

A reporter observed that only a confident person would take on this kind of project. "You mean chutzpah?" Mr. Katz asks with a laugh. "Yes, yes, you're probably right. It's true, I've been obsessed with it. Except for the Sabbath, I work on it night and day."

Mr. Katz recalls that he dealt with evil as a philosophical question in his graduate studies, but he never considered the Holocaust or other historical brutalities. "This really came to me late, maybe when I was ready for it," he observes. "What I've learned has given me humility."

Poll on Doubt Of Holocaust Is Corrected

·······················

Roper Says 91% Are Sure It Occurred

by Michael R. Kagay
The New York Times, Friday, July 8, 1994

Only a small segment of Americans denies that the Holocaust happened, according to a new Roper poll for the American Jewish Committee.

The new poll was conducted to correct a flawed question in an earlier survey that had suggested higher levels of Holocaust denial and, both the researchers and sponsors say, to set the polling record straight.

"Committed or consistent deniers of the Holocaust make up only a small segment of the population, about 2 percent or less," said Dr. Tom W. Smith of the University of Chicago's National Opinion Research Center, which analyzed both the new Roper poll and all other available United States surveys on the Holocaust for the American Jewish Committee.

He added that "there is an additional group of a few percent—under 10 percent—who express some doubts or uncertainty, but do so mainly from lack of information."

The new poll, taken by Roper Starch Worldwide Inc., interviewed 991 adults across the country in person during March. It had a margin of sampling error of plus or minus 4 percentage points.

Question Is Revised

It is a follow-up to a widely publicized Roper poll, taken in late 1992 for the American Jewish Committee, that seemed to indicate that 1 in 5 Americans doubted the Holocaust had happened. The poll question that yielded that earlier finding has been termed flawed by Roper officials as well as by other pollsters.

The revised question in the new poll was: "Does it seem possible to you that the Nazi extermination of the Jews never happened, or do you feel certain that it happened?"

With that new wording, only 1 percent said it was possible the Holocaust had never happened, and another 8 percent said they did not know. Ninety-one percent said they were certain it had happened.

The earlier poll's flawed wording involved a complicated double negative construction that apparently confused many respondents. That question read: "Does it seem possible or does it seem impossible to you that the Nazi extermination of the Jews never happened?"

In response to that wording, 22 percent of adults in late 1992 said it was possible that the Holocaust had never happened and an additional 12 percent said they did not know if it was possible or not; 65 percent said it was impossible that it had never happened.

"The double negative question thoroughly confused people on which answer to give to say what they meant, and many may have given an answer just opposite of what they meant," said Burns W. Roper, the recently retired former chairman of the Roper polling organization.

Mr. Roper expressed satisfaction that the earlier inflated figure had finally been set straight. "The original flawed figure conveyed a misleading impression of the extent of Holocaust doubters. It provided aid and comfort to the skinhead kind of anti-Semites and needlessly scared the Jewish community," he said.

Other findings in the new study included these:

• Detailed knowledge of the Holocaust has shown a modest overall gain, compared with the 1992 Roper poll. Dr. Smith attributed this to the opening of Holocaust museums and the widely viewed film "Schindler's List." That knowledge was still limited, although Dr. Smith said it was comparable to Americans' knowledge of other World War II events, such as the bombing of Pearl Harbor.

• But Americans are less knowledgeable about the Holocaust than the British, French or Germans who answered similar surveys sponsored by the American Jewish Committee. Dr. Smith attributed this to the fact that Europeans were physically closer to the events.

• Education level is a major factor accounting for Holocaust knowledge. Of those with less than a high school education, 55 percent knew what the Holocaust was. This rose to 74 percent among high school graduates, 87 percent among college graduates, and 92 percent among those with advanced degrees.

Dr. Smith's report, "Holocaust Denial: What the Survey Data Reveal," was originally scheduled to be made public by the American Jewish Committee on July 19 [1994].

But some of the findings of the new poll were characterized in the July 1 edition of The Christian Science Monitor in an article by Professor Everett C. Ladd of the University of Connecticut.

In response, the American Jewish Committee accelerated its timetable and disclosed Dr. Smith's full report yesterday.

SURVEY

Denying the Holocaust: A Second Look

· ·

1992: A Flawed Question	1994: The Revised Question
Does it seem possible or does it seem impossible to you that the Nazi extermination of the Jews never happened?	Does it seem possible to you that the Nazi extermination of the Jews never happened, or do you feel certain that it happened?
Not sure 12%	Not sure 8%
Possible 22%	Possible it never happened 1%
Impossible 65%	Certain it happened 91%

Source: Based on Roper polls conducted for the American Jewish Committee

---

Denying the Holocaust

Pseudo-scholars Claim the Gas Was for Delousing,
and the Final Solution a Zionist Myth

by Laura Shapiro
Newsweek, Dec. 20, 1993

The testimony of survivors, the accounts of witnesses, even reports written by the killers themselves haven't convinced everyone that the Nazis murdered 6 million Jews; polls have shown that nearly a quarter of Americans believe it is possible the extermination never happened. For decades, a small but prolific band of anti-Semites and political extremists—first in the United States and Europe, now everywhere from Latin America to Japan—has been poring over the immense documentation of the Holocaust, pouncing on minor inconsistencies to buttress claims that Jewish war victims died of natural causes, the gas chambers were used for delousing, and Hitler's Final Solution was only a Zionist myth devised to bolster support for Israel.

The most dramatic rebuttal to these theories came in September, when Jean-Claude Pressac's "The Crematoriums of Auschwitz: The Machinery of Mass Murder" was published in Paris. Pressac, a pharmacist and amateur historian, has been linked with Holocaust deniers, but he told Newsweek he had never questioned the fact of the Holocaust—merely the methods the Nazis used. "I had questions," he says. "It's normal." Using newly available documents taken by the Soviets from Auschwitz, Pressac explains with chilling objectivity the floor plans and ventilation systems of the gas chambers and reproduces order forms for furnaces. Holocaust experts have hailed his work as definitive.

Holocaust deniers dismiss Pressac's book; they also discount a newly found speech by Nazi propagandist Joseph Goebbels about the "murderous fate" awaiting Berlin's Jews. Deborah Lipstadt, author of "Denying the Holocaust," is appalled by the willingness of some students and the media to see Holocaust denial as simply "the other side"; she refuses to grant deniers the status of "revisionists." "In this relativistic time we live in, Holocaust denial is turned into an opinion, and everyone's opinion is of equal validity," she says. "That's like asking whether slavery happened." But more pernicious than cranks proselytizing the ignorant is simple indifference. When the last survivors cease to bear living witness, will enough people still care to insist that what happened happened? Silence is the ultimate denial.

—Laura Shapiro with Mark Miller in Los Angeles
and Marcus Mabry in Paris

Nazis a Dead Issue? In Argentina, No

by Nathaniel C. Nash
The New York Times, June 25, 1994

For Argentina, which opened its doors to Nazis fleeing postwar Europe, this is the season for exposing war criminals and debating whether, 50 years after the crimes, they should be brought to justice.

Events have once again made this country face its murky history—an arrest of a former SS captain in a southern resort town, interviews with two former Nazis living in the capital and a research project investigating the Government's archives that continues turning up revelations about the numbers of Nazis who entered the country after the war and the Argentine Government's promoting of that immigration.

In May, because of a report on the ABC News program "Prime Time Live," the peace of the alpine town of San Carlos de Bariloche was shaken when the Government placed Erich Priebke under house arrest. The 81-year-old German immigrant admitted having taken part in the killing of 335 Italians, mostly civilians, in the Ardeatine Caves outside Rome in March 1944.

Since that arrest, Argentine television journalists have cornered two former Nazi officials living in Buenos Aires, who expressed no regret over their past.

One, Abraham Kipp, 77, a former Dutch policeman who was sentenced to death after the war on 23 counts of murder, came to the wrought-iron gate at his front door. Refusing to give an interview, he said: "I don't want to talk about the past. It's all over." Then, asked if he felt remorse over the crimes of which he was accused, he said: "What? No."

Mr. Kipp escaped from a Dutch prison after the war, entered Argentina in 1949 and obtained citizenship in 1953. The Dutch Government has repeatedly tried to extradite him, as recently as 1991, but a court here threw out the case.

The judge in the Kipp case, Leónidas Moldes, is now in charge of the Priebke case.

Wilhelm Sassen, 76, a Belgian who ran a newspaper and a radio station for the Nazis in the Netherlands, gave an extensive interview to the Argentine television reporters. He defended his past as a Nazi propaganda officer.

In the years after the war, Mr. Sassen said, he was frequently visited in Buenos Aires by Josef Mengele, the Auschwitz doctor who performed ghastly experiments on inmates in the death camp, and by Adolf Eichmann, the architect of Hitler's "Final Solution."

He described Eichmann as "a bureaucrat" and said of Mengele, who lived freely in Argentina for more than 20 years before fleeing to Paraguay, that he was a "refined" man with a love of classical music and that "his work was academic, to gauge the extremes of physical and mental hardship humans could endure."

Mr. Sassen is not considered a war criminal but a collaborator and would most likely not be subject to extradition.

Argentines debate whether, after 50 years, Nazis should be brought to justice

••••••••••••••••••••••••••

While no one here condones the crimes, there have been some calls for a halt to the continued pursuit of former Nazis. Those who have defended Mr. Priebke echo his own defense, that he was ordered to shoot two victims in the Roman caves or else be shot himself.

The massacre was ordered after 32 German soldiers were ambushed by partisan fighters in Rome and killed. Hitler ordered that 10 Italians die for every German soldier killed. Among the victims were 71 Jews.

Mr. Priebke's defenders say that since arriving in Argentina he has been a model citizen and a leader of the German community in his town, and that his crimes are part of the past. His lawyers also argue that he is too sick to withstand a long trial.

After Mr. Priebke was put under house arrest early in May, a march was called to support him, but in the end it was called off.

"It hurts me to see the cruelty against a man who in that moment was a victim of the system," the Italian Vice Consul in San Carlos de Bariloche, Carlos Botazzi, said in an interview with the daily La Nación. He likened Mr. Priebke to "the pilot who pushed the button and let drop the atomic bomb over Hiroshima," saying they were both victims.

Manfredo Montezemolo, who in an interview with La Nación asserted that his father had been killed in the Roman caves, said: "Die peacefully. I forgive you."

Last week 200 residents of San Carlos de Bariloche signed a petition on behalf of Mr. Priebke, demanding that Argentine courts reject his extradition request. They described him as "a good neighbor and a person of irreproachable conduct since he arrived in this country."

But not everyone agrees. The new Italian Prime Minister, Silvio Berlusconi, said his Government would ask for Mr. Priebke's extradition.

The Argentine Government announced on June 10 that it had received extradition papers from the Italian Government.

Many in the Government of the Argentine President, Carlos Saúl Menem, have voiced support for extradition, including Foreign Minister Guido di Tella and Mr. Menem himself.

And last weekend, Interior Minister Carlos Ruckauf announced that the Menem Government would propose a new law setting up a Government agency that will track down Nazis who fled to Argentina after the war.

But at the same time the President seemed to echo some of the political frustration over the continued pursuit of former Nazis and the waves of adverse publicity that Argentina endures every few months when yet another former Nazi is exposed.

Mr. Menem said that if Mr. Priebke was extradited, then Britain should extradite Lady Thatcher, the former Prime Minister, for the sinking of the Argentine cruiser General Belgrano during the Falkland Islands war in 1982 when the ship was outside the defined areas of engagement.

Italy has warned the Argentine authorities that it fears that a neo-Nazi group might try to free Mr. Priebke. There is also concern here that the legal process might be too slow and that since the case will be handled by the courts, the Government may lose control.

"This man has to be extradited, because extradition represents a no to the idea of impunity," said Beatrice Gurevich-Rubel, research director for Projecto Testimonio, which under the direction of the Daia, the umbrella Jewish organization, is studying the national archives for Nazi migration.

"It is important to delegitimize the idea of obeying orders when it deals with obeying criminal orders," she said. "The issue is not the personal punishment of this man, but that he is put on trial in order to condemn what he represents, make people remember what happened and avoid a repeat of these crimes and conduct."

The discovery of Mr. Priebke and the push to bring him to trial was aided by the Simon Wiesenthal Institute, which tipped off the "Prime Time Live" news program to the existence of another former Nazi, Reinhard Kopps, a former military intelligence officer in Nazi Germany who worked with Vatican officials after the war to get Nazis out of Europe.

Mr. Kopps told ABC News about Mr. Priebke. Mr. Kopps, who the Simon Wiesenthal Institute says finances neo-Nazi activities in Germany, has since disappeared, apparently fleeing to Chile.

According to neighbors, Mr. Priebke did not hide his Nazi past or his participation in the Ardeatine Caves killings. He ran a local deli in the 1950's and 60's and before his arrest was head of the local German-Argentine cultural association.

Wiesenthal officials say they have found not only that Mr. Priebke was in the caves at the time of the executions—he confessed to killing two people—but also that his superior, Lieut. Col. Herbert Kappler, the Gestapo chief in Rome, had said in a confession that Mr. Priebke was assigned to go to Italian prisons to round up prisoners to be shot.

"Opening the archives is important to historians," said Rabbi Marvin Hier, dean of the Wiesenthal Institute, "but it's another thing to clean your house of Nazis that are still alive."

German "Schindler's List" Debut Launches Debate, Soul-searching

by Reuters News Service
published in *The Houston Post*, Feb. 28, 1994

"As countless documentaries written and filmed in Germany show, it is obviously easier to show the gruesome acts than to pay tribute to those who didn't look away. The portrayal of the main character could lead to a new chapter in the way we deal with the memory of the Holocaust."
—Wochenpost, an eastern Germany weekly

Just days before the German premiere of *Schindler's List*, the German press has launched into an uneasy debate over the film about a war profiteer who saved 1,200 Jews from the Holocaust.

Most weekend newspapers enthusiastically praised the acclaimed black-and-white drama directed by Steven Spielberg about hard-drinking wheeler-dealer Oskar Schindler.

But one prominent critic attacked the film as another Hollywood tear-jerker that should be called—in a reference to earlier Spielberg films—*Indiana Jones in the Krakow Ghetto.*

Reflection time

The question "why didn't others react like him?" and the defensive criticism turn the film's debut into a very German occasion for guilt, reflection and polemics over the Nazi era and World War II.

216

Schindler's List will have its premiere Tuesday in Frankfurt's ornate Old Opera House attended by Spielberg, President Richard von Weizsaecker and leading German personalities.

It will be shown in movie theaters throughout the country starting Thursday.

Schindler used his profits to bribe death camp guards to free Jews to work in his factory. He lived out his last years not far from the opera, in a cramped room in the red-light district near a Frankfurt railway station and died in 1974.

Intellectuals who sniffed at the dinosaurs in *Jurassic Park* and space fantasies of *E. T.* wonder why a Hollywood director rather than German dared to film the story of individual heroism in the Holocaust.

"As countless documentaries written and filmed in Germany show, it is obviously easier to show the gruesome acts than to pay tribute to those who didn't look away," the eastern German weekly Wochenpost wrote.

"The portrayal of the main character could lead to a new chapter in the way we deal with the memory of the Holocaust."

A German producer, Artur Brauner, tried for 18 years to film the Schindler story but was refused state financing because official film boards found the story incredible or too sensational.

"Schindler is history that matters today," wrote Munich's Sueddeutsche Zeitung on Saturday, drawing parallels between the silent majority under the Nazis and a tendency it sees now to ignore or play down growing racist violence.

"The world watching us knows this. We hope we do too," it wrote, echoing views widespread among liberals and on the left.

Will Tremper, 65, veteran film critic of the conservative daily Die Welt, said *Schindler's List* was a horrible film and no movie had ever upset and angered him so much.

The survivors who told Schindler's story to Australian writer Thomas Keneally were mostly children who could not have understood what was going on, he wrote in Saturday's Welt.

Tremper reserved his sharpest barbs for Spielberg himself, the "hard-boiled director of Hollywood adventure films" he first met in the early 1970s when Spielberg was making horror films.

Filming disgusting

The thought of seeing him calling out "action! action" to start the filming of the brutal Krakow Ghetto round-up was disgusting, he wrote.

Tremper recalled Spielberg told viewers at the Hollywood premiere of *Schindler's List* that it was only in making the film that he really understood his Jewish background and thought of relatives who must have died in the Holocaust.

"That's how far California is from the reality of Europe," the critic remarked.

Good Germans: Honoring the Heroes. And Hiding the Holocaust

by Diana Jean Schemo
The New York Times, June 12, 1994

In Europe, some celebrate saviors, around whom they can rebuild an ugly history.

In the half century since Allied soldiers first stumbled upon the mass graves and gas chambers that sketched the broad, dark outlines of the Nazi annihilation of European Jewry, histories of that period have largely remained faithful to the Holocaust's over-arching themes of abandonment, complicity and devastation. But a tendency in recent years to focus on the rescue of Jews by gentiles is alarming some survivors and scholars, who complain that the enthusiasm for rescue may spill over into the distortion of history.

"Schindler's List," the Stephen Spielberg film that portrays the Holocaust through the life of a Nazi businessman-turned-savior, is but the most visible illustration of the shift in perspective. A spate of conferences, books and films have sprung up to tell the story of Jews who survived thanks to Christian heroism.

The American Jewish Committee, which hired Theodor Adorno to conduct a study titled "The Authoritarian Personality" in the years immediately after the war, more recently asked Samuel and Pearl Oliner to interview rescuers for another study, "The Altruistic Personality." A conference on "The Holocaust in Southern Europe" at the New York University Law School last month, sponsored by the National Italian American Foundation, focused neither on the role Italian fascism may have played in setting the stage for Nazism's rise in Germany nor on the genocide of Jews throughout Southern Europe. The conference's purpose, rather, was to highlight the decency of ordinary Italian citizens, soldiers and diplomats who protected Jews in Italy and elsewhere until Germany occupied northern and central Italy in 1943 in the face of Allied advances.

An Odd Moment

As "Schindler's List" illustrates, however, anointing heroes often involves weighing personal, and, in the case of a country, historical records that are ambiguous, and choosing on the side of faith. As much of Europe flirts with fascism and the former Yugoslavia remains locked in ethnic killing, it seems an odd moment to embrace the anomaly and call it history.

While the academics and survivors at the Holocaust conference took pains to avoid a wholesale exoneration of people and political regimes, the questions from the audience revealed broader undercurrents that can eventually engulf any nuance: one woman asked why it took 50 years to learn the "true story" of Italy's behavior during the war, as if the favorable history Italians were credited with that day canceled out the rest of its wartime role; another listener, apparently unaware of the Vatican's silence about the genocide, stated that wherever the Vatican had tried to intercede on behalf of the Jews, conditions became worse for them, and asked when the "true story" of the Christian schools and convents that had sheltered Jews would be told.

The problem is symptomatic. Holocaust history, as perhaps any history, goes through fashions that may reveal as much about the contemporary era as the past it is peering into. Currently, three distinct classes of students, some of whose interests are mutually antithetical, are studying overlooked heroes with particular interest: leaders of Jewish organizations, for whom rescuers serve as both role models for resistance and vehicles to convey the Holocaust to non-Jews; the newly established or newly freed states of Eastern Europe, which are writing their histories of the wartime years; and historical revisionists eager to prove that there was no Holocaust, or to play down the slaughter.

Perhaps one enduring legacy of the Holocaust is the ratcheting down of moral standards across the last half of the century. Hannah Arendt, in her treatise on Adolf Eichmann's trial in Jerusalem 30 years ago, condemned countries like France for deporting foreign Jews with the rationale that they were sparing French Jews; in doing so, she argued, they had accepted the principle of persecution of the innocent, and were later powerless to argue when the Nazis ignored their distinction and demanded French Jews as well. Susan Zuccotti, a Barnard College history professor, interviewed French Jews for her 1993 book "The Holocaust, the French, and the Jews" and reached an opposite judgement. Given the rabid anti-Jewish temper of the time, she argued, the French were to be commended for the "generosity, tolerance, and fundamental humanity" that permitted 76 percent, or 250,000 French Jews, to survive.

Leaders of Jewish organizations say they do not reject, indeed they encourage, studies of those who rescued Jews. "I don't think it's an attempt to deny or revise history, but an attempt to convey that we're not all powerless in a world where we may feel powerless," said David A. Harris, executive director of the American Jewish Committee.

But Raul Hilberg, the Holocaust historian, said he finds the emphasis on rescue misleading, if a sign of the very human hunger to find meaning and community in the bleakest places. He said he knows there were truly righteous rescuers, but that the current fascination with them inflates their historical role. "There is *nothing* to be taken from the Holocaust that imbues anyone with hope or any thought of redemption," he said, "but the need for heroes is so strong that we'll manufacture them."

Developing as the newly emerging states of Eastern Europe are writing their own histories of the Holocaust, the climate has opened the way for claims to heroism that seem an assault on memory itself. For if the survivors live to tell their personal stories of the odd kindly farmer, or of the neighbor who hid a hunted family, there is nobody left to speak in the voice of the millions who could find no haven, and precious little that they left behind: the dairy of Anne Frank, the Holocaust museum's chimney stack of photos from Eishishok, Lithuania, whose inhabitants were slaughtered in September 1941, the photos of Roman Vishniak's "Vanished World." To be a student of the Holocaust is, above all, to be a humble student of silence.

Claude Lanzmann, the French film maker who toiled 10 years on "Shoah," asserts that even survivors—much less those who rescued them—cannot relate the full tale. There is an essential contradiction, he feels, in telling the story through the eyes of the living, when the essence of the

Holocaust was industrialized slaughter. This, he said, creates a special burden for those who would tell any part of the history. Speaking by telephone from Paris, the director said his subjects "wanted to testify for the majority of people—they would have found it scandalous" to focus on how they had survived. (None uttered the word "I" during the film, he said.) "The project of telling Schindler's story confuses history," he said.

He expressed fear that the movie inadvertently gave fodder to revisionists and moral relativists. "All of this is to say that everything is equal, to say there were good among the Nazis, bad among the others, and so on. It's a way to make it not a crime against humanity, but a crime of humanity."

The clearest illustration of the moral confusion these overlapping visions produce may have come when the lawyer for Paul Touvier, an official of the Vichy secret police who was charged in France with crimes against humanity, tried to invoke "Schindler's defense." True, the lawyer said, Mr. Touvier had seven Jews executed near Lyons, but he claimed that the Gestapo demanded he execute 100 and he bargained them down to 30. By his logic, he saved 23 lives. "In reality, Touvier is Schindler," said the lawyer, Jacques Tremolet de Villers. (In the end, Touvier was convicted; there was no corroborating evidence for his tale of bargaining the Germans down.)

Each land likes to tell of the Jews it saved, as so many more died
....

It should not have been surprising that Germans, too, were drawn to Oskar Schindler's tale. From Frankfurt to Berlin, people lined up to see Mr. Spielberg's film when it opened; some told journalists they welcomed a film that finally told the story of a good German, and—apparently oblivious to the larger message—they wondered why no German had made such a film. Der Spiegel, the news magazine, delved into the archives of Yad Vashem, the Holocaust memorial in Jerusalem, for a five-page story on Max Liedtke, a Wehrmacht officer who ordered his troops not to hand over Jews despite demands from the SS. "The most they can do is shoot us," read the headline, quoting him.

Moving down the continuum from the sterling example of Denmark, to the largely favorable record of the Italians, a reader of history enters regions progressively more ambiguous, where the late-born emphasis on heroes becomes more startling.

'Hungary? My God!"

Thus Hungary, where 70 percent of the Jews were deported or murdered under German occupation, claims that Adm. Miklos Horthy only agreed to deport Jews when he had no choice. ("Hungary? My God!" exclaimed Elie Wiesel, the Nobel laureate who as a child was deported to Auschwitz. "If ever there was a total collaboration." In his town, Mr. Wiesel said, "it was the Hungarian gendarmes who rounded up the Jews.") Or Slovakia, where anti-Jewish legislation accompanied independence, and where 58,000, or 75 percent of all Jews, were deported. Or Croatia, where the puppet Ustashe regime ran the notorious Jascnovac concentration camps.

David Singer, research director of the American Jewish Committee, said his organization is often approached by cash-poor East European countries eager to play down their role in the Holocaust. "They think Jews in this country control the banks and government, and if they can win us over, the money will flow," he said. "It really is prototypically anti-Semitic in that way."

He said all three sides in the Bosnian war had approached his group to discuss their behavior during the Holocaust. "In the middle of killing each other, they want to be scrupulously careful about who was killing the Jews," he said. "Obviously none of it has anything to do with creating or correcting the historical record. It's all being played out for an American Jewish audience."

Mr. Harris, his boss, agreed: "If one solely listened to statements made to us, one would have to assume that virtually every country in Europe and every major institution was struggling on behalf of Jews."

Mr. Hilberg, who has lately been studying what happened to the personal effects of Jews who were murdered, proposed filling out the historical record with his own "anti-book": a catalogue of shoes, pillows, shirts, slips, books and beds, with the names of the bystanders who came to inherit them.

Nazi Hunter Raves about "Schindler's List"

·······················

by Reuters News Service
published in *The Houston Post,* Jan. 26, 1994

Stephen Spielberg's movie *Schindler's List* is the best Holocaust film ever made, says veteran Nazi-hunter Simon Wiesenthal.

"It gave me goose bumps over my whole body," said Wiesenthal, who recently saw a preview of the film in a special screening.

"Of course I have seen many Holocaust films, but none of them can compare with this. The others always lacked something, to those of us who had experienced it," the 85-year-old concentration camp survivor said.

Wiesenthal, interviewed by the Vienna weekly magazine Kurier Freizeit, said he hoped many young people would see the film, which depicts how a plundering, brandy-swilling skirt chaser, Oskar Schindler, saved 1,200 Jews from massacre.

"The film is especially important at this time, when we are experiencing a regrowth of neo-Nazism in Europe," he said.

Wiesenthal said he met the real Schindler twice after World War II. "He was a playboy and a ladies' man who shortened his life by drinking too much, a real go-getter," he said.

"Naturally that impressed the SS. In times when you could not get anything, he even managed to lay hands on French cognac."

Schindler started out as a convinced Nazi, Wiesenthal said, "but he was one who changed."

Instead of profiting from forced labor and discarding Jews to their fate in Auschwitz, Schindler got them out. "I cannot remember there being ever such a case again," said Wiesenthal.

He recounted how he had personally experienced many of the scenes depicted in Spielberg's film of how the Nazis murdered 6 million Jews in Adolf Hitler's "final solution of the Jewish problem."

"Once we had to dig up the corpses in the concentration camp and burn the dead and strew their ashes," he said. "The stench of the corpses was terrible."

The incident occurred in September 1944 "when the Russians were already quite close." A camp "capo" ripped gold teeth from the dead, Wiesenthal recalled.

He also remembered a forced march to the Mauthausen concentration camp—because Auschwitz was too full.

"God helped us," he said. "He sent us snowflakes and we stood with our mouths open and drank."

Wiesenthal, who is urging Israel and the United States to ask Syria to hand over Nazi fugitive Alois Brunner, said Spielberg had promised to come to Vienna to meet him in February.

Wiesenthal's documentation center in Vienna has helped compile evidence and bring many Nazi war criminals to justice, but Brunner, whom he describes as one of the most evil, was never caught and is believed to be still alive in Damascus.

Wiesenthal said he knew Spielberg's mother—but not from the dark days. "I've known her for ages," he said. "She has a kosher milk bar in Los Angeles. A rabbi in our center there always drags me off to it."

"Schindler's List" and the Politics of Remembrance

....

by Richard Wolin

In These Times magazine, March 21-April 3, 1994

With the opening of the Holocaust museum last year in Washington, D.C. (an institution fashionably derided as a "Holocaust theme park" in European circles), and Steven Spielberg's powerful film *Schindler's List,* the Holocaust has once again become newsworthy.

It wasn't always so. At Nuremberg, Nazi higher-ups (all 22 of them) were brought to trial both for launching an "imperialist war of aggression" as well as the better known charge of "crimes against humanity." In neither indictment, however, did Hitler's genocidal assault against European Jews—which cost the lives of two-thirds of European Jewry and one-third of world Jewry—figure explicitly. And should one visit Auschwitz today, nowhere will one find reference to the fact that the primary, though in no way exclusive, targets of the Nazi extermination process were the European Jews.

More than any other event in the postwar era, it was probably the 1961 Eichmann trial in Jerusalem that focused world attention on Hitler's notorious *Endlosung,* or the Final Solution to the Jewish question.

But of equal importance over the years have been a number of cultural events and spectacles that have stirred popular awareness concerning what was historically unprecedented about the Holocaust: that Hitler's Germany put into effect a plan to negate the existence of an entire people.

The annals of history are replete with brutal massacres and extermi-
nations, often bordering on genocide. As a rule, however, most of these—
from the Roman sack of Carthage to the Crusades to the more recent
genocidal carnage of Stalin and Pol Pot—were at least tangentially related
to strategic and political goals.

The Holocaust broke definitively with the terms of earlier human history. In the words of Trotsky biographer Isaac Deutscher, all of these earlier crimes possessed some "human logic." But it was precisely such logic
that was absent from the Holocaust. The Jews posed absolutely no strategic or political threat to Hitler. Most German Jews were wholly assimilated and considered themselves to be more German than Jewish. Only in
historical retrospect do we see how tragically mistaken they were in this con-
viction.

The attempted annihilation of Jews was unique insofar as they were
chosen as victims primarily because of their "ideological" status as Jews.
So foreign were these events to the common run of human experience that
one can, with reason, assent to historian Nora Levin's contention that
"Auschwitz was a foreign planet."

First among the cultural breakthroughs was the publication in the
'50s of *The Diary of Anne Frank*. Another milestone of sorts occurred with
the 1978 television miniseries *Holocaust*. Regardless of its aesthetic qualities,
which indeed were few, *Holocaust* had the merit of turning the unassimil-
able events of the Final Solution into a tidy, palatable narrative. It contained
the standard (and standardized) elements of prime-time melodrama that
had become familiar to a postwar generation for which TV had become
the family hearth: protagonists with whom one could readily identify, an
upbeat, pro-Zionist ending, and the necessary psychological reprieve of regular commercial breaks. But therein lay the rub: "Ah! At last we understand!"—all the better to trivialize and forget.

Schindler's List is certainly a far cry from *Holocaust*.... It will supplant
the latter as a popular point of reference for our understanding of the
Third Reich's boundless capacity for inhumanity. It contains two scenes that
are destined to qualify as among the most disturbing in cinematic history:
the brutal liquidation of the Cracow ghetto at the hands of sadistic SS
men; and the wrenching "selection" episode at a nearby work camp, where
Jews deemed unfit for labor were surveyed like cattle by Nazi medical personnel and then shipped off to a local death installation.

Throughout the narrative, Spielberg displays a consummate attention to historical detail. The random, everyday character of the violence perpetrated by the Nazis against Jews is fully captured, as is the chaos and harshness of ghetto life. The deaths we are shown, and there are many, are hard, graphic—in a word, "uncinematic."

At one point, where it appears that Schindler may no longer be able to protect his Jewish laborers from the Nazi predators, Schindler promises his beloved accountant, Itzhak Stern, that he will make sure that Stern receives "special treatment." In a marvelous touch, Stern slyly demurs: after all, "special treatment" (in German: *Sonderbehandlung*) was the official Nazi euphemism for the fate awaiting the Jews at the death camps.

One of the film's central themes concerns the Nazis' phobic, ideological preoccupation with exterminating the Jews, even when such policies conflicted with the attainment of more "rational" goals pertaining to the waging of war.

The Schindler Jews, as they were called, were spared for a time since they were engaged in productive labor essential to the German war effort. Yet their status as productive laborers was never a sufficient guarantee against the Nazis' genocidal zeal. For it was common practice for the SS to divert resources vital to the conduct of war to be used for annihilating the Jews. Thus, in 1944, when Germany's fortunes in the war had already declined precipitously, the Lodz ghetto was liquidated, despite the fact that Lodz was Poland's major industrial center and that its workforce consisted primarily of Jewish ghetto residents. As it became clear that the European war was unwinnable, the Nazis thought that they could at least triumph in their war against the Jews.

A magisterial achievement, *Schindler's List* still has its faults. Of all the stories one could tell about the Holocaust, why was Schindler's the one worth transforming into a three-and-a-half-hour epic? Schindler's tale, as rendered by novelist Thomas Keneally, is dramatic and compelling. Yet, upon reflection, one can't help but wonder about those elements of the Schindler profile that make Spielberg's film so ripe for success.

Could a partial answer be that the protagonist is a non-Jew; and that, more generally, his is a story that would have patent appeal to non-Jewish audiences? Is it because Schindler himself is a figure with whom a mass audience could readily identify, even sympathize?

With Schindler, are we not in fact presented with a genuine Christian martyr, a classical case of the "holy sinner"? Far from being a friend of the Jews, Schindler employs them, at least initially, because theirs is the cheapest labor to be found—even less expensive than that of the local Poles. He is a debauchee, a rake, with a marked appreciation for the fineries of life. A more unlikely suspect for selfless acts of heroism could hardly be found.

All the more glorious and unexpected, then, will be his final transfiguration as "savior" of the Jews. In the process of rescuing his workers—of literally purchasing their freedom from an eminently venal SS overlord—Schindler, we are told by faithful accountant Stern, has gone broke. In the movie's postscript, we learn that his postwar business ventures came to naught and that his marriage soon dissolved.

In stark contrast to Schindler, the film's Jewish characters are, as a rule, underdeveloped. The only exception is the sidekick accountant Itzhak Stern, played by Ben Kingsley as a sort of Ashkenazi Sancho Panza. Stern displays all the foibles of the Jewish *Untermensch:* abject, circumspect, yet shrewd. We see the Jews as tragic victims and servile accommodators. But they are devoid of personality. They are the film's supernumeraries and huddled masses, waiting to be saved. It is not really their story that has been told. It is Oskar Schindler's.

Then there is the detestable and psychotic SS lieutenant Amon Goeth. Carbine in hand, he picks off Jews from his balcony window before breakfast with about as much conscience as a child killing flies. The word "sadistic" doesn't do justice to the depths of his psychopathological derangement.

Goeth is both attracted and repulsed by his Jewish housekeeper. In between savage beatings, he fantasizes about bringing her back to his native Vienna after the war. Schindler, the voice of reason even among Nazis, brings him back to his senses. Of course, all sexual contact between Germans and Jews had been forbidden by law. Goeth longs to taste the forbidden fruit, then hates himself for it. The housekeeper becomes the victim of his sublimated self-hatred.

But there is a danger in allowing a pathological figure like Goeth to personify the evils of Nazism. It suggests that all Nazis—or the ones we really have to worry about—suffered from personality disorders. At least, this is what we would like to think—insofar as it spares us the real burdens of contemplating how things like Nazism and Auschwitz were possible.

To pathologize the Nazis and Nazism is to provide a balm for our innate human narcissism. If it's only the Amon Goeths of the world we need worry about, then our tasks of comprehension and prevention are relatively simple. The question of how you or I or our neighbor might have responded in a similar situation is never addressed.

But Goeth and his kind could not have successfully placed in motion the Final Solution without a vast amount of assistance. None of the evil perpetrated by the Nazis would have been possible without the support and cooperation, on a truly massive scale, of "ordinary men": bureaucrats, engineers, railway personnel, members of the German foreign office, *Wehrmacht* foot soldiers, repair crews, as well as men and women throughout Europe who either stood to profit from the Jews' so-called "disappearance," or who, more often, just did not care. As a historian once remarked, the road to Auschwitz was built with hate but paved with indifference.

By pathologizing Nazi crimes, we spare ourselves the distasteful thought that, were it not for the avid participation of people very much like ourselves, the whole enterprise would have foundered early on. By isolating it as an event that occurred seemingly in a different galaxy, by considering the camps as some kind of inverted Disneyland, we set up a barrier between the evil of yesteryear and that still present among us.

In Jerusalem they have a saying: "There's no business like Shoah business." This suggests that we must constantly second-guess ourselves lest the Holocaust become fashionable, lest it be turned into kitsch. In shifting to present-day Jerusalem at the end of his film and showing us the real "Schindler Jews," Steven Spielberg has done us a service by pointedly reminding us that there *is* a difference between art and real life. Will such reminders, though, be sufficient? In seeing *Schindler's List* are we moved by the cinematography, by the actors, by its epic visual qualities? Or is it for the actual victims of the Holocaust that we shed our tears?

What precisely does *Schindler's List* help us to remember? Will it simply be recalled as an Academy Award-winning motion picture and as one of the 10 top-grossing films of 1994? Now that Hollywood has paid homage to the greatest crime of the modern era, can it return in good conscience to its normal "blockbuster" mode?

These are more than idle questions. Ours is an era that has a special difficulty in distinguishing appearances from reality. Our comprehension of the past is less and less shaped by the complexities of the written word and the intimacy of human dialogue. Increasingly, our understanding of history is transmitted via the fleeting imagery of mass media. Whether we like it or not, these media have become primary vehicles of socialization. They dictate the way we see the world.

None of these remarks are meant as a specific criticism of *Schindler's List*. They pertain more to the informational structure of late capitalist society, which applies to the production and reception of virtually all films. More specifically, they imply that we can't allow such media to educate us; and that, at best, films such as *Schindler's List* can only be part of a more general process of individual and collective coming to terms with the past.

A key historical irony here is that the Third Reich was one of the most aesthetically self-conscious regimes the world has known. It is common knowledge that Hitler himself was a failed artist. An inveterate admirer of Wagner, he at some level envisioned the Third Reich as a gigantic Wagnerian *Gesamtkunstwerk*—a "total work of art." From *Triumph of the Will* to *Jud Suss* to the weekly newsreel footage, regime operatives knew well how to bend cinematic art to their purposes. Goebbels' entire ministry of propaganda would be inconceivable apart from its expert demagogic employment of mass media such as radio and film.

In fact, as the war ground to its conclusion in 1945, Goebbels, in order to boost sagging morale, made the following telltale appeal couched in revealing, cinematic terms: "Gentlemen, in a hundred years still another color film will portray the terrible days we are undergoing now. Do you want to play a role in that film which will let you live again in a hundred years? Every one of you has to choose the person he wishes to be in a hundred years. I can assure you that it will be a tremendous film, exciting and beautiful, and worth holding steady for."

Let us make sure that we in no way become the heirs to this prototypical Nazi confusion between art and life, an ever-present temptation in our society.

"Schindler" Reaction:
Thinking, a Few Snickers

······························

by Jeffrey A. Roberts
The Denver Post, May 24, 1994

The movie ended, the credits began to roll across the screen, and 18-year-old Kelli Trotsky sobbed in her chair at the United Artists Continental Theatre in southeast Denver.

"Schindler's List" has that effect on a lot of people. But it wasn't just Steven Spielberg's stunning tale of the Holocaust that had Trotsky in tears yesterday afternoon. The senior at Thomas Jefferson High School was upset by the way a few of her classmates had reacted to the film.

"I just couldn't handle the laughing," Trotsky said. "I just couldn't handle it when someone was shot and they burst into laughter, like this was something funny. Like it was a 'Rambo' movie or something. They just don't realize ... There's so much hatred and there's so much ignorance among people my age."

Whether it was ignorance or restlessness—they wouldn't talk about it—some kids snickered at nearly every graphic example of Nazi brutality in "Schindler's List." They laughed, for instance, when a Jewish construction foreman at a forced labor camp was shot in the head for pointing out a critical structural error in a building. And they laughed when a Nazi commandant shot a boy for failing to remove a bathtub stain.

But most Denver high school students sat silently during a free screening of the 3½-hour film, one of several for Colorado teenagers this week.

And afterward, many spoke thoughtfully and intelligently about the lessons they had learned from the movie, which tells the story of a Czech-German industrialist who saved 1,100 Polish Jews from Nazi gas chambers.

Just as Gov. Roy Romer hoped when he and Spielberg announced the showings, several teens made a connection between the hate-bred violence of Nazi Germany and today's senseless gang violence in Denver and other American cities.

"It shows that hatred for no cause is really stupid," said Philip Hernon, a 17-year-old junior at Abraham Lincoln High School who saw the film for the second time. "The Nazis hated the Jews and people were dying for no reason. And the same thing is going on in this city. People are going out and killing each other for no cause."

Meant to teach

At a Denver news conference two weeks ago, Spielberg said he made "Schindler's List" not to be a commercial success, but as a tool for educators to "teach on the subject of racial hatred, tolerance and just getting along."

For teachers at Jefferson, Lincoln, Manual and the Zuni Alternative High School yesterday, the screening was a chance to show their students something they've tried to address in the classroom through books, documentaries and research assignments.

Phil Wade, an English teacher at Manual, said his sophomore students just finished writing papers on the Holocaust and the movie "made the death and destruction more three-dimensional for them." Manual Principal Linda Transou called the film "a must for all human beings, just like 'Roots' is."

Emphasizing lessons

Kids are sometimes jaded because they have grown up seeing so many episodes of violence," Transou said, "and I'm not sure that all of them actually realized how true this is until (the movie)."

Following the film, about a dozen Manual sophomores and juniors discussed it with Wade in the school lunchroom.

Ellis Jackson, 17, said he had expected to be bored by the film but found himself "really into it, especially when they started shooting people for no cause." It reminded him of the recent death of his classmate, Geronimo Maestas, who was shot and killed for his Denver Broncos jacket.

"That was senseless," Jackson said. "It's the same thing."

Myisha Barr, also 17, said the movie erased all doubt in her mind that the Holocaust really happened. "There are so many people who say it never happened and us being so young, sometimes we don't know who to believe." A Jewish student, 16-year-old sophomore Jay Pepper, said he really hadn't realized what happened during the Holocaust until "Schindler's List" opened his eyes.

"I went to see it to teach myself what happened to my people," he said. "When I saw the movie, I could see that it was real."

But some minority students had a mixed reaction to "Schindler's List." While not criticizing the movie or its message about racial hatred, they said they wished the historical and present-day plight of blacks, Hispanics and Native Americans could receive the same amount of attention.

"When people think of (black) slavery, they don't think of anybody who died," said Abeni Thomas, a 17-year-old junior. "They just think about cotton picking ... They want sympathy for how many people died (in the Holocaust). But they have to give sympathy to all people."

Similar feelings kept at least one teen from seeing "Schindler's List" with her class yesterday.

Eighteen-year-old Micah Cook and other students at Zuni Alternative High in north Denver school prepared for the screening last week with an emotional talk by Felix Sparks, a former state Supreme Court Justice who commanded the U.S. forces that liberated the Dachau concentration camp and whose 16-year-old grandson was killed in a drive-by shooting last year.

Cook, who is black, listened respectfully. But Sparks' talk did nothing to pique her interest in seeing the movie.

"We have our own problems," she said. "It seems to me that the Holocaust is overpublicized. There were 100 million Africans that died on slave ships and you never hear about that. Blacks and Mexicans die every day. But everyone's worried about the Holocaust."

Emphasis on Holocaust Film in Fighting Racism Criticized

....

by Iver Peterson
The New York Times, Feb. 19, 1994

A program by Gov. Christie Whitman to combat racism drew criticism from some black residents of New Jersey on Friday for its emphasis on screenings of the Holocaust movie *Schindler's List* as a response to an inflammatory speech by a Black Muslim last fall.

Callers to the governor's office objected that the movie about Jewish concentration camp victims should be augmented with films about black suffering from injustices as well.

Whitman said Thursday that screenings of the movie, which will be lent to the state for five showings by its maker, Steven Spielberg, are in response to a speech last November at Kean College by Khalid Abdul Muhammad, an officer of the Nation of Islam.

In his speech, Muhammad characterized Jews as oppressors of the black community and also attacked Roman Catholics and homosexuals.

The governor said that the screenings, near state college campuses before college students and community members, would be followed by a month-long public school initiative to teach tolerance.

She said the initiative was aimed at combating all forms of bigotry, not only the anti-Semitic attacks but also attacks on other religions and homosexuals expressed in the speech by Muhammad.

Callers on Friday complained that the governor should have balanced the film program with such movies of black triumph over prejudice as the public television series about the civil rights movement *Eyes on the Prize* and *Roots*, said Rita Manno, Whitman's deputy press secretary. There were about 350 calls, many of which supported the governor, Manno said.

Many callers said they were responding to criticism of the governor's initiative broadcast Friday morning by Mary Mason, a black Philadelphia radio talk show host, who invited listeners to complain to the governor's office.

The stress on the Holocaust movie was also criticized by Walter Fields, political action director for the New Jersey National Association for the Advancement of Colored People.

"I don't believe it's an appropriate response to the problem of racism," Fields told The Associated Press. "It rings hollow unless there is a policy response."

Muhammad was demoted as top aide to the leader of the Nation of Islam, Louis Farrakhan.

Bracher's Letter

by Carol Rust
Houston Chronicle, Feb. 2, 1994

The 11-mile journey on the autobahn in early summer ... was a pleasant ride over rolling, verdant hills, punctuated at regular intervals with cedars planted in perfectly straight rows as far as the eye could see.

The three American officers felt the wind rush past their faces as their Jeep traveled from where they were stationed in Leipheim, Germany, to the Bavarian market town of Dachau.

A mid-16th century castle topping a hill at the scenic town's entrance had long attracted landscape painters, but the Americans weren't artists.

They'd heard accounts of German concentration camps—they'd even read about them in The Stars and Stripes—but the general public was mostly skeptical, attributing the stories to wartime hysteria or propaganda. The Americans decided to take the afternoon to drive to Dachau and see for themselves if the news that eventually would shake the world was true.

"We were just curious," says Houstonian Roy Bracher, who served in the 876th Airborne Aviation Battalion during World War II. "It seemed kind of far out—it was hard to comprehend what humans would do to each other."

What he saw changed his life, he says today. The normally stoic Bracher wept when he saw the film *Schindler's List* recently. Whenever the retired engineer rereads the letter he wrote his parents on June 10, 1945, he starts shaking inside like the day he walked past the walls of corrugated metal that housed hell itself.

Today, Bracher is appalled by the resurgence of neo-Nazis and their claims that the Holocaust never happened. He plans to donate the letter, which recently was excerpted in the locally circulated Jewish Herald-Voice, to the Holocaust Education Center Memorial Museum of Houston when it is completed this spring [1994].

If it helps to keep memories of Adolf Hitler's atrocities alive, Bracher will be satisfied.

Mom, I took a trip to Dachau the other day out of curiosity. Do you re-member the name?

It was a concentration camp, or rather I should say, slaughterhouse. No, Mom, it isn't war propaganda. I thought for a while the human being was above such things until I went through this camp. Can you possibly conceive thousands of human beings being slaughtered? Not without seeing one of these places.

The U.S. soldiers guarding the camp let the officers enter, but they advised one of them, who was Jewish, against going. He insisted; they shrugged and said OK.

About 200 prisoners were left, mostly Polish Jews—skeletonlike peo-ple whose eyes seemed disproportionately large in their thin, thin bodies.

"I couldn't stand to look in their eyes," Bracher says. "They were like dark holes on a flat plate—they'd been through so much."

The remaining prisoners carried typhus, which had run rampant in the camp before the Germans were defeated. Although they were liberated, they were quarantined there until they got well or died.

The former inmates were eager to show the Americans around the camp, where the smell of death still hung in the air. What they couldn't con-vey in German, they demonstrated with their hands.

When the Poles showed the American officers their cramped sleeping quarters, Bracher thought it was a miracle that all the prisoners didn't have typhus or another communicable disease.

I went through the camp and saw row on row of barracks where slave la-borers were packed in like animals. There was one aisle in each barracks and the rest of the space was taken up by double and triple bunks, jammed one against the other.

Typhus ran wild through the camp. This was all pretty handy because the butchers had all they could do.

The Poles explained nonchalantly that the little trolley that ran from the barracks area to the crematory was used to haul away the dead and dying; historians estimate that the bodies of 238,000 prisoners were burned there. "The troublemakers had the privilege of going into the furnace alive," Bracher wrote to his parents.

Dachau was the first of Hitler's concentration camps, established in 1933 five weeks after Hitler was named chancellor of Germany. It became the model and training center for other concentration camps.

There was a room about 12 by 20 feet next to the furnace room where the dead were stacked, and after many scrubbings, the blood ring is 6 feet high on the walls.

Blood ran out under the door, down the steps, down the walks, leaving a stain that will never be cleaned up.

The whole place had an ungodly stench that you can never forget.

There were furnaces with trays to feed the bodies three at a time. I saw all this and there is absolutely no doubt as to the fact of the matter.

When the Americans arrived, the guards were in the process of slaughtering the entire camp. There were 14 freight cars on the siding loaded with bodies. Bodies were stacked like cordwood all over camp, and scattered and sprawled everywhere.

Bracher found the letter among his parents' belongings after his father died in 1973. He recognized his youthful scratch, and reread his chronicle of the concentration camp.

He and Fay, his wife of 20 years, went to Europe four years ago to retrace his steps while in the military.

They had planned to visit Dachau.

The night before they were to go, Bracher changed his mind.

Two on Schindler's List Recall Horror

······················

by Jeremy Simon
The Fort Lauderdale Sun-Sentinel, Dec. 19, 1993

During the Holocaust in 1944, Helen Beck saw a grave that had been dug by Nazi soldiers. It was meant for her.

"It had enough room for 1,000 people. Out of curiosity, I went out to see it one day," Helen said about the trench behind the factory where she and other Jewish prisoners worked.

"It made me numb."

But thanks to a Nazi businessman named Oskar Schindler, she and her husband outlived the grave.

Kuba and Helen Beck of Delray Beach, Fla., were two of the names on Schindler's list, a roster of about 1,100 Jews who were saved by Schindler from near-certain "liquidation" in Nazi-run death camps in Poland during World War II. The story is receiving attention thanks to the movie *Schindler's List,* directed by Steven Spielberg. Many movie critics have called the film a top candidate for an Academy Award.

Schindler pulled Jews out of the camps and ghettos they were in and put them to work in his own factory in Brunlitz, Czechoslovakia. Schindler was able to keep the Jews away from those who wanted them exterminated.

"There are no words to describe the thanks and true feelings of compassion we have for Schindler," Helen, 68, said. "He was a man with a human heart. The rest (of the Nazis) were beasts."

Although the Becks did not meet until 1945, their story began when World War II broke out in 1939, when they were teen-agers.

Kuba Beck, 71, had lived in Krakow, Poland, a city the Nazis turned into a ghetto for Jews at the beginning of the war. In 1942, his parents and his two brothers were taken to concentration camps. They were not seen again.

A year later, he was sent to a labor camp.

"I got to go. The rest were killed in the ghetto, buried in mass graves," Kuba said.

Kuba was working in a metal shop when he was ordered to go to Emalia, Schindler's factory. Kuba, who worked producing black-market pots and pans for Schindler, did not know why he was chosen. He just went.

Kuba's future wife, Helen, was one of 10 children. She was sent to Schindler's factory in 1943 when one day she was pulled from her job building roads at Krakow-Plaszow under Nazi commandant Amon Goeth. Goeth was a sadist who would shoot at random people whom he saw from his balcony, Helen said.

"I have no idea why I was chosen," she said. "There were some brave ones who asked questions. They are no longer here."

She was sent to work for Schindler, who was born in Czechoslovakia. Schindler joined the Nazi party, but his business interests led him to Poland when Germany invaded it. Jewish labor was cheap there, so he took over a factory.

"He was a master at bribery, entertaining, gaining influence. He had an unusual charm," she said.

But he soon sympathized with the Jews and decided to try to save them after seeing the Nazi practices, Helen said.

Schindler managed to gain Nazi permission to use Jews for labor by opening up a munitions factory that would make parts for German V-2 missiles. By making German missiles and black-market items, Kuba said, Schindler became rich, satisfied the Nazi party, and protected his Jewish workers from the SS.

In the summer of 1944, Schindler was forced to disassemble his factory because of Russian advances in the war. Kuba was sent to Gross-Rosen, and Helen was sent to Auschwitz. But Schindler wanted to reestablish the factory in Czechoslovakia, so he compiled a list of the people who had already worked for him.

He wanted the same workers because they had already been trained, and he used his influence to win their release. Thanks to Schindler, Kuba and Helen were spared such practices as the death-camp number tattoos on most Holocaust survivors.

In May 1945, the camp was liberated by the Russian Army, and they both went to then-free Krakow to try to find living relatives—Kuba alone, Helen with her sister, Cecilia. Helen found three sibling survivors, Kuba none.

"Schindler did a lot, but he couldn't save everybody. Unfortunately, we lost our families, but life goes on," Kuba said, sadly.

Helen and Kuba met in Krakow in 1945. They were married the next year. The couple came to America in 1949. They live in Poughkeepsie, N.Y., most of the year and have two sons and four grandchildren.

As for Schindler, he was considered a traitor by many in Czechoslovakia. Jews smuggled him out of the country. Schindler left the country dressed in a prisoner's uniform. All his belongings were stolen, and he died poor in 1974, leaving a request that he be buried with *meiner yuden*—his Jews.

Japan's Schindler

....

Consul General Saved Thousands of Jewish Lives in WWII

by Teresa Watanabe
The Los Angeles Times
(Republished in the *Houston Chronicle* March 20, 1994)

The making of the man known as "Japan's Oskar Schindler" started this way:

At 5:15 on a chilly summer morning in 1940, Chiune Sugihara awoke to the sound of a low rumble outside. He was no industrialist, like the German Schindler who saved more than 1,000 Jews by employing them in his factories, a story captured in the movie *Schindler's List.*

Rather, Sugihara was Japan's consul general in Lithuania.

On this particular morning, he peeked outside the curtained windows of the consular building and was startled to see the quiet street choked with a crowd of more than 200 strangers.

Unnerved and afraid, Sugihara woke his wife and three children and hid them in a closet. But when he took a closer look, he saw that the people outside were not hostile. They were desperate.

Their eyes were bloodshot. They looked fatigued. There were older men in beards and hats, young boys, mothers holding infants. When they saw him, some put their palms together in prayerful entreaty. Others, excited, tried to climb over the fence.

They were Polish Jews fleeing the encroaching German army, and

Sugihara was their last hope to avoid the Nazi death camps.

As war rumbled through Europe, all escape routes from Poland had been cut off except a treacherous journey through the frozen hinterlands of the Soviet Union via Lithuania. From the eastern port of Vladivostok, the refugees could sail to Japan and, from there, try to flee to China or North America. But they needed a transit visa through Japan. So they lined the streets, waiting for days, outside the Japanese mission.

The pleas presented Sugihara with the kind of searing dilemma that confronts few people in a lifetime: a choice between individual conscience and national duty, between life and death. To issue the visas, he would have to defy orders from his government not to accommodate the Jews.

Three times the 40-year-old official sent urgent cables to the Japanese government seeking permission to proceed; three times he was refused. Japan was on the verge of entering a military alliance with Germany and Italy and was being pressured to cooperate in addressing "the Jewish problem."

"I had to do something," Sugihara told the U.S. military newspaper Stars and Stripes a year before his death at age 86 in 1986. "Those people told me the kind of horror they would have to face if they didn't get away from the Nazis, and I believed them. There was no place else for them to go.

"I had to look at it from the standpoint of humanity. I could only be fired and returned to Japan. What else were they going to do?"

Chiune Sugihara, Japan's consul general in Lithuania, managed to write an estimated 1,600 visas, which the Israeli government and various scholars credit with saving the lives of 2,000 to 6,000 Jews.
....

He decided to defy his government, a choice that would change his life forever. He was in fact fired by the Foreign Ministry upon returning to Japan seven years later. Paradoxically, he remained a diplomat during the war, serving in various postings.

For 28 days, from July 31, 1940, until the Japanese government ordered Sugihara out of Lithuania to Berlin, the consul general feverishly wrote transit visas. From morning to night, he interviewed one applicant after another and wrote one visa after another. He lost weight and grew weak with exhaustion. His wife, Yukiko, also suffered from stress; she became unable to nurse their newborn son.

But Sugihara kept writing permits, even after he closed the consulate and moved to a hotel for a few days to wait for the train that would take him and his family to Germany. He kept writing even on the train, thrusting the precious pieces of paper through the window to waiting hands outside.

In the end, he managed to write an estimated 1,600 visas, which the Israeli government and various scholars credit with saving the lives of 2,000 to 6,000 Jews (an entire family could travel on one visa).

As the train rolled slowly out of the station, Sugihara bowed deeply to the Jewish refugees still crowding the platform and apologized; "Please forgive me. I can't write any more. I will pray for your safety."

Yukiko still recalls the look of shock on the faces of the remaining refugees. Nevertheless, as the train pulled away, one shouted; "Banzai, Japan!"

"Sugihara, we will not forget you!" the refugee shouted as he ran alongside the departing train. "We will see you again."

Most of the refugees never did see him again. But few forgot him.

One who remembers is Samuiel Minski, 73, a retired hosiery salesman living in Farmington, Mass. Thanks to a visa from Sugihara, the Polish native managed to escape to Japan with his mother and two siblings and, from there, join his father in the United States.

The Minskis braved capture by the Lithuanian police as they crossed the Polish border. They took a two-week Trans-Siberian train journey over Russia and spent three months in Japan on an expired visa, departing on one of the last boats to leave before the Japanese attack on Pearl Harbor. Today, Minski is a father of three and grandfather of six.

"Everyone is talking about Schindler, but he used people as slave labor and made money off of them," Minski said. "I'm not minimizing what he did, but I feel we are forgetting the people who did these acts for pure good.

"Mr. Sugihara didn't get any money for what he did, and he suffered greatly for it. If it were not for his generosity and humanity, I am sure I would not be here today."

For nearly half a century, Sugihara's case remained virtually unknown in his own nation, although Israel gave him its version of the Nobel Peace Prize, the Yad Vashem Prize for Righteous Gentiles, in 1985.

No such laurels were bestowed upon him in Japan. Part of the reason was Sugihara himself: A modest man, he did not tell even his siblings about his heroic deeds in Lithuania.

In a nation that honors obedience to authority more than individual conscience, Sugihara's acts were not viewed as particularly honorable by many top officials.

Those who knew Sugihara say he would squirm under the limelight, for he believed he had done nothing extraordinary.

The Real Schindler

·······················

*Why did this unlikely hero—a Nazi informer and war profiteer—
take the risk? He said, 'There was no choice.'*

by Mark Miller
Newsweek, Dec. 20, 1993

Who was the real Oskar Schindler? "Schindler's List" leaves the audience with a puzzling mix of a man—Nazi Party member, womanizer, gambler and savior. When the movie is over, the mystery remains. Why did such an unlikely hero spend his fortune and risk arrest to protect 1,200 Jewish prisoners from the Nazis?

After the war, when asked, the real Schindler would simply say, "There was no choice." His answer to Moshe Bejski, a former prisoner, was more revealing, perhaps in an unintended way: "If you saw a dog going to be crushed under a car, wouldn't you help him?"

Schindler came to occupied Cracow to make his fortune. Gradually he saw what was happening to the Jews. Simple kindnesses such as handing out extra food turned into his dangerous practice of declaring unqualified Jews as workers essential to the war effort. In autumn 1942, Schindler agreed to a secret meeting with Jewish leaders in Budapest to tell what he knew of impending plans to deport Jews.

He seemed to thrill at such danger. He had a near "manic" attraction to the black market, says Thomas Keneally, author of the book on which the movie is based. Undoubtedly, Keneally says, Schindler liked his life in

Poland and spent lavishly to keep it going. He was, after all, a slave-camp profiteer. "You add up all the elements—the expediencies and the decency—and you don't get the sum of what happened," Keneally says. "Ultimately, he had no motive except the desire to create a haven."

Schindler seemed lost after the war. He moved to Argentina in 1949 with his wife, Emilie, and his German mistress to start a nutria farm. When it failed, he abandoned both women (today they are close friends) and went back to Germany and more bankruptcies and alcoholism. In 1961 Schindler traveled to Israel. Each year thereafter he spent six weeks in Israel, at the expense of the *Schindlerjuden*. "When he was here it was easier for us to help him," says Janek Dresner. The ring made for him from a prisoner's gold teeth at the end of the war disappeared. "Ah," Schindler said, "That went to schnapps." He died in Frankfurt in 1974 at 66.

Some survivors are uncomfortable with any attempt to canonize Schindler. "We owe our lives to him," says Dr. Danka Dresner Schindel. "But I wouldn't glorify a German because of what he did to us. There is no proportion." Emilie once said Schindler had lived an unremarkable life before and after the war. Somehow, in the six years in between, he reacted in remarkable ways to the extraordinary events of his world.

—Mark Miller with Caroline Hawley in Jerusalem

Spielberg's Hero Died Alone and Forgotten

by Rachel Fixsen
Reuters News Service, Feb. 10, 1994

A street name and the memories of a few close friends are all that remain in Frankfurt of Oskar Schindler, the Holocaust hero brought to life in director Steven Spielberg's new film "Schindler's List."

Few people in Frankfurt, the German banking capital where he lived for the last 16 years of his life, had ever heard of the man who saved 1,300 Jews from the gas chambers until reports of the film began appearing in the press.

A middle-aged taxi driver is typical: "Oskar Schindler, hmmm ... there's a street with that name near here, but I'm afraid I couldn't tell you who he was."

The street sign reads "Oskar-Schindler-Strasse" and a small plaque underneath says, "Oskar Schindler, 1908-1974. Savior of many Jews from extermination in concentration camps."

Schindler, a hard-drinking bon vivant and womanizer in Nazi-occupied Poland when he shielded his Jewish factory workers from the death camps, died alone, impoverished and practically forgotten in his post-war home town.

He passed his final years in an attic apartment in the seedy quarter near the central railway station, relying on handouts from friends to supplement a meager pension.

Germany swept the memory of Schindler under the carpet because he reminded Germans of their own failure to resist the Nazis, Schindler's friends say.

"If you emphasize Oskar Schindler's deeds, then it immediately becomes clear just how many did not help," says Dieter Trautwein, a retired clergyman.

Spielberg pulled Schindler back from obscurity with his film, which has been nominated for 12 Academy Awards. The German-dubbed version will have its premiere in Frankfurt on March 1 [1994].

The film is based on the book 'Schindler's List" by Australian novelist Thomas Keneally, which reconstructs the German industrialist's life from accounts of more than 50 Jews that he rescued.

Schindler never joined the military but hobnobbed with high-ranking SS officers. He saved the Jews by using his charm and connections to convince the Nazis they were vital as workers in his Polish enamelware factory.

He employed far more than he needed. Babies born in the camp housing the workers were kept alive despite Nazi laws saying they should be killed.

Spielberg, along with some who knew Schindler during the war, are hard pressed to explain how the man who went to Poland as a war profiteer ended up selflessly saving lives while his money ebbed away.

Many of the ethnic Germans who lived in Sudetenland—a part of former Czechoslovakia until its annexation by Germany in 1938 and where Schindler was from—were fervently pro-Nazi.

"To this day I cannot explain where he found the courage," Elisabeth Tont, Schindler's secretary in Poland during the war, told a local newspaper.

"He could only say the terrible thing happening to the Jews made him suddenly feel he just had to help," Trautwein says.

He made a success of his business during the lean war years, but had failed later—first as a fur breeder in Argentina. Then he saw both a slipper factory and a cement factory he ran in Germany close in failure.

After the war, he seemed to lose energy and purpose.

"He was a burned-out soul," says 73-year-old Trude Simonsohn, who met Schindler after he moved to Frankfurt in 1958 and began working with her at the Frankfurt Friends of the Hebrew University of Jerusalem.

"It was as if all the energy which he had in his life was exhausted in this rescue action ... You could sense this from him. A person who had so much strength in those terrible times couldn't find his feet again."

Schindler's wife Emilie stayed behind in Argentina, where the couple had gone after the war. He lived alone then in Frankfurt, frequenting various pubs where he was known and, true to character, had a series of love affairs.

From the 1960s on, he spent several months every year in Israel visiting people he had saved. Frankfurt's Jewish and church communities often invited him to discussions about the war and what he had done.

Richard Hackenberg, former head of the Ackermann Community of former Sudetenland residents in Frankfurt, says Schindler probably used up a life's worth of energy just rescuing the workers who still refer to themselves as "Schindler Jews."

"A person who has done something like this will always be in the shadow of his deeds," he says.

Schindler's remarkably humanitarian acts were first publicized in April 1962 when he was received in Israel by a crowd of 800 people. He was one of the first 10 Gentiles to have a memorial tree planted for them in the "Street of the Just" at the Yad Vashem Holocaust memorial in Jerusalem.

But recognition in Germany was scant.

"To soothe a bad conscience, he got the order of the Federal Republic, a ridiculous pension of $115 a month and in Frankfurt now, a narrow lane in a distant suburb is named after Schindler," Hackenberg says.

"There were probably too many people who were themselves shamed because of what he had done," says Trautwein.

Trautwein said Schindler did not shy from confronting others about their behavior during the war.

"He asked nearly everybody, 'What did you do?'"

Annotated Bibliography

Further readings about the Holocaust

Abzug, Robert H. *Inside the Vicious Heart: Americans and the Liberation of Nazi Concentration Camps.* New York: Oxford University Press, 1985. What the Allies found when they opened the infamous camps.

Adler, Jerry. "The Last Days of Auschwitz." *Newsweek,* Jan. 16, 1995. Cover story in *Newsweek,* 50 years after Auschwitz and other death camps were liberated. That issue also contains 6 other accompanying articles about the death camps, including a memoir, "Stay Together, Always" by Elie Wiesel.

Amery, Jean. *At the Mind's Limit.* Bloomington: Indiana University Press, 1980. Thoughts on survival by a Holocaust victim.

Anger, P. *With Raoul Wallenberg in Budapest.* New York: Holocaust Library, 1981.

Arad, Yitzhak; German, Yisrael and Margaliot, Abraham. *Documents of the Holocaust: Selected Sources on the Destruction of the Jews of Germany and Austria, Poland and the Soviet Union.* Jerusalem: Yad Vashem, 1981.

Barnouw, D., and Van der Stroom, G. *The Diary of Anne Frank: The Critical Edition.* New York: Doubleday, 1969.

Bauer, Yehuda. *American Jewry and the Holocaust.* Detroit: Wayne State University Press, 1981. What American Jews were doing during World War Two.

———. *Flight and Rescue.* New York; Random House, 1970. How almost 300,000 Jews who survived the Holocaust escaped from eastern Europe, 1944-1948.

———. *A History of the Holocaust.* New York: Franklin Watts, 1982.

———. *The Holocaust in Historical Perspective.* Seattle: The University of Washington Press, 1978.

Bauer, Yehuda, and Rotenstreich, Nathan. *The Holocaust as Historical Experience.* New York: Holmes & Meier, 1981. Twelve scholarly essays about the Holocaust.

Berenbaum, Michael. *The World Must Know.* Boston: Little Brown and Co., 1993.

Bergmann, Martin S., and Jucovy, Milton E. *Generation of the Holocaust.* New York: Basic Books, 1982. The psychological effects of children of Holocaust survivors.

Berkovits, Eliezer. *With God in Hell: Judaism in the Ghettos and Death Camps.* New York and London: Sanhedrin Press, 1979.

Bettelheim, Bruno. *The Informed Heart.* New York: The Free Press, 1960. Bettelheim was a prisoner in Dachau and Buchenwald before coming to the United States and becoming a psychiatrist; here he explains what type of personality would survive best in a death camp.

———. *Surviving and Other Essays.* New York: Alfred Knopf, 1979.

Bierman, J. *Righteous Gentile: The Story of Raoul Wallenberg.* New York: The Viking Press 1981. There are at least six major books about Raoul Wallenberg (Anger, Bierman, Lester, Marton, Rosenfeld and Werbel-Clarke) who saved more people than Oskar Schindler and who was arrested by the Soviets at war's end and disappeared into the Soviet prison system, never to be seen again.

Block, Gay, and Drucker, Malka. *Rescuers: Portraits of Moral Courage in the Holocaust.* New York: Holmes & Meier, 1992. Recent interviews with people like Schindler who saved those they could save. Highly recommended.

Bor, Josef. *The Terezin Requiem.* New York: Alfred Knopf, Inc., 1963. The story of how an orchestra of Jewish prisoners was assembled in the Terezin concentration camp and how the orchestra played Verdi's "Requiem" for Nazi commanders, including Eichmann. In the end, the camp commander agreed that the orchestra should not be broken up—all the musicians were sent together to be destroyed. The author survived not only Terezin (Theresienstadt), but Auschwitz-Birkenau and Buchenwald as well.

Brecher, Elinor J. *Schindler's Legacy: True Stories of the List Survivors.* New York: Plume Books (Penguin), 1994. Schindler's List survivors relate their first encounters with Schindler, their experiences after the war and their emotional reunions with him over the next 20 years. Highly recommended.

Breitman, Richard. *The Architect of Genocide: Himmler and the Final Solution.* New York: Alfred Knopf, Inc., 1991.

Brenner, R.R. *The Faith and Doubt of Holocaust Survivors.* New York: The Free Press, 1980.

Bullock, Alan. *Hitler: A Study in Tyranny.* New York: Harper & Row, 1964.

Cargas, Harry James. *Harry James Cargas in Conversation with Elie Wiesel.* New York: Paulist Press, 1976. Interviews with Wiesel; each chapter has an excerpt from a Wiesel publication, followed by a commentary by Cargas.

———. *The Holocaust: An Annotated Bibliography.* Chicago: American Library Association, 1985.

———, ed. *When God and Man Failed: Non-Jewish Views of the Holocaust.* New York: Macmillan, 1981. Twenty sections about various aspects of the Holocaust.

Charny, I. W. *How Can We Commit the Unthinkable? Genocide, the Human Cancer.* Boulder, Co.: Westview Press, 1982.

Chartok, Roselle, and Spencer, Jack, eds., *The Holocaust Years: Society on Trial.* New York: Bantam, 1978. An anthology about the Holocaust.

Dawidowicz, Lucy S. *The War Against the Jews, 1933-1945.* New York: Holt, Rinehart & Winston, 1975.

——, ed. *A Holocaust Reader.* New York: Behrman House, 1976. Over 60 selections, including Nazi documents and material about the condition of those inside the ghettos.

Des Pres, Terrence. *The Survivor.* New York: Oxford University Press, 1976. In part a personal story of survival and in part a survey of survivors in literature. The author cites Donat, Primo Levi and others.

Dimsdale, Joel, ed. *Survivors, Victims & Perpetrators.* New York: Hemisphere, 1980. Essays on the emotional effects of the Holocaust on survivors, their children and Nazis alive in the 1970s. Dimsdale is a medical doctor.

Dinnerstein, Leonard. *America and the Survivors of the Holocaust.* New York: Columbia University Press, 1982.

Donat, A. *The Holocaust Kingdom: A Memoir.* New York: Holt, Rinehart & Winston, 1965.

Epstein, Helen. *Children of the Holocaust.* New York: Putnam, 1979. Epstein was a Holocaust survivor, as a child.

Ezrachim, Sidra. *By Words Alone: The Holocaust in Literature.* Chicago: The University of Chicago Press, 1980.

Feig, Konnilyn. *Hitler's Death Camps.* New York: Holmes & Meier, 1981. A study of all the death camps established by the Nazis.

Fein, Helen. *Accounting for Genocide.* New York: The Free Press, 1979.

Feingold, H. *The Politics of Rescue: The Roosevelt Administration and the Holocaust, 1933-1945.* New Brunswick, N.J.: Rutgers University Press, 1970. Similar to the Arthur Morse book, below.

Feldman, Shoshana, and Laub, Dore. *Testimony: Crisis of Witnessing in Literature, Psychoanalysis and History.* New York: Routledge, 1991.

Fenelon, Fania. *Playing for Time.* New York: Atheneum, 1977. The story of a member of a women's orchestra assembled in Birkenau.

Fleming, Gerald. *Hitler and the Final Solution.* Berkeley: University of California Press, 1984.

Fogelman, Eva. *Conscience and Courage: Rescuers of Jews During the Holocaust.* New York: Doubleday Anchor Books, 1994.

Fogelman, Eva, and Wiener, V.L. "The Few, the Brave, the Noble." *Psychology Today*, Vol. 19, No. 8, August, 1985.

Frank, Anne. *Anne Frank's Tales from the Secret Annex*. New York: Doubleday, 1984. Anne Frank's fiction, essays, fables and vignettes of her life. Not as widely known as her *Diary*.

——. *The Diary of a Young Girl*. New York: Doubleday, 1967. Classic autobiography of a young woman hidden from, then found by, the Nazis.

Friedlander, Albert, *Out of the Whirlwind*. New York: Shocken, 1976. A collection which includes Wiesel, Donat, Levi, Anne Frank and others.

Friedman, A.J., ed. *Roads to Extinction: Essays on the Holocaust*. Philadelphia: Jewish Publication Society, 1980.

Friedman, Philip. *Their Brothers' Keepers*. New York: Holocaust Library, 1978.

Furet, Francois, ed. *Unanswered Questions: Nazi Germany and the Genocide of the Jews*. New York: Schocken Books, 1989. 15 essays edited by a French historian.

Geis, M., and Gold, A. *Anne Frank Remembered: The Story of the Woman Who Helped Hide the Frank Family*. New York: Simon & Schuster, 1987.

Gilbert, Martin. *Auschwitz and the Allies: A Devastating Account of How the Allies Responded to the News of Hitler's Mass Murder*. New York: Henry Holt, 1981. How and why the Allies ignored what was happening in Auschwitz.

——. *The Holocaust: a History of the Jews of Europe During the Second World War*. New York: Henry Holt, 1985. A major one-volume encyclopedia of the Holocaust.

Goldstein, B. *Five Years in the Warsaw Ghetto*. Garden City, N.Y.: Doubleday & Co., 1961.

Green, Gerald. *Holocaust*. New York: Bantam, 1978. This book was the basis of a nine-hour NBC mini-series of the same title.

Grobman, Alex, and Landes, Daniel, eds. *Genocide*. Los Angeles: Simon Wiesenthal Center, 1983. Published as a companion to the film of the same title.

Guttman, Y. *Encyclopedia of the Holocaust* (4 vols.). New York: Macmillan, 1990.

Guttman, Y., and Zuroff, Efriam, eds. *Rescue Attempts During the Holocaust*. New York: KTAV Publishing House, 1974.

Harman, Geoffrey H., ed. *Holocaust Remembrance: The Shapes of Memory*. Cambridge, Mass.: Blackwell, 1994.

Hass, Aaron. *In the Shadow of the Holocaust*. Ithaca, NY: Cornell University Press, 1990.

Hellman, P. *The Auschwitz Album*. New York: Bantam Books, 1981.

———. *Avenue of the Righteous: Portraits of Uncommon Courage of Christians and the Jews They Saved from Hitler.* New York: Atheneum, 1980.

Hersey, John. *The Wall.* New York: Knopf, 1967. A long, wrenching novel about the Warsaw Ghetto.

Heymont, Irving. *Among the Survivors of the Holocaust—1945.* Cincinnati: American Jewish Archives, 1982. What happened to death camp inmates immediately after World War Two. President Truman once said, "As matters now stand, we appear to be treating Jews as the Nazis treated them except that we do not exterminate them."

Hilberg, Raul. *The Destruction of the European Jews.* New York: Holmes and Meier, 1985 (3 vol. set); Chicago: Quadrangle Books, 1961 (single volume edition). Major analysis of the Holocaust. Hilberg relied upon German documents as his major source.

———. *Perpetrators Victims Bystanders: The Jewish Catastrophe, 1933-1945.* New York: Harper Collins, 1992. The book is divided into three sections, which can be read in any order.

Iranek-Osmecki, K. *He Who Saves One Life.* New York: Crown Publishers, 1971.

Jacobson, Ken. *Embattled Selves: Jewish Identity and the Holocaust.* New York: Grove/Atlantic, 1994.

Klee, Ernest; Dressen, Willi; and Reiss, Volker. *The Good Old Days: The Holocaust as Seen by Its Perpetrators and Bystanders.* New York: The Free Press, 1988.

Korman, Gerd, ed. *Hunter and Hunted.* New York: Delta Books, 1974. A collection that includes Wiesel, John Toland, Donat and many others.

Kosinski, Jerzy. *The Painted Bird.* New York: Pocket Books, 1966. The story of a young boy abandoned by his parents who witnesses the war alone. Very violent and graphic.

Kuznetsov, Anatoly. *Babi Yar.* New York: Dell, 1967. This is the story of the massacre of thousands of Jews near Kiev, Russia. The author calls it a "documentary novel." This book caused a sensation when it was first published in Russia.

Langer, Lawrence L. *Admitting the Holocaust: Collected Essays.* New York: Oxford University Press, 1994. *Publishers Weekly* magazine called his essays "gripping, often profound" (Nov. 7, 1994, p. 60).

———. *The Holocaust and the Literary Imagination.* New Haven: Yale University Press, 1975. How Holocaust survivors had to invent new literary forms to describe the experiences they had gone through. The author examines the works of Wiesel, Kosinski and many others.

———. *Holocaust Testimonies: The Ruins of Memory.* New Haven: Yale University Press, 1991. This book won a National Book Critics Circle award in 1991.

——. *Versions of Survival: The Holocaust and the Human Spirit.* Albany: State University of New York Press, 1982.

Lanzmann, Claude: *Shoah: An Oral History of the Holocaust.* New York: Pantheon Books, 1985. The complete text of the film *Shoah.*

Laqueur, Walter. *The Terrible Secret: Suppression of the Truth about Hitler's Final Solution.* New York: Little Brown, 1981. How much most Germans knew about Hitler's "Final Solution" and how much the rest of the world knew. The "terrible secret" was no secret at all.

Lester, E. *Wallenberg: The Man in the Iron Web.* Englewood Cliffs, N.J.: Prentice-Hall, 1984.

Leuner, H.D. *When Compassion was a Crime: Germany's Silent Heroes, 1933-1945.* London: Oswald Wolf, 1966.

Levi, Primo. *Survival in Auschwitz.* New York: Collier, 1961. One of the best known of the Holocaust memoirs; previously published under the title *If This Man Is a Man.*

Levin, Nora. *The Holocaust: The Destruction of European Jewry 1933-1945.* New York: Schocken Books, 1973.

Lifton, Robert J. *The Nazi Doctors: Medical Killing and the Psychology of Genocide.* New York: Basic Books, 1986. A psychological analysis of how German physicians could willingly aid the Nazis.

Lipstadt, Deborah. *Beyond Belief: The American Press and the Coming of the Holocaust, 1933-1945.* New York: The Free Press, 1986. How journalists in the U.S. ignored (or could not believe) the Holocaust despite substantial evidence available at the time.

——. *Denying the Holocaust: The Growing Assault on Truth and Memory.* New York: The Free Press, 1993. How some groups are now charging the Holocaust did not happen.

Lookstein, Haskel. *Were We Our Brothers Keepers?* New York: Hartmore House, 1985. The response to the Holocaust by the American Jewish press. Interesting to compare and contrast with Robert Ross's *So It Was True: The American Protestant Press and the Persecution of the Jews.*

Marrus, Michael R. *The Holocaust in History.* Hanover, NH: The University Press of New England, 1987.

Marton, Kati. *Wallenberg.* New York: Random House, 1982.

Mayer, Arno J. *Why Did the Heavens Not Darken? The "Final Solution" in History.* New York: Pantheon, 1990.

Medoff, Rafael. *The Deafening Silence: American Jewish Leadership and the Holocaust.* New York: Shapolsky Publishers, 1987.

Meltzer, K. *Rescue: The Story of How the Gentiles Saved Jews in the Holocaust.* New York: Harper & Row, 1988.

Morse, Arthur D. *While Six Million Died: A Chronicle of American Apathy.* New York: Random House, 1967. How the Franklin Roosevelt administration knew about the Holocaust and did little to save victims of the Nazis, because rescuing victims of the death camps was not a high priority of the war.

Oliner, Samuel, and Oliner, Pearl. *The Atruistic Personality: Rescuers of Jews in Nazi Europe—What Led Ordinary Men and Women to Risk Their Lives on Behalf of Others.* New York: The Free Press, 1988.

Paldiel, Mordecai. *The Path of the Righteous: Gentile Rescuers of Jews During the Holocaust.* Hoboken, NJ: KTAV Publishing House, 1993. Profiles of many who rescued Jews during the Holocaust, country-by-country throughout Nazi-occupied Europe.

Penkower, Monty. *Jews were Expendable.* Urbana, IL: The University of Illinois Press, 1983.

Rabinowitz, Dorothy. *New Lives.* New York: Alfred Knopf, 1976. Biographical information about Holocaust survivors 25-30 years after the end of the war.

Reitlinger, Gerald. *The Final Solution.* Norvale, NJ: Jason Aronson, 1988.

Roiphe, Anne. *A Season for Healing: Reflections on the Holocaust.* New York: Summit Books, 1988.

Rosenberg, Alan and Myers, Gerald E. *Echoes from the Holocaust: Philosophical Reflections on a Dark Theme.* Philadelphia: Temple University Press, 1988.

Rosenfeld, H. *The Swedish Angel of Rescue: The Heroism and Torment of Raoul Wallenberg.* Buffalo, Prometheus Books, 1982.

Ross, Robert. *So It Was True: The American Protestant Press and the Nazi Persecution of the Jews.* Minneapolis: Univ. of Minnesota Press, 1980. How much American Protestant church leaders knew of the Holocaust.

Roth, John, and Berenbaum, Michael. *Holocaust: Religious and Philosophical Implications.* New York: Paragon House, 1990.

Rubenstein, Richard L. *The Cunning of History: The Holocaust and the American Future.* New York: Harper Colophon Books, 1975.

Rubenstein, Richard L., and Roth, John. *Approaches to Auschwitz.* Atlanta: John Knox Press, 1987.

Ryan, Michael, ed. *Human Responses to the Holocaust.* Lewiston, NY: Edwin Mellen Press, 1981.

Sachar, Abram L. *The Redemption of the Unwanted.* New York: St. Martin's, 1983. What happened to the approximately 400,000 Jews who survived the war.

Schaeffer, Susan Fromberg. *Anya.* New York: Macmillan, 1974. A novel about one woman's survival of the Holocaust.

Schwartz-Bart, Andre. *The Last of the Just.* New York: Bantam, 1961. This novel is based on the Jewish tradition that the world is being preserved because of the existence on earth of one Just Man. The author traces that legend from the twelfth century to the Holocaust era.

Sherwin, Byron, and Ament, Susan, eds. *Encountering the Holocaust.* Chicago: Impact Publications, 1981. A collection of fourteen chapters in an interdisciplinary approach to Holocaust studies.

Shirer, William L. *The Rise and Fall of the Third Reich.* New York: Simon & Schuster, 1960.

Silver, E. *The Book of the Just: The Silent Heroes Who Saved Jews from Hitler.* London: Weidenfeld and Nicholson, 1992.

Singer, Isaac Bashevis. *Enemies, a Love Story.* New York: Farrar, 1972. A novel of Jewish life in Poland and New York; characters in the book are affected by their previous Holocaust experiences.

Spiegelman, Art. *Maus: A Survivor's Tale.* New York: Pantheon, 1986. The story of one Polish family caught in the Holocaust, told as a cartoon. The Jews are mice, the Germans are cats, and that makes Nazi Germany a giant mousetrap. Highly lauded book; not a Disneyesque version. (Based on Spiegelman's father's story.)

——. *Maus: A Survivor's Tale. And Here My Troubles Begin.* New York: Pantheon, 1991. A continuation of the *Maus* story, also told as a cartoon.

Steiner, Jean Francois. *Treblinka.* New York: Simon & Schuster, 1967. A non-fiction novel, written much like *Schindler's List,* which describes how 600 Jews revolted against their murderers and burned a Nazi death camp to the ground. Steiner's father and other relatives were Holocaust victims.

Steinitz, Lucy, and Szonyi, David, eds. *Living After the Holocaust.* New York: Bloch, 1976. The editors are children of Holocaust survivors—and write about what it means to be the second generation of Holocaust survivors.

Styron, William. *Sophie's Choice.* New York: Random House, 1979. A controversial novel, with basis in the Holocaust.

Suhl, Uri, ed. *They Fought Back.* New York: Schocken, 1975. This book refutes the commonly-held belief that there was no Jewish resistance to the Nazis.

Szonyi, David M. *The Holocaust: An Annotated Bibliography and Resource Guide.* New York: National Jewish Resource Center, 1985.

Thomas, Gordon, and Witts, Max Morgan. *Voyage of the Damned.* New York: Stein and Day, 1974.

Uris, Leon M. *Exodus.* New York: Doubleday, 1958. An epic novel tracing the history of European Jewry from the end of the 19th century to the establishment of Israel.

Wallenberg, Raoul. *Letters and Dispatches: 1924-1944.* New York: Arcade Books, 1995. This newly published collection of Wallenberg's letters, largely to his grandfather, may spur international interest in how and why Wallenberg disappeared inside the Soviet Union toward the end of World War Two, never to be seen again, despite diplomatic protests which continued sporadically for years.

Waite, Robert G. L. *The Psychopathic God: Adolf Hitler.* New York: Basic Books, 1977.

Werbell, Frederick. E., and Clarke, Thurston. *Lost Hero: The Mystery of Raoul Wallenberg.* New York: McGraw-Hill, 1982.

Wiesel, Elie. *The Gates of the Forest.* New York: Holt, 1966. An awesome novel about a young child who survives by posing as a mute.

———. *Legends of Our Time.* New York: Avon, 1970. Fifteen stories about the Holocaust. The first is about Wiesel's father, who was killed by the Nazis.

———. *Night.* New York: Hill & Wang. A classic memoir. Wiesel lost his parents and younger sister in Auschwitz when he was 15. He survived Birkenau, Auschwitz, Buna and Buchenwald. *Night* was a world-wide best seller. Wiesel won the Nobel Peace Prize in 1986.

———. *One Generation After.* New York: Random House, 1970. Wiesel's thoughts about the first generation after World War Two: "Nothing has been learned; Auschwitz has not even served as a warning. For more detailed information, consult your daily newspaper."

Wiesel, Elie; Dawidowicz, Lucy; Rabinowitz, Dorothy; and Brown, Robert McAfee, eds. *Dimensions of the Holocaust.* Evanston: Northwestern University Press, 1977. This is a collection of lectures in response to a speech given at Northwestern University, of which the premise was that the Holocaust never happened.

Wiesenthal, Simon. *Justice Not Vengeance.* New York: Grove Weidenfeld, 1989. Wiesenthal's accounts of some Nazis that he and his organization brought to justice after the war and some that escaped or died before justice was served.

———. *Max and Helen.* New York: Morrow, 1982. A nonfiction novel about the consequences of the Holocaust; a love story with no happy ending.

Wundheiler, L.N. "Oskar Schindler's Moral Development During the Holocaust." *Humbolt Journal of Social Relations,* Vol. 13, No. 1-2, 1985-1986.

Wyden, Peter. *Stella: One Women's True Tale of Evil, Betrayal and Survival in Hitler's Germany.* New York: Simon & Schuster, 1992. A horrific story of how one woman was tortured into becoming a "catcher," who hunted down Jews for the Gestapo; she became a black reversal of what Oskar Schindler was. A compelling book.

Wyman, David S. *The Abandonment of the Jews: America and the Holocaust, 1941-1945.* New York: Pantheon, 1984.

———. *Paper Walls.* Amherst: University of Massachusetts Press, 1968. Why the United States granted only 150,000 visa to Jews fleeing Europe, 1938-1941.

Wytwycky, Bohdan. *The Other Holocaust.* Washington, DC: Novak Report on the New Ethnicity, 1980. Without diminishing the experiences of the Jews in the Holocaust, this book covers other ethnic groups also lost: the Gypsies, the Poles and others.

Yahil, Leni. *The Holocaust: The Fate of European Jews.* Oxford and New York: Oxford University Press, 1991.

Video

Blair, Jon, producer. "Schindler." Contains interview with Schindler's widow Emilie, Amon Goeth's mistress, Leopold and Herman Rosen, and other *Schindlerjuden.* Color and black-and-white, approx. 82 minutes. Released in England by Thames Television, about 1983. Re-released in the United States by HBO (Home Box Office), 1994. See also Blair, Jon, "Spielberg Comes of Age," *Esquire* (British edition), March, 1994, Blair's memoirs of his documentary. Especially interesting glimpses of Amon Goeth's mistress, suffering from emphysema as Blair interviewed her in 1982. She committed suicide shortly thereafter.

Appendix

Cast, Credits and Awards of Steven Spielberg's film "Schindler's List"

Oskar Schindler	Liam Neeson
Itzhak Stern	Ben Kingsley
Amon Goeth	Ralph Fiennes
Emilie Schindler	Caroline Goodall
Poldek Pfefferberg	Jonathan Sagalle
Helen Hirsch	Embeth Davidtz
Directed by	Steven Spielberg
Screenplay by	Steven Zaillian
Based on the novel by	Thomas Keneally
Produced by	Steven Spielberg
	Gerald R. Molen
	Branko Lustig
Executive Producer	Kathleen Kennedy
Director of Photography	Janusz Kaminski
Music by	John Williams

Running time: 197 minutes

VCR available through: MCA Universal, 100 Universal City Plaza, Universal City, CA, 91608.

"Schindler's List" won:

U.S. Academy Awards for: Best Picture; Best Director (Spielberg); Best Screenplay (Zaillian); Best Cinematography; Best Music; Best Editing and Best Art Direction.

British Academy Awards: seven.

Best Picture awards from: the New York Film Critics Circle; the National Society of Film Critics; the National Board of Review; the Producers Guild; the Los Angeles Film Critics; the Chicago, Boston and Dallas Film critics; a Christopher Award, the Hollywood Foreign Press Association Golden Globe Awards.

Steven Spielberg also was honored with the Directors Guild of America Award.

Photo Credits

1., 2., 3. and 4. Main Commission for the Investigation of Nazi War Crimes, Warsaw, Poland, courtesy of U.S. Holocaust Memorial Museum, Washington, D.C.

5. Archives of Mechanical Documentation, Warsaw, Poland, courtesy of U.S. Holocaust Memorial Museum, Washington, D.C.

6. Professor Leopold Pfefferberg-Page, courtesy of U.S. Holocaust Memorial Museum, Washington, D.C.

7. Main Commission for the Investigation of Nazi War Crimes, Warsaw, Poland, courtesy of U.S. Holocaust Memorial Museum, Washington, D.C.

8. Courtesy of Herbert Steinhouse.

9. Thomas Fensch.

10. and 11. Courtesy of Herbert Steinhouse.

12. Archives of Mechanical Docmentation, Warsaw, Poland, courtesy of U.S. Holocaust Memorial Museum, Washington, D.C.

13., 14. and 15. Professor Leopold Pfefferberg-Page, courtesy of the U.S. Holocaust Memorial Museum, Washington, D.C.

16. Courtesy of Herbert Steinhouse.

17. Professor Leopold Pfefferberg-Page, courtesy of the U.S. Holocaust Memorial Museum, Washington, D.C.

18., 19., 20., 21. and 22. Al Taylor, courtesy of Herbert Steinhouse.

23. Courtesy of the U.S. Holocaust Memorial Museum, Washington, D.C.

Acknowledgments Continued from page iv

The Chronicle of Higher Education, "Making Novels of Life's Ethical Choices" by Pedro E. Ponce and "The Uniqueness of the Holocaust" by Liz McMillen, copyright © 1994 *The Chronicle of Higher Education,* Reprinted with permission;

Cineaste magazine, review of "Schindler's List" by Thomas Doherty, first appeared in *Cineaste,* Vol. 20, No. 3, 1994, reprinted with permission of *Cineaste;*

The Columbus Dispatch, "Redemption amid tragedy," reprinted with permission of *The Columbus Dispatch;*

The Denver Post, "'Schindler' Reaction: Thinking, a Few Snickers," reprinted with permission of *The Denver Post;*

The Detroit News, "Spielberg Triumphs with His Forceful Epic of the Holocaust's Unlikely Hero" by Susan Stark, reprinted with permission of *The Detroit News;*

Entertainment Weekly, "Making History: How Steven Spielberg Brought 'Schindler's List' to Life," © 1994 Entertainment Weekly Inc., reprinted with permission;

Fort Worth Star-Telegram, material reprinted courtesy of the *Fort Worth Star-Telegram;*

Houston Chronicle, "Keneally's Luck," "Spielberg Tells Powerful Holocaust Tale" and "Bracher's Letter," reprinted with permission of the *Houston Chronicle;*

Gannett News Service, articles from the Gannett News Service copyright © 1994, Gannett Co., Inc. Reprinted with permission;

In These Times, "*Schindler's List* and the Politics of Remembrance," reprinted with permission from *In These Times,* a biweekly news magazine published in Chicago;

Knight-Ridder Tribune News Service, "Holocaust Movie Lost on Laughing Students," reprinted with permission;

Los Angeles Times, "Japan's Schindler" by Teresa Watanabe copyright 1994, *Los Angeles Times.* Reprinted by permission;

Stephanie Mansfield, "Liam Neeson Puts the Kettle On" by Stephanie Mansfield, reprinted by permission of International Creative Management, Inc. Copyright © 1993 by Stephanie Mansfield;

The New Republic, "Spielberg Revisited" by Stanley Kauffmann and "Close Encounters of the Nazi Kind" by Leon Wieseltier, reprinted by permission of The New Republic, © 1994, by The New Republic, Inc.;

Newsweek, "Spielberg's Obsession," by David Ansen; "After the Survivors" by Jonathan Atler; "The Real Schindler" by Mark Miller and "Denying the Holocaust" by Laura Shapiro, from *Newsweek* Dec. 20, 1993 © 1993 *Newsweek,* Inc. All rights reserved. Reprinted by permission;

The New York Times, "Journal: Extras in the Shadows" by Frank Rich; "Buenos Aires Journal: Nazis a Dead Issue? In Argentina, No" by Nathaniel Nash; "Emphasis on Holocaust Film in Fighting Racism Criticized" by Iver Peterson, "Good Germans: Honoring the Heroes. And Hiding the Holocaust" by Diana Jean Schemo and "Poll On Doubt of Holocaust Is Corrected" by Michael H. Kagay, copyright © 1994 by *The New York Times.* Reprinted by permission;

Terrence Rafferty, "A Man of Transactions" originally published in *The New Yorker*, reprinted with permission of Terrence Rafferty;

The Orange County Register, "'Schindler's' Author Gives Film a Standing Ovation" by Valerie Takahama, reprinted with permission of *The Orange County Register,* copyright © 1994;

Reuters News Service, "Nazi hunter raves about 'Schindler's List'"; "German 'Schindler's List' Debut Launches Debate, Soul-searching" and "Spielberg's Hero Died Alone and Forgotten"; reprinted with permission of Reuters News Service;

San Francisco Chronicle, "Spielberg's 'List': Director Rediscovers his Jewishness while Filming Nazi Story" by Edward Guthmann, copyright © 1993 *San Francisco Chronicle,* reprinted by permission;

The San Francisco Examiner, "The Paradox of a Candle" by Scott Rosenberg, reprinted with permission from the *San Francisco Examiner* © 1993 *San Francisco Examiner;*

Stephen Schiff, "Seriously Spielberg" originally published in *The New Yorker,* reprinted with permission of Stephen Schiff;

The Seattle Times, "Spielberg's 'List': A Commanding Holocaust Film" by John Hartl, reprinted by permission of *The Seattle Times;*

Sight and Sound magazine, "Witness" by Simon Louvich, reprinted courtesy of *Sight and Sound* magazine;

Herbert Steinhouse, "The Man Who Saved a Thousand Lives," reprinted with permission of Herbert Steinhouse;

The Sun Sentinel, "Two on Schindler's List Recall Horror" by Jeremy Simon, reprinted with permission from the *Sun Sentinel,* Fort Lauderdale, Florida;

Al Taylor photographs reprinted with permission of Herbert Steinhouse;

David Thomson, "Presenting Enamelware," first published in *Film Comment,* reprinted with permission of David Thomson;

United States Holocaust Memorial Museum, Washington, D.C., photographs reprinted with permission of the United States Holocaust Memorial Museum.

Index